TOKYO

T O K Y O
City of Stories

by Paul Waley

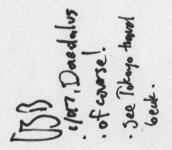

BB
· for, Daedalus
· of course!
· See Tokyo travel
  book.

New York · **WEATHERHILL** · *Tokyo*

Woodblock illustrations are from the collection
at the National Museum, Tokyo.

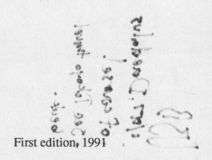

First edition, 1991

Published by Weatherhill, Inc., New York, with editorial offices a
Tanko-Weatherhill, Inc., 8–3 Nibancho, Chiyoda-ku, Tokyo 102
Copyright © 1991 by Paul Waley; all rights reserved. Printed in Japan

Library of Congress Cataloging in Publication Data: Waley, Paul.
Tokyo: city of stories   / by Paul Waley. / p.   cm. / 1. Tokyo
(Japan)–History.   2. Tokyo (Japan)–Description. / I. Title.
DS896.6W35   1990 / 952'.135–dc20 / 89–25092 CIP / ISBN
0–8348–0227–9

Contents

Preface

A few years back, I wrote a historical guidebook to Tokyo called *Tokyo Now and Then*. My intention had been to give meaning to the modern city by describing its past, so little of which remains for us to see today, and by relating past to present. It was really two books stitched into one, an attempt to write all manner of things about Tokyo that had not been written before in English. Tokyo, however, changes quickly, and so it is time now to unstitch the two books and offer what I hope is a more rounded picture of Tokyo's history. The present volume comprises for the main part material from *Tokyo Now and Then*. However, I have added several new chapters, revised or rewritten several more of the old ones, and, more drastically, cut those sections of the earlier book that were intended as guides to a tour of the city. What is left is, I hope, a more cohesive introduction to the fascinating history of a rather extraordinary city.

I have attempted to cover all those parts of the city with a substantial history to their name. But Tokyo has moved the axis of its activity westward. Nowadays, many people, especially foreigners, find themselves spending most of their time in districts that are not even mentioned in this book. You will look in vain through its pages for Ochiai, Ikebukuro, Kōenji, Shimo Kitazawa, Jiyūgaoka, and Gotanda, to name but a few. It is not that these places do not have a history. I am sure that the story of these and similar districts is an intriguing one, but to do them justice would mean writing a disquisition on Tokyo's urban expansion in the last fifty years, not the stuff for a book of this sort. A balanced portrayal of Tokyo's history takes us inevitably east, to the banks of the Sumida River. The result might seem like bias to the Shitamachi area of craftsmen, merchants, and industry, but once upon time, indeed not so long ago, this was the center of the city. If it seems like bias, perhaps I should admit to my own preference. I find even in the modern city much more that is appealing in Shitamachi than in the more predictable beat of the hills of the west of the city. Shitamachi has been in cultural and industrial decline for several decades now, and it is not much helped by the patronizing approach adopted by television and the newspapers.

Swimming against the tide is not regarded as rewarding work in Japan. In Tokyo, Japan's capital, the cultural mainstream of the nation's life shifted some years ago to the west, to Akasaka, Roppongi, Aoyama, and Shinjuku. As the city builds its way into the bay, it might move back again to the east. But by now, there is little pattern to the shifts in the city's dynamic. Money seems to control all. Both in its mercantilism and its presumption, Tokyo has become something of a monster city. It seems to have set itself the task of outstripping all other cities on earth without really having worked out what that entails—like the nation in microcosm, if that is the right term for the world's biggest conurbation. By most physical standards, it left nearly all other cities in its wake long ago. If development continues at its present pace—and until the year 2000, it is sure to—the nature of the city will become more and more problematic as it tries to reconcile the power it wields with its own inherent weaknesses. Tokyo has become so large, such a devourer of resources, that it pushed its most intractable problems beyond metropolitan borders and, more importantly, beyond national borders. In other words, *Tokyo mondai,* the "Tokyo issue," is rapidly becoming the concern of people outside Japan.

The problem takes shape from the serious distortions that exist in Tokyo. These manifest themselves, I would suggest, in a deterioration in living standards at the very time when the nation as a whole is becoming richer and more powerful than ever before. In the vacuum caused by a lack of serious public debate on what sort of city Tokyo should become, the commercial and administrative manipulators can chart out their own strategy, which rests on the premise that whatever pronouncements are made in public, property prices must never be allowed to fall, and on a refusal to tamper with the complicated regulatory environment, claiming that to do so would be to infringe personal rights.

Pious comments from manipulators on high and a general exasperated wringing of hands among the public seem to be leading to acceptance of what should be an unacceptable situation. Clusters of new high-rise developments are being undertaken in various parts of the city: in Tsukudajima, Ōjima, Ueno, Akasaka, and elsewhere. Most of these are a mixture of offices, shops, and apartments. Given their central location, the apartments tend to be very expensive, far beyond the range of the ordinary household. The main roads connecting these and the existing high-rise clusters are now lined with pencil buildings, eight- to ten-story, wobbly, windy structures that afford room only for hole-in-the-wall offices and apartments, and often expensive ones at that. Houses in the back streets are giving way to three-story tiled apartment buildings with bizarre, magpie names and comical archways. The whole visage of residential Tokyo is being redrawn in the design rooms of the estate agents, the new arbiters of the city's face. For those without land, Tokyo offers little hope except something "smart" and high and no less cramped than what it replaced. For those with land, Tokyo offers little peace: the pressure to use one's home as a commercial investment is great and inheritance tax is murderous for some.

Now, in the summer of 1988, the explosion in property prices of 1986 and 1987 has fizzled out. But it would be wrong if Tokyo fell back into old habits of unthinking expansion. What is needed is less redevelopment, not more. Such a policy of suppression would require careful control by people who genuinely care more for the individuals living in the city than they do for the business corporations that claim they best represent collective interests. It needs a less patronizing attitude on the one hand and a more engaged one on the other. Above all, it requires a more disinterested approach from all.

A historical introduction to Tokyo, which is what I hope this book to be, might not seem like the best place for a *cri du coeur* about planning policies in the modern city. But Tokyo's dynamism makes it all too easy to consider the problems of the present without putting them in the context of the city's historical development. It is easy to forget that housing conditions have always been exceptionally cramped in the city. It is easy to forget, too, the receptacle nature of Tokyo and before it Edo, its function as a physical, not a spiritual, home, that role being played by the *furusato*, the hometown. Nor should we forget that, for the first time ever, a substantial proportion of Tokyo's inhabitants were born in the city.

These younger generations have different requirements. Perhaps it is in part a result of their concerns that, even as so many people despair at the state of the property market, the last few years have seen such a welter of writings on the city. The momentum had already started when, a few years ago, I wrote *Tokyo Now and Then*. I trust that, despite all that has been written in the meantime, there is still something left to say.

A Morning View of Nihombashi under Snow. This and the following illustrations are taken from Hiroshige's woodblock print series *One Hundred Views of Famous Places in Edo* (1856-58).

Tōri 1-chōme in Nihombashi. These stores belong to wealthy dealers in cotton goods.

The Site of the Gate at Teppōsu Tsukiji. The temple roof behind
the entrance to the Edo quays is that of Tsukiji Honganji.

Ryōgoku Bridge and the Riverside. Some of the Ryōgoku streetside entertainers' stalls are in the foreground.

Shitaya Broadway. Matsuzakaya is on the
right, Ueno hill in the background.

Ōji Inari Shrine. The twin peaks of Mount Tsukuba were invariably shown in views from the northern part of Edo.

The Hashiba Ferry and Tile Kilns along the Sumida River.
On the far bank are the cherry trees of Mukōjima.

The Paulownia Plantation at Akasaka. On the
hill to the left stood the Sannō Hie Shrine.

TOKYO

1
From Edo to Tokyo

Tokyo is a difficult city to get to know. It hides its secrets in temple graveyards, down tortuous lanes, and in the backyards of factories. It is not a beautiful city. Its buildings are modern, put up by people who have given a lot of thought to cutting costs and very little to good looks. Two disasters that destroyed most of the city in the first half of the twentieth century are sometimes put forward as explanations for the prevailing architectural bleakness, but it is unlikely that very many old buildings would still be standing even if there had been no earthquake and no air raids.

"Ah, you see," people protest, "but wooden houses are not made to last long. How could they be?" True, and yet there are plenty of ways of constructing something presentable in materials other than wood. "Tokyo is such a crowded city," they continue. "It is no good any more building long, rambling houses that adhere to traditional lines. There are far too many people to house, to find work for, to feed, and to clothe."

People—now we're getting somewhere. Tokyo is a city not of buildings but of people, and not so much of great, farsighted individuals who left their stamp on the city's appearance and its culture, but of people living out their lives in the countless different ways that people have of living out their lives. Tokyo is, therefore, as much a city of stories as a city of sites. The stories are seldom tales of heroic deeds carried out by men and women of destiny. They are quiet, whimsical vignettes, anecdotes that follow a logic of their own, divorced from the straight, angular lines of Fact and Verisimilitude. They are stories that have accumulated like dust on the leaf of a plant, like lichen on a garden rock. They reflect a delight in whimsy and quirkiness and a love and a respect for places that are and things that exist precisely because they are and because they exist. The people of Tokyo have not lost their native appreciation for the natural order and their feeling of spiritual affinity with all things animate and inanimate.

The Japanese sense of urban living is different from that prevalent in the West. It does not recognize our polarities of town and country, of the wicked pleasures and pollution of the city set against the spiritual and natural purity of the countryside. This is why it took the Japanese so long to cotton on to the Western concept of an urban park as a fenced-off home for nature in the city and why there are still far fewer parks in Tokyo than in most large Western cities. This is also why Tokyo, or at least the more traditional parts of the city, has such a profusion of vegetation, of potted plants growing in all the narrowest and most precipitous of places. The city of Tokyo adheres much more closely to the rhythms of nature than Western cities do.

Cities, however, are social places. It is all very well to follow the natural spirit and order of things, but it might not go over very well with the next-door neighbor. Cities need a structure if people are to live harmoniously together. And capital cities require not only a social structure but also a governmental network. Herein lies the dynamic of Tokyo. Over the centuries, men and clans and factions have moved east—from Mikawa near Nagoya in the case of the Tokugawa, and from the far-flung provinces of the south and west in the case of the men and their factions who took over the city and the country after the fall of the shoguns. Ever since Ieyasu, the first Tokugawa shogun, made this his capital city and the military hub of the nation, Tokyo—or Edo, as it was called before 1868—has had imposed on it the plans and the culture of the rulers of the country to a much greater degree than is common among capital cities.

So it is that the city has been, ever since it was born, the scene of a dialogue, a debate, and occasionally a struggle between its rulers, who have wanted to impose on it their ideals and their way of life, and the natives, who want to let things be as they have always been, accordance with the natural laws. But "native" is a relative term in a city as young as Edo/Tokyo, a city where the flow of immigrants, and sometimes of emigrants, has been so swift.

It was inevitable, really, that immigrants would come in large numbers and settle in the eight provinces of eastern Japan, in the flatlands known as the Kantō Plain. Not only is this the largest of Japan's three principal alluvial plains, it is also farthest from the likely direction taken by a potential invader from the continent; it contains the largest expanse of fertile, well-irrigated rice land; and it is good country for the exercise of horses, an important factor in the rise of the warriors of the east. That Edo of all the towns and villages of the eight provinces should have become the site of the chief city in the east would have been less easy to predict. It had certain advantages. It stood at the entrance to the plain for anyone traveling along the sea road to the north of the country. Its five ridges that stretched like fingers from the hills of Tama and the Musashi grasslands to the waters of the bay were just about the last tracts of elevated ground that the traveler passed before entering the Kantō Plain proper. And it stood conveniently close to several mouths of the Tone River, the greatest river of the east, whose many tributaries and courses served as vital transport arteries.

These no doubt were among the considerations that led a junior member of the Taira clan who had settled in Chichibu to build himself a house and fortified compound here by the mouths of these rivers in the latter part of the twelfth century. He named his family Edo, Mouth of the River, after the location of his house. There is some disagreement about the actual situation of the Edo homestead, but it is generally believed to have been built on the central one of the five ridges. Despite his Taira descent, Edo Shigenaga was well disposed to aiding Minamoto no Yoritomo in his attempts to defeat the Taira family and establish the Minamoto as military overlords of the country. After Shigenaga's death, the Edo family expanded its territory, but it split up, with different sons taking on the names of the localities where they held land. Among these names we find Shibuya, Maruko, and Ikura, names that have survived to this day.

In the next few centuries the land by the bay where Edo Shigenaga had built his house became, it is thought, part of the estates of the wealthy Hie Shrine near Kyoto. At any rate, little is heard of the place until a man by the name of Ōta Dōkan built a castle there in 1457 (see map on page 254). At this time two contending representatives of the Ashikaga shogun in Kyoto both claimed dominion over the eight provinces. One of the two controlled the five easternmost of the provinces (Awa, Kazusa, Shimōsa, Hitachi, and Shimozuke). The other claimed control of provinces in the west of Kantō (Kōzuke, Musashi, and Sagami). In both cases, however, their control was only nominal. The provinces of Musashi and Sagami were under the sway of the powerful Uesugi family, which itself had splintered into rival branches.

It was in these confused and fluid circumstances that Dōkan built his castle at Edo. The site had the additional advantage for him that it lay in the front line of Uesugi fortifications, near the border between the land of the two claimants to the position of shogunal representative. Dōkan's castle consisted of three fortresses, and in the principal one was situated his own residence. What little we know about the castle derives principally from the descriptions of poets who stayed there on occasion, seeking refuge from the wars that were afflicting Kyoto and the home provinces. Dōkan himself was a poet and a man of taste and culture, and he has become over the centuries something of a legendary figure, the wise and prescient founder of the city. He is also the subject of one celebrated story, so celebrated indeed that many parts of the modern city claim it as their own. While out on a hunting trip one spring day, he was caught by a cloudburst and repaired to a nearby hut to ask for a straw raincoat. A beautiful young peasant woman appeared at the door, and, instead of giving him what he had asked for, she offered him one yellow rose. Mystified, he left, and, soaked to the skin, returned to his castle. Still puzzled, he asked one of his advisers, who told him what he should have known all along, that the allusion was to a poem by Prince Kemmei from a Heian-period anthology:

> Sad indeed am I
> That I have not one straw raincoat
> Like the seven-petaled, eight-petaled
> Blossom of a yellow rose.

Dōkan swallowed his pride, and resolved from that day to dedicate himself to the study of poetry.

As well as his achievements in poetry, Ōta Dōkan was an extremely able military strategist and administrator. In his castle he built a drill ground for his small conscript army, which was given training in archery and other military techniques. That he was able to do this suggests that he raised levies on goods in transit at the mouth of the river. Dōkan was murdered in 1486 at the command of his own lord, head of one of the branches of the Uesugi family, who was suspicious and jealous of his vassal.

Although Dōkan's stronghold was occupied for most of the next hundred years, when the Hōjō family held power in the eight provinces, its importance was eclipsed by Odawara Castle in Sagami, the Hōjō headquarters.

The Hōjō unwisely attempted to resist the all-conquering Toyotomi Hideyoshi. In 1590 Hideyoshi laid siege to Odawara, a siege that was brought a swift and successful conclusion. He now offered the Hōjō territory, the eight provinces of the east, to his most powerful ally (and therefore his most powerful potential adversary), Tokugawa Ieyasu, whose father, Matsudaira Hirotada, had been lord of Okazaki Castle in the province of Mikawa (Aichi Prefecture). Through a mixture of cunning and patience Ieyasu had won control of the three strategic provinces that lay astride the East Sea Road from Kyoto to the east—Mikawa, Tōtōmi, and Suruga (the latter two in modern Shizuoka Prefecture).

When Hideyoshi offered him the eight provinces of the east in exchange for his strategic domain along the East Sea Road, Ieyasu's senior retainers all spoke out against the move. They thought Hideyoshi was shunting them into a siding. Furthermore, Hideyoshi had suggested that Edo would make a better site for a castle than Odawara, and Ieyasu had agreed, much to their surprise and dismay. It is not hard to see their point. Edo, with its tiny strip of land between the hills and the sea, had only very limited room for expansion. In front of it were the swamps of the coast of the bay, behind it stretched the hostile and unproductive Musashi Plain, good for rearing horses but not much else. In addition, despite all the rivers, there was an insufficiency of natural spring water. Ieyasu saw things differently. The marshy coastline might make mooring a problem, but Edo was still preferable to an ocean port, both for military and natural reasons. It was far less susceptible to storms than Odawara, say, or Kamakura and, standing at the top of a bay with a narrow mouth, it would be easy to defend. It stood at the point where the road to the mountain province of Kai (the Kōshū Kaidō) branched off from the main road from Kyoto to the east and north. This was a further advantage.

It is easy to look back with the wisdom of hindsight and praise

Ieyasu for his foresight, but at the time it was certainly a gamble. It was a gamble taken in the knowledge that the various disadvantages could be overcome as a result of the great advances made in engineering in the last few decades. Ieyasu made his formal entry into the little town that was to become the nation's military capital on the first day of the Eighth Month of 1590, and he had his retainers at work on construction projects straightaway—on the construction of a fortress, of a moat to its main gate, of a canal from the nearby salt flats around the bay, and of a conduit for the city's drinking water.

Together with his senior vassals and his skilled surveyors and engineers, he devised an ingenious form of defense for his castle. The plan involved not a conventional moat around the fortress but a long swirl of moats that wound round the boundaries of his town ever inwards, with the main fortress of the castle inside the innermost ring. Because part of this system used existing waterways, it was not quite as graphic as it sounds. Nevertheless, the basic plan—from Asakusabashi round via Yotsuya Gate, Toranomon, Sukiya and Tokiwa gates, and on into the castle grounds—can still be quite easily traced today. Gates and bridges with lookout towers (*mitsuke*), of which there were thirty-six, stood where roads into and out of the city crossed the moats. In the center of this maze stood the castle, which itself was composed of several fortresses, with the keep and principal fortress in the middle.

Part of this plan for the defense of the castle involved the disposition of the houses of the feudal lords (*daimyō*, or "great names"). The feudal lords were men whose land holdings exceeded an area assessed at 10,000 *koku* (50,000 bushels) of rice a year. (The Tokugawa were feudal lords themselves and had holdings of over 2.4 million *koku*.) There were a little over two hundred feudal lords throughout the country. Ieyasu divided them into two groups: the *fudai daimyō*, "dependent lords," who had fought on his side in the final showdown with the Toyotomi forces at the Battle of Sekigahara in 1600; and the *tozama daimyō*, "outside lords," who had taken sides against him. Perhaps as a result of his own experience as a hostage when he was a child, Ieyasu decided to have the lords spend a certain amount of the time in Edo, with their wives and children remaining in the city on a permanent basis. This meant the construction of houses where they could stay. Ieyasu leased them land, and he did it in a way that fit in with his system of moats. Those nearest to the main gate of his castle were his own chief vassals and the dependent lords (in modern Ōtemachi and Marunouchi), while a little further round the swirl (in Hibiya and Kasumigaseki), the outside lords were given land (see map on page 255). In these early days of the city, the houses of the feudal lords were grand and beautiful buildings in the sumptuous Momoyama style. The decoration on the gates and the gables on the roofs was like that on the buildings of Tōshōgū, the shrine to Ieyasu in Ueno, or the nearby Nezu Shrine. The gardens, too, were large and elaborate, as can be seen today in the garden of the lords of Mito, Kōrakuen.

Not all the feudal lords were in Edo at the same time. The outside lords had their commuting season in the Fourth Month, with about half arriving for the following year and half returning to their domains. The dependent lords commuted in the Eighth Month, while the lords whose domains lay within the eight provinces spent six months in Edo and the rest of the year at home. They all brought with them a retinue, often quite large, of both higher-ranking and lower-ranking samurai retainers.

Even with the lords in Edo, a close watch had to be kept on them, and for this purpose the office of censor was created. The censors reported back to the shogun or his "cabinet," which consisted of a grand councillor, four or five councillors of state (both ranks chosen from among families like the Ii and Sakai, who had followed Ieyasu from their home province to Edo), and five assistants to the councillors. All these officers worked according to a rotation system. Some way under them, in the strict hierarchy of the shogun's government, came the two city commissioners, or magistrates. The magistrates were, in a very approximate sense, mayors of the city, and they had a good number of deputies working under then. They were chosen from among the shogun's own retainers and were therefore samurai, members of the military class, although it was only over the townspeople that they had jurisdiction. Whenever it was necessary, they could rely on the cooperation of the three families of the townsman (chōnin) class who had followed Ieyasu to Edo from Mikawa. Taruya, Naraya, and Kitamura were their names, and they settled in the center of the townspeople's part of the new city, in Honchō 2-, 1-, and 3-chōme, respectively. Under them came the nanushi, "district chiefs." This, too, was a hereditary title, and it involved looking after the interest of the inhabitants of anywhere from five to eight quarters (machi or chō).

When Ieyasu founded his new capital, the town at the foot of Ōta Dōkan's old fort was small and rudimentary. But townspeople soon arrived from various parts of the country to provide services and goods for the shogun, the feudal lords, and the other members of the military class (for it must not be forgotten that this was a feudal society, with its own classes and division of labor). The merchants and craftsmen, the two classes that together made up the townspeople, were accommodated mainly along a stretch of land, most of it reclaimed from the sea, between the castle and the coast. The merchants congregated around Nihombashi and along the waterways of the port in the immediate vicinity of the bridge. Many of them came from Ise and Ōmi in central Japan, and not a few of them managed soon to acquire considerable wealth. The craftsmen for the most part inhabited the districts to the north of Nihombashi in Kanda and to the south in Kyōbashi. The original idea was that each quarter should be inhabited by craftsmen engaged in the same occupation. Traces of this system can still be seen in some of the district names in Kanda: Kon'yachō, "Quarter of Dyers," and Kajichō, "Quarter of Smiths." Other districts belonged to plasterers, carpenters, lacquerers, and candlestick makers. Each of these quarters had a gate at the entrance, which was closed at night, and a little guardhouse. Various duties of the quarter, such as manning the guardhouse and putting up notices, would be carried out by one of the five members of the district's neighborhood association.

This was, as it were, the city in theory. In practice, the various quarters soon lost their exclusive identity in the townspeople's part of town, and in the military districts outside lords soon found they had dependent lords as next-door neighbors and vice versa. The original plan had to be severely modified after the Furisode ("Long-Sleeves") Fire of 1657, also known as the Great Meireki Fire. This was less one fire than a whole series of conflagrations that raged for three days, blown about willy-nilly by gale-force winds. At least a quarter of the four hundred thousand inhabitants of Edo died in the flames, and most of the city's buildings, including the castle keep, were burnt to ashes.

For eighty days there had been no rain. From the first night of the new year, the third year of Meireki, 1657, nine years before the Great Fire of London, the bells had rung warning of fire. They had rung every night, and the inhabitants of this new city, which within a little over half a century had grown to be even larger than the emperor's capital, Kyoto, had spent seventeen restless nights. On the night of the eighteenth, gusts of wind were blowing, depositing an indiscriminate layer of dust and sand on people and buildings. In these circumstances, fire might have started anywhere. In fact, the first flames rose from Hommyōji in Hongō. The fierce northwesterly winds blew the flames south and east through Yushima and Kanda as far as Ginza, and then across the river to Fukagawa. Nothing stood in their way. Frail wooden houses were covered with invitingly combustible thatched roofs, and the only firefighters in the whole of the city were those organized for their private protection by powerful lords like the Maeda of Kaga. One of the tragedies within the catastrophe that was unfolding occurred when the keepers of the Asakusabashi Gate misunderstood a message that had been passed on to them concerning the inmates of the city's prison at nearby Kodemmachō. The prisoners had in fact given an assurance (and all who lived were true to their word) to rendezvous at a certain temple, and this was the message conveyed. However, for some reason lost in the fog of history and the heat of the fire, it was taken to mean that the prisoners had escaped and were on the rampage. The gate was kept firmly closed. Over twenty thousand people died in the stampede and the crush at the unyielding gates. The Kanda River, whose course had been carved out of the land not many years earlier, was piled so high with corpses that it appeared just like dry land. If the gate had been opened, the crowd could have fled across the bridge. But then where would they have gone? The nearby Sumida at this time had no bridges, and thousands more died attempting to swim to safety.

The day after that, gale-force winds were still blowing, and a new fire broke out, in one of the houses of the keepers of the shogun's falcons outside Denzūin in Koishikawa. Once again, the flames spread quickly: past Tayasu and Tokiwabashi gates to the mansions of the feudal lords in Marunouchi. From here the fire wound its wicked way into the shogun's castle, where it claimed its most vaunted of victims, the castle keep. The following night, a third fire broke out, in Kōjimachi, west of the castle, burning to cinders the magnificent Momoyama-style palaces of Sakurada and then moving on to Hibiya, Shiba, and finally Shibaura by the sea. The result of this terrible conflagration: three-quarters of the new city destroyed; roughly 108,000 people killed; most of the castle, over 500 of the mansions of the feudal lords, nearly 800 houses of the shogun's retainers, and 350 temples and shrines razed to the ground; and almost all the popular quarters were a ruin of smoldering timber.

The next day it snowed, and the survivors huddled under straw mats, afraid to light a fire even though there was nothing left to burn. Many died of cold and starvation. Nevertheless, the authorities were prompt in enacting relief measures, including the distribution of rice from the shogun's granaries. When it came to reconstructing the city, the complicated system conceived as a defense for the castle was to a large extent abandoned. It was no longer necessary. Instead, precedence was given to fire precautions, for that was where the danger now lay. First, the castle must be protected from fire. This was accomplished, among other things, by the creation of a firebreak on the land that lay directly to the north and west of the castle. Secondly, the size of the city was expanded to relieve the overcrowding. This was effected in part through the displacement of temples and shrines, a move that is still reflected in the modern city. Honganji was moved out of crowded Bakurochō to newly reclaimed land east of Ginza; Reiganji was moved out to Fukagawa; and other temples were moved to Fukagawa, Asakusa, Yanaka, Yushima, Hongō, Ushigome, Yotsuya, Azabu, and Shiba. And that is why, to this day, there are so many temples in these areas. Thirdly, swamps and ponds in Koishikawa and Ushigome were filled in; land was reclaimed from the sea, chiefly east of Ginza, in Tsukiji; the areas east of the Sumida River, Fukagawa and Honjo, were developed; and a bridge, Ryōgokubashi, was built to link them to the main body of the city. In addition, a long embankment, over seven meters high, was built along the Kanda River on top of which pine trees were planted, and a number of firebreaks were created—in Ueno and Asakusa, and by Sujikaibashi Gate—with whole districts being removed to make room.

Last, the configuration of the residences of the feudal lords was considerably altered. Land was made available for them on the outside of the outer moats on which to build their secondary residences, and most of them built an additional, third compound. The second of the three was for their children and womenfolk and for their own recreation. The third was either situated along a waterway and used for storing all of the goods needed to maintain the other two and their inhabitants, or it was a villa in the city's outer suburbs, a country retreat and at the same time a place to repair to if fire destroyed the main residence. However, in return for this greater latitude in the number of residences allowed, strict regulations controlled and limited the size and appearance of the buildings. Gone were the magnificent Momoyama palaces of before the fire, uncomfortable reminders of the suppressed ambitions of powerful families that had been defeated not so long ago. The new residences were stern, austere buildings with a surrounding wall formed by the quarters of the lords' retainers. Only the garden was spared from these restrictions, although it, too, was informed by the spirit of restraint. Edo Castle itself was rebuilt with less of the lavish decoration that had characterized it before, and the keep was never rebuilt at all.

The reconstruction of Edo was followed by a period of consolidation, leading up to the rule of the "dog shogun," to the Genroku era, and to the first flowering of culture in Edo. The much-maligned fifth shogun, Tsunayoshi, distressed at his inability to produce an heir, thought this must be punishment for sins committed in an earlier life. He was born in the year of the dog, and so he ordered that dogs should be given special consideration and should be referred to with respect. He built a compound for strays and decreed that anyone found killing a dog should themselves be sentenced to death. At the same time he adopted measures to improve the quality of life for the human inhabitants of the city. He was much under the aura of his mother, who was a compulsive founder of temples. A large part of Tsunayoshi's rule as shogun coincided with the Genroku era, 1688 to 1704, a period of great cultural activity, much of which was centered in Osaka and Kyoto. Edo had still to develop a distinctive culture of its own.

It took the administrators time to catch up with the city's expansion. Not until the second decade of the eighteenth century were the area east of the river and the suburbs like Asakusa, Yotsuya, Akasaka, and Azabu brought within the administrative jurisdiction of the city magistrates. This was one of the measures carried out by Yoshimune, the "falcon shogun," and his wise assistant, Ōoka Tadasuke, most celebrated of all Edo's magistrates. Together, these two men introduced a number of reforms that made Edo a safer and more tolerable city, the last successful, large-scale reforms until the fall of the Tokugawa. They addressed themselves first to the "flowers of Edo," the city's greatest scourge, its fires. There were no fewer than ninety-seven major conflagrations between 1603 and 1868, and an inhabitant of one of the crowded townspeople's quarters would consider it highly unusual if two consecutive years passed without his being driven out of house and home at least once by fire.

The number of fires and the damage they wrought was something that invariably impressed foreign visitors to the city during the last years of Edo and the first of Tokyo. In the middle of the nineteenth century, Sir Rutherford Alcock, first British minister to Japan, had this to say on the subject: "It is impossible to ride through the streets of Yeddo without noticing one of the most striking and constant features of the city, no matter what the season of the year—large gaps where charred timber and rubbish mark the scene of a recent fire.... It is certainly very rare that the night passes without the fire bell of the quarter ringing a fearful alarm, and rousing all the neighborhood."[1] Two objects are needed, before anything else, to fight a fire: water and men. Of the first there seems always to have been a lack. But of the second, Alcock writes that there was "an elaborate and apparently well-organized system of fire brigades, which are formed of a large number of the able-bodied in every ward."

The man responsible for this "well-organized system of fire brigades" was the magistrate Ōoka. He created a system of forty-eight brigades for the townspeople's quarters, each one of which was given its own syllable in the native Japanese syllabary—with the characters for "hundred," "thousand," "ten thousand," and "book" in place of the uneuphonious or semantically inappropriate *he, ra, hi,* and *n.* He had watchtowers erected in each quarter and equipment installed in the district guardhouse. From then on the brave city firemen, the *tobi,* became the cynosure of the citizens of Edo, the embodiment of flair and derring-do, who inspired storytellers and playwrights and starry-eyed children.

Fires and the firemen were a part of Edo culture, the culture of the townspeople's part of the city. Each of the blocks of the townspeople's quarters had originally been laid out to a prescribed size, about 120 meters square. The main city streets were to be 18 meters wide, and the streets running off them, 12 meters. The area in the middle of each block was to be kept open and free from encumbrance. In the city's early years, these measurements and regulations were adhered to, as best as geography permitted. However, from the last decades of the seventeenth century, when Edo began to prosper and the influx of people went on increasing, it was no longer possible to preserve the open space behind the houses of each block. Ramshackle tenement huts began appearing, and before long there was scarcely an open space left in the central townspeople's districts of Kanda, Nihombashi, and Kyōbashi.

These back streets were slums. Their tenement houses, normally one story high, were known as *ura nagaya,* "rear long-houses." The alleys on which they fronted were often less than a meter wide, with a drain running down the middle. The houses themselves consisted typically of a three-meter frontage on the alley and a small kitchen leading into a four-and-a-half tatami mat room (nine square meters). And that was all. The toilet was communal. The residents of the long-houses were often single men, or men who had left their family behind in the country—clerks in the great shops of Nihombashi, day laborers, litter-bearers, tinkers, hawkers, mendicant entertainers and sometimes mendicant priests, the occasional masterless samurai, and all the riffraff of the city. But among them, too, were many families, Edo precursors of the modern "nuclear family." Women being in the minority, especially in Edo's back-street slums, they were accorded much more respect than they were elsewhere at the time. So much so, indeed, that a special term was coined to describe this unusual state of affairs: *kaka-denka,* "rule of the missus."

The houses of the townspeople's quarters belonged to three different structural categories. The most rudimentary of the three were those built entirely of wood, which included almost all of the long-houses. Weatherboarding formed the walls of these houses, which have not entirely disappeared from the streets of Tokyo (although the ones we see now are of more recent construction). The sturdiest, and the smartest, of the three styles were the houses built of thick earthen walls. These were the houses with a frontage on the main streets of the city. They were two stories high, fire resistant, and had roofs covered with a special light form of tile whose use was promoted by Ōoka. Their stucco walls were painted a lustrous black. Unlike the long-houses, they were owned by their occupants. These were normally wealthy merchants and shopkeepers or craftsmen working on commission for the shogunate who, unlike their poorer neighbors, had to pay tax in kind or in cash. The middle category of structural style was a type of house that was semi fire resistant, being built of lath and plaster. This type of house was to be found both on main streets and on side streets. The occupants normally owned the house but not the land it stood on, unlike the residents of the lustrous black stucco houses, who owned both land and house. They, too, tended to paint their houses black (the paint was made from the ash of burnt oyster shells, lime, and India ink), and so the townspeople's quarters had an eerie but elegant black sheen.

"*Edo wa tenka no hakidamari*" ("Edo is the nation's rubbish heap"). Such was said of the shogun's capital. Edo had grown from almost nothing at the beginning of the seventeenth century to a city the equal of Kyoto and Osaka by the middle of that century. But by the 1720s, despite all the fires, it had left its rivals far behind and had become the most populous city in the world. Thereafter, its population was stable at about 1.3 million. London's, on the other hand, stood at 850,000 in 1801 and rose dramatically to exceed Edo's by the middle of the nineteenth century.

It was no easy job compiling the Edo census. In the case of the townspeople, one particular problem was posed by the 60,000 shopkeepers and tradesmen who lived outside the townspeople's districts in the grounds of temples and shrines. Including them and the 10,000 inhabitants of the licensed quarter at Yoshiwara and the 25,000 or so social outcasts in the city, the number of townspeople residents of Edo stood at about 600,000. This was almost half the city's population, crowded into only 16 percent of its area. It represented a population density of 69,000 people per square kilometer, which compares with 22,000 in Toshima Ward, the most densely inhabited part of the modern city. Life was much more comfortable for the military classes. Here, too, an accurate calculation of the population was difficult, but somewhere either side of 600,000 is the normally accepted figure. They were spread over 69 percent of the city's area, which represented a population density of 14,000 per square kilometer, a little more than the 10,000 per square kilometer of modern Minato Ward. The temples and shrines, most of which were in the suburbs, had a population density of 4,500 per square kilometer, almost the same as that of a modern suburb of Tokyo, Tama City.[2]

The imbalance of the sexes gradually lessened during the second half of the eighteenth and first half of the nineteenth centuries (from almost two men to one woman in 1733 to ten men to nine women in 1845). The proportion of the townspeople resident in the city who were born there stood at 76 percent in 1832, but if one applied the traditional criterion for distinguishing the Edokko, "Child of Edo"— that is to say, residence in the city over three generations—then only about 10 percent of the townspeople, some 60,000 souls, qualified. Nevertheless, the city had developed its own peculiar ethos.

About this ethos, this culture of the Edokko, academics in modern times have written monographs, essays, books, and all manner of lucubrations. They have compiled complicated equations to prove that penury + style + Buddhist world view = mystique of Edokko culture. The whole business of the Edokko badly needs rescuing from the fustian research of the academics and the antiquarian mentality of the sentimentalists. For it is undoubtedly true that a special approach to life developed in Edo among the townspeople, an approach that was based inevitably on the bedrock of communal living in the back-street slums. It was nourished by the city-dweller's sense of style (*iki*) and chic (*sui*), and his wit, which expressed itself in a love of comic verse, whether whimsical, satirical, or downright ribald. And it was starved and then again replenished by the Edokko's proverbial and endemic inability to hold onto his money from one day to the next.

On those mornings when he did have some money left over from the night before, the Child of Edo would go for a wash and a soak in the public bathhouse (of which he had 523 to choose from in 1810). There he might well find himself taking a bath in the company of his women neighbors (mixed baths were banned, without much effect, by the prurient Matsudaira Sadanobu in 1791). From the bathhouse, he might make his way—always providing that his purse was well stocked—to one of the city's three officially licensed Kabuki theaters. Here the performances lasted all day, and he could chat with friends and drink and doze off. If he was planning to make a day of it, he might feel tempted to cross the river and indulge himself in one of the seven unlicensed quarters of Fukagawa. If, however, he had struck it lucky in one of the temple lotteries, or if he was a little wealthier than he had at first thought (the owner, perhaps, of one of the smart black houses on a main road), then the chances are he would choose to be entertained at the licensed quarter of Yoshiwara, in the paddy fields north of Asakusa.

He would most likely make the trip by boat, which he would board at the moorings near Asakusabashi Gate, and he would go in the company of his friends. There, in one of Yoshiwara's smarter houses, he and his fellows would be treated to music and jokes and dancing performed by the women of the quarter, and they would end up perhaps with a few party games, and so to bed—or back to the missus.

If anyone could be said to embody the spirit of Edo, then that person would surely be Karai Senryū, of whom we know little from contemporary documents but a lot from the sort of poetry he chose for his anthologies. So closely associated did he become with this form of poetry that it came eventually to be known by his own name. The great age of *senryū*, when the genre escaped farthest from the twin dangers of coarseness and overrefinement, was between 1757 and 1790, during which time anthologies of the seventeen-syllable verses selected by Karai Senryū were published. The son of a *nanushi,* or "district chief," from Asakusa, Karai Senryū did not write the verses himself, but he exercised his skill in shaping the art by selecting those verses that best expressed the humor inherent in Edo life. Verses like this are part of the poetry of the city:

> The flowering-plant market:
> A grasshopper chirps,
> All confused.[3]

When considering the world of the Edo townsman, one is struck by the importance given to the pursuit of pleasure. This was in part the consequence of wealth newly acquired in a semimercantile society wedded to a profound appreciation of the evanescence of all things in the "floating world," the *ukiyo.* A society informed by the ethos of living for the pleasure of the moment militates against the creation of art and literature with an abiding appeal. Nevertheless, in their depictions of the floating world, the artists of Edo gave life to scenes and people in prints (*ukiyo-e*) whose beauty has ensured their continued popularity. It was a happy coincidence of circumstances: that of the merchant desirous to act as patron or to make money through printing and publishing; that of the craftsman stimulated by technical developments into extending the fields of his talent; and that of an increasingly large, avid, and affluent public.

Another important ingredient in the flowering of the city's culture was the gradual blurring in class differences between the wealthier townsmen and the middle- and lower-ranking members of the military class, who were often forced by poverty into spurning the privilege of carrying two swords and into becoming simple townsmen. A classic case is that of the writer Takizawa Bakin, son of a minor retainer of a not very powerful lord, who married a shopkeeper and later lived off royalties. Toward the end of his life, in 1840, Bakin (reluctantly, as he was an unsociable man) threw a great party for eight hundred people in one of the pleasure houses of Yanagibashi. Among those invited were the scholar and painter Watanabe Kazan, the painter Tani Bunchō, the *ukiyo-e* artists Hokusai and Hiroshige, the popular writers Ryūtei Tanehiko and Tamenaga Shunsui, numerous publishers and booksellers, and several officials of the shogunate. It was just the sort of mixed gathering that one might expect in modern Tokyo, or London, or New York.

The shogunate as a rule was hostile to these developments. After a period of laxity and cultural freedom under the easygoing, corrupt, but economically stimulating rule of the councillor Tanuma Okitsugu in the 1770s and 1780s, there followed a sharp, chilly period of retrenchment and attempts to restore fiscal, cultural, and moral rectitude (all regarded as being much the same thing). This painful remedy (painful for writers like Santō Kyōden, who was manacled in his house for fifty days, and for publishers like Tsutaya Jūzaburō, who had half his property confiscated) was administered in 1790 by Matsudaira Sadanobu, statesman and scholar and unsuccessful reformer. Later, in 1843, after another period of cultural and economic laissez-faire, the whip was cracked once again, and this time the unlicensed quarters of Fukagawa and the licensed Kabuki troupes were among the victims.

By then, however, Edo society was in the grip of a disease— manifested in decadence, crime, disasters, and epidemics— that was to prove terminal. In 1854 and again in 1855, the city was rocked by powerful earthquakes, the second of which killed four thousand people and was followed by incessant downpours that flooded the low-lying parts of town. There was also a cholera epidemic, recalled many years later by the wife of Katsu Kaishū, a prominent official at the time of the shogunate's demise. "I was so anxious," she told Clara Whitney, who recorded the old woman's words in her diary. "Every night when all had retired I would take a candle and go the rounds, looking carefully into each face to see if there was any change. In the morning I was up first and went into each room, thankful to the goddess of mercy on finding that none of my large family...had fallen prey to that dreadful disease. Ah! Indeed it was terrible—a terrible time!"[4]

This concatenation of disasters was blamed by many on Commodore Perry and his Black Ships, which had arrived at the country's front door in the summer of 1853 and anchored at the mouth of the bay. Half a year later, he returned, and a treaty was signed, thereby officially ending a period of over two hundred years when Japan had been cut off from the rest of the world and when the only Westerners to set foot in Edo had been the Dutch traders during their quadrennial visits from the seclusion of their trading post off Nagasaki.

What struck the foreigners who made their way gingerly into Edo over the next fourteen years (apart from fires) was the city's greenness: "The capital itself," wrote Sir Rutherford Alcock, "though spreading over a circuit of some twenty miles, with probably a couple of millions of inhabitants, can boast what no capital in Europe can—the most charming rides, beginning even in its centre, and extending in every direction over wooded hills, through smiling valleys and shaded lanes, fringed with evergreens and magnificent timber."[5] The expanses of green were soon to increase, for in 1868 the shogunate fell, and the houses of the feudal lords were abandoned. The Meiji emperor moved into Edo in a formal procession and proclaimed that the city was henceforth to be known as Tokyo, the Eastern Capital. The chance had existed to return the capital to the west, to Kyoto or to Osaka, but it was decided that Edo's size, importance, and central position in the country made it the obvious choice.

One of the earliest measures the leaders of the Meiji government took bore a striking resemblance to the policy of the Tokugawa. They surrounded the castle, now the Imperial Palace, with government offices, army barracks, and parade grounds. Later, the military facilities were moved away, leaving gaping green spaces in the center of the city like the craters on the moon. In 1878, the emperor's new capital was divided into fifteen wards: Kōjimachi, Kanda, Nihombashi, Kyōbashi, Shiba, Azabu, Akasaka, Yotsuya, Ushigome, Koishikawa, Hongō, Shitaya, Asakusa, Honjo, and Fukagawa. Eleven years later, a new municipal entity, Tokyo City, was born as part of Tokyo Prefecture, but like Osaka and Kyoto, it was denied its own mayor and municipality. There were strong protests against this state of affairs, and in 1898 the government capitulated and granted the country's capital a mayor and a municipal office, where the metropolitan government's headquarters now stands, in Marunouchi 3-chōme.

In the meantime, great changes had been occurring in the city's transport network. Waterways had ceased to be the principal corridors of transportation. Roads had taken their place. Rickshaws suddenly appeared on the scene in tens of thousands, and for the wealthy there were horse-drawn carriages. The first regular form of public transport in the city (excluding the trains that had been carrying passengers between Yokohama and Shimbashi since 1872) was the horse-drawn bus, whose conductor's bugle was so well imitated by a comedian named Tachibanaya Entarō that it was named in his honor the Entarō Cart. In 1882 tracks were laid down from Shimbashi through Ginza over Nihombashi to Asakusa, although whether this was a help or a hindrance to the horses is unclear. The horses and rickshaw-pullers soon found themselves competing for space with bicycles, and then finally, in the first decade of the twentieth century, the tram appeared, soon to sweep all before it and occupy center stage until its sad decline in the 1960s. By then railways, overground and underground, had taken over not only as the chief conveyors of people but also as one of the main elements in people's lives—dominating principally their choice of a house or apartment.

Tokyo, the emperor's capital, has had a strange way of imitating in its development the conformation of Edo, the shogun's capital. Those parts of the city on either bank of the Sumida River, but particularly on the far bank where the poorer townspeople and the impecunious samurai lived, were the first parts of the city to attract factories and yards in the Meiji era. Housing conditions in these areas continued to be bad, as they had been under the shoguns. Later a second industrial zone appeared, stretching south along the banks of the bay from Tsukishima through Shibaura to Shinagawa. Big business moved into land at the palace gates, with the biggest business of all, Mitsubishi, leading the way. Asakusa was the kaleidoscopic center of the city's insatiable quest for diversion, but in the decades between the death of the Meiji emperor in 1911 and the declaration of war against the Allies it found itself an increasingly potent rival in Ginza, which was the first part of town to abandon wood for brick and was to remain flagbearer for the culture of the West.

In the years 1923 and 1945 two disasters occurred, roughly equal in their magnitude and in the number of victims they claimed, the like of which no other modern city has suffered in such close succession. The earthquake occurred at one minute and sixteen seconds before noon on 1 September 1923, when children were returning home for lunch after their beginning-of-term school ceremony. A typhoon had just passed out to sea north of Kyoto. The winds were strong and it was drizzling. The quake measured 7.9 on the Richter scale, and it was followed by over seventeen hundred after-tremors during the next three days. Fires broke out in several places in the low-lying districts (the old towns-people's quarters), and over the next three days they burnt their way through all the most crowded part of Tokyo on both banks of the river, destroying 20 to 30 percent of the city's houses. Most of the hundred thousand or so victims died not in the earthquake itself but in these fires that followed it. After the disaster, draconian plans were drafted, and a huge relief budget allocated, but the main change that occurred was, as it were, spontaneous. Many of the former residents of Shita-machi, the plebeian quarters, moved to higher ground, to Nakano, Shinjuku, and other parts of the expanding western suburbs. In 1932, as the culmination of a series of reforms that had seen the disappear-ance of many of the city's old place-names, twenty wards—including Edogawa, Adachi, Suginami, and Setagaya—were added to the original fifteen.

Tokyo paid heavily for the folly, the muleheadedness, the sheer wickedness of the country's military rulers. The atmosphere in the city during the war was an eerie one. It is captured by the correspondent for *Le Monde,* Robert Guillain: "Tokyo, which had never been a beautiful city, had now become a dirty city. The capital woke up each morning a little more sordid, as if tainted by the doom-laden night in which it had bathed.... The raids had still to begin, and yet, night after night, an obsession gripped the city plunged into darkness by the blackout, an obsession that debilitated and corroded it more than even the appearance overhead of the first enemy squadrons was able to do.... Tokyo was a giant village of wooden boards, and it knew it."[6] In the summer of 1944, Saipan fell to the advancing American troops. Tokyo was now within range of the B-29s. From January 1945 until the Japanese surrender in August, Tokyo was the victim of 102 raids, the worst one of which, on the nights of 9 and 10 March, destroyed almost half the city, including the areas that had been razed by the 1923 disaster. Again the number of casualties was hard to calculate but was reckoned to be around a hundred thousand.

This time no grand plan was devised to restructure the city. No one had the money or the energy. It was all people could do to scrape a living from one day to the next. Sweeping reforms occurred, however, in the city's administration and in its structure. In 1946 elections were held for the post of governor of what had become the metropolis of Tokyo, Tokyo-to. In the following year, the city's thirty-five wards became twenty-three. Of the fifteen old wards founded in 1878, the new Chiyoda Ward absorbed Kōjimachi and Kanda wards; Nihombashi and Kyōbashi became Chūō Ward; Shiba, Akasaka, and Azabu became Minato Ward; Yotsuya and Ushigome became a part of Shinjuku Ward; Koishikawa and Hongō made up the new Bunkyō Ward; Shitaya and Asakusa formed Taitō Ward; Honjo became a part of the new Sumida Ward; and Fukagawa, a part of Kōtō Ward. Later, direct elections were instituted to fill various ward posts.

The Tokyo Metropolitan Government functions as administrative overseer of Tokyo Prefecture, which stretches as far west as the Tama mountains and includes such satellite towns as Hachiōji and Tachikawa and the islands that reach down in two long strands to the south, the Izu and Ogasawara chains. It also serves as municipal organ for the twenty-three wards. It tackles all those affairs that need to be organized on a city-wide basis: fire, refuse, water, and the like, as well as construction projects, health insurance, and aid for small-scale enterprises. In 1978, the deficit in the budget of the metropolitan government stood at ¥101 billion, but ten years later, the picture was different. The budget was safely in the black, with 78 percent of revenues being provided by municipal taxes. Education and cultural facilities accounted for 18 percent of expenses in the draft 1988 budget, but only 4 percent each to new housing and the environment. Fourteen percent was earmarked for public works, 11 percent for police and fire, and 8 percent for social welfare and health insurance.

A large part of the deficit had been run up by arguably the city's most popular governor, Minobe Ryōkichi. Minobe was mayor for three terms, from 1967 to 1979. During his tenure of office, he introduced many necessary social reforms and was an especially effective supporter of improved facilities for the elderly. Before then, private enterprise had been given a relatively free hand. During the Korean War, when the citizens of Tokyo were anticipating more traumas, this time at the hands of rampant Communists, the rate of annual industrial production in the city more than tripled. In the following decade, the policy of putting growth and economic priorities first found concrete expression in the expressways that cast their shadow over so much of the city.

There has in the years since the war been yet another rationalization, so called, of the names of the city's districts, with the result that now there are very few districts (*machi* or *chō*) that are not subdivided into *chō* (written differently)—1-chōme, 2-chōme, and so on. The city's population has almost doubled since 1950, when it stood at 6.75 million, but in recent years it has been more or less steady. And there is, of course, the "doughnut phenomenon" to reckon with, according to which the daytime population of Chiyoda, Chūō, and Minato wards is six times higher than the population at night. The preponderance of tertiary industry is an important element in today's Tokyo. Sixty percent of industry in the city is tertiary, with bars and eating houses accounting for 30 percent of the outlets of the service industry. Printing and publishing stand out among other industries for their concentration in Tokyo.

Many of the inhabitants of the city who do not work in shops and restaurants commute every day to offices. However, to suggest that Tokyo is therefore a "middle-class" city in the way some Western cities are would be misleading. After all, 40 percent of houses and apartments have a floor space of under twenty-nine square meters, which is approximately the space covered by fifteen tatami mats. The city's inhabitants live in the modern Tokyo equivalent of the long-houses of Edo. The difference is one of degree, perhaps, rather than substance. What has changed, however, is where they live. The typical inhabitants of the modern city, if there are such persons, live not in the area that had once formed the townspeople's Edo, but in the hills to the west and to the south. They live as close as possible to one of the railway lines that link so smoothly nowadays with the subway network. So the city has completed its own sort of march from river to road to railway.

Rivers, roads, and railways—but above all people. This is modern Tokyo. A crazy profusion of people, and an apparently infinite capacity to absorb more. A vast pullulation, delighting in the sheer fun of intense activity.

2
Central Tokyo: Chiyoda Ward

The Imperial Palace

In Tokyo there is a story for everything, and of the founding of Edo Castle, on the hill where now the Imperial Palace stands, the following story is told. The goddess Benten, one of whose oldest shrines stands on the little island of Enoshima near Kamakura, guided Ōta Dōkan, wise and prescient constructor of the first Edo Castle, up the bay toward the spot she had chosen This she revealed through the medium of a fish, of a species known as *konoshiro,* which appeared out of the waters of the bay and dived through the air in front of the appointed hill. The goddess's message was quite clear, for *kono shiro,* written with different characters, means "this castle."

Ōta Dōkan fell victim to the machinations of his own lord. After his murder, in 1486, the castle lost its prominence and eventually fell into disrepair. When Tokugawa Ieyasu chose it as the site of his new headquarters in 1590, there can hardly have been a building still standing. Ieyasu was not deterred. The site offered him certain advantages, and it also answered the requirements of Chinese geomancy—more or less. To the east, in the direction of the green dragon, there must be a river. This there was, the Sumida River. To the south, in the direction of the red bird, there must be a pond—and there was, more or less, in the form of the waters of the bay. To the west, there should be a road, domain of the white tiger. The Tōkaidō filled this requirement. To the north, there should be a mountain, the domain of the black warrior (represented by a turtle and a snake). Mount Fuji answered this requirement more or less. Finally, the problem caused by the unwillingness of the topographical features to take up their allocated places (Mount Fuji, for example, lies to the west) was easily solved by placing the main gate, Ōte, in the east, instead of its proper position to the south. Thus, Mount Fuji fell to the "north," and the problem was solved.

If ever one was searching for an illustration of the difficulty of adapting Chinese concepts to Japanese soil, then Edo Castle provides it. The lofty geomantic Chinese vision, with its dragons and tigers, its sweeping river, towering mountains, and broad plain, was like a beached whale on Japan's cramped and steeply sloping terrain. Having cunningly contrived to propitiate the black warrior and the red bird, Ieyasu next set about devising a plan in harmony with the lay of the land to make the castle unassailable. The scheme he and his advisers hatched was the "*no*" plan, so named because it involved the construction of canals and moats and the use of existing rivers to form a continuous web of water like the whorls of a fingerprint, or like the Japanese character "*no*" (の). Improvised and sinuous, so different from the stately, square Chinese grand plan, these whorls were crossed by bridges, many of which still exist, and guarded by fortified gates. The two inner whorls of water enclosed the castle itself and its dependent buildings, which included the palaces of family members and the residences of collateral families and senior administrators.

The castle walls were built of granite and other types of volcanic rock, which were quarried from the cliffs of the Izu Peninsula, a full hundred kilometers down the coast. The largest rocks were given a boat to themselves for the journey to Edo, sometimes being suspended through a hole in the hull. Some three thousand ships were involved in this work, making the return journey to Izu an average of twice a month. Accidents were not rare, and in the worst of them 196 ships belonging to three powerful lords from Kyushu were lost in a storm. When the rocks reached Edo's port, they had to be hauled up to the site of the construction work. Oxcarts supplemented human muscle power on this last stretch, but the largest rocks were heaved along the streets by teams of a hundred and more men. The rock was placed on a primitive sort of sledge, and seaweed was laid out underneath its path to help the sledge slip along. The most remarkable feature of these processions was the troupe of entertainers—banging drums, blowing into conches, and dancing around in imitation of southern barbarians (that is, of Europeans)—who cheered the men on from their vantage point on top of each rock.

Where did Tokugawa Ieyasu find the enormous resources of men and money needed for a project of this magnitude? The answer is that it was all done for him. After Ieyasu's triumph over the troops from the west of Japan at the Battle of Sekigahara in 1600, all the most important feudal lords were determined to impress on him the extent of their support. The larger their holdings the more men they were able to send. Sometimes the haulage and construction work took on the appearance of a sporting contest, with each lord vying to outdo his rivals by having his men work harder and finish faster. Fights broke out, resulting in the imposition of strict rules of conduct: no gambling, no contact with men from other fiefs, and so on. The stakes were high, in terms of human life, too. When part of the wall they were building collapsed, over a hundred men supplied by Asano, lord of Tajima, were crushed to death. Seeing this, Katō Kiyomasa, the famous general who had led the Japanese invasion forces in Korea and who was himself noted for his skill as a constructor of castles, had his men cut down reeds from the wild plains west of the new castle and convey them to that part of the wall whose construction he was responsible for. He then rounded up all the children he could find and had them dance and play and jump on the reeds, which had been laid down like a carpet over the soggy topsoil. This ploy proved a great success in overcoming the problems posed by the unsuitable nature of the terrain.

The castle was built, burnt, and rebuilt, reduced and expanded, decorated, burnt again, and then redecorated. Finally, in 1640, fifty years on, it was complete—the largest and most magnificent castle in the land. Too good, indeed, to last; in 1657 nearly all the castle buildings were burnt to ashes in the Long-Sleeves Fire, and they had to be rebuilt once again. Like other large Japanese castles, Edo Castle consisted of various *maru,* or fortresses. There were four of them in Edo Castle, each one containing a group of buildings enclosed within fortifications contiguous with those of one of the others. In the center, on the highest ground, was the Hon Maru (the principal fortress), which included the halls where affairs of state were conducted, the shogun's own residence, and the inner chambers, where the shogun's ladies lived. At the foot of the Hon Maru was the Ni no Maru (the second fortress), with its gardens and teahouses, a palace for the shogun to retire to after stepping aside for his successor. To the southwest, on the site of the present palace, was Nishi no Maru (the western fortress), to which the shogun repaired when fire drove him out of his own quarters. To the north was Kita no Maru, now a park of the same name. All this was enclosed within and intersected by mighty stone revetments and walls, punctuated by a total of ninety-nine gates. At strategic points along the revetments were placed *yagura,* large watchtowers, twenty-one of them, of which three still stand. Between the watchtowers, there were *tamon,* long storehouses where munitions were kept. Of the twenty-eight original *tamon,* two can still be seen. This great fortified whorl of a castle encompassed an area of 1.8 square kilometers.

Not a flagstone nor a charred pillar, not a tile nor a tatami mat remains to help kindle our imagination and suggest what the buildings of the Hon Maru must have looked like. Detailed drawings and plans based on historical records show a concatenation of halls of a far greater complexity and intricacy than surviving castle buildings like those at Himeji. There were three groups of buildings in the Hon Maru. The first, situated in the southern part of the grounds, nearest Fujimi Tower, consisted of the halls where affairs of state were conducted and audiences with the shogun held. The largest of these halls, and the one most often used for public business, was the Ōhiroma, the Hall of a Thousand Mats. It was here that once every four years the head of the Dutch trading mission in Nagasaki paid obeisance to the shogun. "The whole ceremony [wrote warehouse-master Fischer about the audience granted in 1822] consists in making the Japanese compliment upon the appointed spot, and remaining for some seconds with the head touching the mats, while the words *Capitan Holanda* are proclaimed aloud. A stillness as of death prevails, broken only by the buzzing sound made by the Japanese to express profound veneration."[1]

On those two days of the month, the first and the fifteenth, when all the feudal lords resident at that time in the city presented themselves at the castle, there was great congestion, and several of the main halls were used, including the White Study and the Black Study. Each lord was allotted a place in a certain hall, and woe betide him if he should move to a different spot. Beyond these halls were the rooms used by the secretaries to the councillors of state. Some of the secretaries exercised great power, and their in-tray was known as the "box of hell." Maybe it was for fear of the secretaries or maybe of the official censors, the *metsuke,* that when the councillors of state (*rōjū*) met in conference in a nearby hall they would converse on paper, writing down what they had to say with specially prepared magnolia-wood charcoal and then burning their comments afterwards. Intrigue and intrigue's bedfellow, paranoia, were rife.

Edo Castle cannot have been a happy place, and for no one less so that the shogun himself, whose personal rooms occupied the second group of buildings in the middle of the Hon Maru. From the moment his page woke him up with a "*Mō*"—"already" (time to get up)—at six o'clock in the morning, the shogun's activities for the day were strictly regulated. He ate a spartan breakfast during which his hair was set. The morning was given over to study (which normally meant long and often tedious lectures) and the martial arts, while the afternoon was dedicated to affairs of state. At last, come evening time, the shogun was able to abscond from his ritualized duties and disappear into the inner chambers, where, apart from his ladies' doctors and a few guards and officials, he was the only man allowed to enter. Even here among his own ladies, however, the shogun had to adhere closely to convention. (The Japanese have never subscribed to a system where he who holds power wields it.) At few times were the shoguns who succeeded the able Yoshimune (shogun from 1716 to 1745) capable either by temperament or talent of rising above the everyday circumstances of their life and impressing their will on those around them. Power came increasingly to reside in the hands of an official known as *gosoba yōnin,* "official in honorable attendance"—a chamberlain, in other words. The two most scandalously corrupt wielders of power in the last century or so of the shogunate, Tanuma Okitsugu and Mizuno Tadaakira, both started their careers as pages and went on to become chamberlains who acquired unrivaled power and wealth in no small measure by manipulating and currying favor with the shogun's ladies in the inner chambers.

The inner chambers made up the third, and indeed the largest, of the three sections of the Hon Maru. They occupied that part of the castle nearest the site of the keep and furthest from Fujimi Tower. What were they like, these inner chambers? In Japanese, they are called *ōoku,* the "large interior," not a very descriptive term. In English, we can follow George Sansom, be exotic, and call them the seraglio, or we can be coy and conservative and opt for the inner chambers, a term with fewer Byzantine connotations. In all, including even the lowliest servants and cooks (one rank of whom was called *oinu kodomo,* "honorable whelps"), there were between five hundred and one thousand women in the inner chambers. The most important person of them all was the shogun's wife, to whom profound respect was shown at all times. However, as in the outer apartments, so in the inner chambers: the shogun's wife seldom had occasion to exercise the power she held. This was particularly the case since all but the third shogun, Iemitsu, and the last shogun, Yoshinobu, were born to concubines. Procreation was the business of the inner chambers (business, not pleasure), and success was measured in those terms.

Power in the inner chambers was exercised by two ranks of aides, the *otoshiyori* and *jōrō,* most of whom had themselves once been concubines. Their power derived mainly from their role as sponsors of suitable bedmates for the shogun, who often had no more than a final veto on the matter. The concubines themselves belonged to a rank one notch down, that of *chūrō.* There were normally seven or eight *chūrō* "within reach," but the extravagantly debauched eleventh shogun, Ienari, had at least forty. In Ienari's day potential concubines seem to have been accepted from all quarters on presentation of a suitable gift, but it had once been the practice to select girls principally from the aristocracy of Kyoto. Girls from the imperial court were brought up in a highly refined, rather etiolated atmosphere and so did not always prove the best of child-bearers. They were not helped by two customs: first, they were to retire from their nuptial duties when they reached the age of thirty; the other was still more constricting—a second lady from the chambers was to remain in wakeful attendance beside the shogun and his partner for the night (but no peeping allowed, asserts one historian), and one of the senior ladies was to keep vigil in an adjacent room. Thus it could be ensured that no requests of a political nature were made to the shogun during his more susceptible moments.

It comes as little surprise to learn that the shogun soon began to spend longer in the bath, which he took in the company of a solitary female attendant. The resultant child was known as *oyudono no ko,* "child of the honorable bathroom." The shogun found himself forced by the senior ladies, however, to take baths on his own, and lesbianism became an increasingly common outlet for the frustrations of the concubines. Conditions, and standards, deteriorated rapidly in the nineteenth century. Political intrigue was rampant, and repeated attempts to cut the prodigal levels of spending all met with failure. The inner chambers abounded with stories of ghosts and strange happenings. These culminated in the disappearance, in 1854, of one of the higher-ranked ladies. Her body was found, still dripping blood, slung into a palanquin in one of the garages. The murderer was never apprehended. When the inner chambers were dissolved and their occupants disbanded in 1868, the secrets of the palace were never divulged.

Perhaps there was something appropriate in the location of the inner chambers, symbol of family perpetuation, immediately in front of the castle's keep. Largest in the country, the keep at Edo Castle was built and rebuilt three times. For seventeen short years, its golden roof-dolphins and glittering lead tiles towered over the fledgling city. Unlike the other buildings of the castle, which, during the last phase of construction between 1637 and 1640, had been given gorgeously and intricately decorated interiors designed and executed by the most famous artists and craftsmen in the land, including the Tokugawa "court" painter Kanō Tan'yū, the keep was left bare, its role being purely military. It soared eighty-four meters over the town and a full forty-four meters over the grounds of the Hon Maru. Like a pagoda, with which it had several points of architectural resemblance, it had five floors above ground. Beneath it, a cellar was built containing coffers and arms. All the other castle buildings had been plastered white. Only the keep was black. The other halls of the Hon Maru had roofs of gray tiles, austere and serene. Only the five-tiered roof of the keep glittered golden in the sun. The view of the castle from outside its walls must have been exceedingly beautiful: the massive stone walls with their white-plastered parapets, pine trees stretching their necks elegantly into view, waves of gray-tiled roofs rising layer on layer over the walls, and, soaring above them like a phoenix or like Mount Fuji, the castle keep.

The keep had been built using every possible defense against fire. To no avail. On the nineteenth day of the First Month of 1657, fires raged throughout the city. By the time the flames reached the castle they were of such a heat and intensity that they were creating whirlwinds, one of which blew open the windows of the keep. So fierce was the fire and so thorough its work that it melted the gold buried in the keep's cellar. The shogun escaped death in the flames by a whisker. The scenes of panic and terror were recorded by the son of one of the chief stonemasons. "We rushed into the castle to knock down some of the most fire-prone buildings, but no sooner were we about to leave again in the direction of Ōte than the fire seemed to have suddenly spread throughout the castle. All around us it grew darker and darker, and people were lighting lanterns to show them the way. About then, the gunpowder stored in the towers began to ignite, and the sound of the explosions rent heaven and earth. With a thunderous roar, the towers crashed burning to the ground. The sight of the flames flickering through the dense smoke was too terrible to describe."[2] The whole of the Hon Maru and the Ni no Maru was burnt to a cinder. Two years later, it had all been rebuilt. The base of the keep had been restored to its former appearance, and construction work on the main structure was about to begin when it was suggested to the shogun that the keep, as a symbol of raw military might, was inappropriate in a time of peace. So for the next two hundred years the solid stone base stood there naked behind the inner chambers.

Through its very success, Edo Castle soon made itself redundant. It was such a mighty conglomeration of buildings, its construction so galvanized the former enemies of the Tokugawa, the system of repression of which it formed the pivot was so effective that within a few decades of its completion it had outlived its military purpose. It became not a castle so much as a series of fortified palaces on a scale that can have had few parallels anywhere in the world. It was worthy of Edo, the world's largest city. So powerful was its appeal as symbol of a unified land that, despite its all but exclusive association with the much-derided Tokugawa regime, it was chosen in 1868 as the site of the new Imperial Palace, a choice whose wisdom the years continue to reveal. But the castle buildings themselves were a different matter.

Many had been burnt down in the last years of the shogunate, others succumbed to fire in 1872, still others were deemed no longer relevant to the new order and destroyed, so that little was allowed to remain of the old castle.

The new palace built for the emperor Meiji was finished in 1889. It was built "of wood, a light fawn-colored wood, giving out the most delicate aroma" and "floriated gables...and richly painted eaves, ... broad corridors lined, dado fashion, with shining orange and cedar woods, golden colored and scented," and rooms with glass sliding doors that "get all their light and air from the wide surrounding corridors." So much wood was the downfall of this enchanting palace. Among the millions of bombs that were dropped on the city in the air raids of 1945, a few scored direct hits on the Imperial Palace.

In the dark days of the war, the view of the two bridges and the fortifications that led to the palace symbolized the imperial ideal for which the Japanese were fighting. If ever a view stood for a national sense of purpose, this was it. Families came to take photographs of their young fighting men here, and all the panoply of flag-waving, song-singing nationalism was displayed here. Parades were held, one of the largest of them (on 10 November 1940) marking the 2,600th anniversary of the foundation of the imperial house. Even passengers on board trams passing along the outer moat rose to their feet and bowed in the direction of the invisible palace, "trying not to lose their balance in the jolting vehicle, which would have been absurd and inappropriate at such a solemn moment."[3] In the days after the emperor made his unprecedented broadcast announcing surrender, the ground in front of the bridges became the site of a macabre spectacle: that of the disemboweled bodies of young officers and other recalcitrants who refused to submit. Japan's new overlord, General MacArthur, established his headquarters on the far side of the open space, in the grim building that now houses the head offices of the Daiichi Life Insurance Company.

The precarious psychological and geographical balance between the occupation forces, with their headquarters on one side, and the emperor, in his invisible palace on the other, was upset in the open space in between, just three days after the ratification of the San Francisco Treaty ending the occupation. On 1 May 1952, a group of May Day demonstrators broke away from the main procession and marched across Tokyo to the Concourse in Front of the Palace, where May Day rallies had been held each year since the end of the war. It had become Jimmin Hiroba, the Concourse of the People, and the people wanted it back. But the police were waiting. In the ensuing disturbances, two demonstrators were killed and eighty-three policemen and about one hundred demonstrators seriously injured, not to mention thirteen American cars, which had been parked in the vicinity, overturned and burnt.

The modern Imperial Palace, completed in 1968, is ferroconcrete but adheres to traditional architectural style in its long, low, sweeping lines. To mark its completion, that part of the grounds where the Ni no Maru and Hon Maru once stood was opened to the public and made into a park.

# # #

Ōtemachi, Marunouchi, Yūrakuchō, and Hibiya

The history of Tokyo is one of changing names and shifting water courses. In the early days the district now called Ōtemachi was known as Shibasaki, while Hibiya was the name of an inlet of the bay. Hibiya Inlet extended inland as far as Ōte Gate and the Palace Hotel (before the day, that is, of castle gates and Palace Hotels). It seems to have got its name from the rows of bamboo stakes and nets, known as *hibi,* that were set out in mudflats of this sort to trap oysters and seaweed. Most of modern Marunouchi and Yūrakuchō was under water. To the east there was a headland, which petered out in the bay somewhere around Kyōbashi. This headland was known as Edomaejima, the "Island in Front of the Mouth of the River." On this peninsula there were several hamlets of fishermen, but the largest of the settlements in the area was probably at the head of Hibiya Inlet, the settlement known as Shibasaki.

The earliest settlers at Shibasaki built a shrine which they dedicated, some historians say, to a god of the sea, as they themselves had first reached the east by boat and were fishing folk. In the tenth century, after the defeat of the rebel Taira no Masakado, who had conquered the eight provinces of the east and declared himself emperor, the inhabitants of Shibasaki worshiped Masakado alongside their god of the sea at the same shrine. Kanda Myōjin was the name given to this shrine, the very same Kanda Myōjin that was later moved to a hill not far north, where it became the tutelary shrine of the children of Edo.

Shibasaki stood by the mouth of a stream called the Hirakawa. One reason why Ōta Dōkan decided to settle at Edo and build his castle here in the middle of the fifteenth century was his success in improving the moorings and navigation courses. This he accomplished by diverting the course of the Hirakawa, which flowed into Hibiya Inlet where Ōte Gate now stands. Dōkan diverted its course at Kandabashi (between Ōtemachi and Uchi Kanda) and set it flowing due east into the bay at the mouth of the Sumida. This waterway later became one of the central arteries of the city, Nihombashi River, straddled by Nihombashi, the great little bridge itself, and it was only recently, this century, when the Ginza subway line was being built, that the inhabitants of the city were reminded of the fact that their Nihombashi River was a fifteenth-century feat of engineering. This was the first of many instances when the course of rivers was to be changed, along with their names, the first of so many instances that the history of the city now known as Tokyo becomes not so much the march of time that Westerners have been trained to expect but a subtle geographic and historical flow on whose current we should float, but whose waters we would be wiser not to try to chart.

With the construction of the river's new course, Takabashi, the "Tall Bridge," which had once carried the road to the north of Japan over the Hirakawa at its mouth, became redundant. The main bridge of the little town at the feet of Edo Castle was now Tokiwabashi, which carried the same road to the north over the new Nihombashi River. Tokiwa Bridge came to be called simply Ōhashi, the "Great Bridge," and in later years a sword market was held on the bridge. The sword market grew in fame, and before long there were more buyers than there were swords to buy. The result was an increase in the number of imitation products, swords with forged inscriptions. The market was thrown into bad repute. It became a byword for fakes and forgeries, and *ōhashi-mono* was coined as a term meaning a counterfeit object. In the way of these things, a new Tokiwa Bridge, Shin Tokiwabashi, has been built a hundred meters downriver from the old bridge. Proper, old Tokiwabashi is the oldest stone bridge in the city, and its granite paving stones form an elegant sleeping surface for the tramps who take shelter under the expressway that obscures this bridge like most of the other famous Tokyo bridges. The Nihombashi River here was later to become part of the outer moat (*sotobori*) that constituted the perimeter of the Tokugawa castle. On the inside of the moat was a gate, the Tokiwa Bridge Gate, and the stone base of this gate still stands, providing a test of rock-climbing skills for businessmen in their lunch hour.

Tokugawa Ieyasu followed the example of his illustrious predecessor. One of his first acts after moving into his new home, Edo Castle, was to indulge in some river-diverting and build a canal that went straight to Ōte Gate, his front door. The construction of his front-door canal, Dosambori, was one of the principal tasks of engineering that Ieyasu addressed himself to after his arrival in Edo in 1590. The canal flowed from Ōta Dōkan's Nihombashi River, branching off at Ichikoku Bridge and heading straight toward Ōte Gate along a route that lay roughly parallel to the modern Eitai Street. The Nihombashi River still exists, although, with its expressway accompaniment, it is but a specter of its former self. Ieyasu's Dosambori canal, however, has long since disappeared.

The earth that was dug up to make the canal was put to use: it was used to reclaim the Hibiya Inlet. A little later on, the Tokugawa were at it again, constructing yet another new mouth for the poor Hirakawa. This time the river's course was diverted up near Suidōbashi and made to flow due east through the north of Kanda into the Sumida River, thus forming the outermost of the castle's defences. Previous river diversion projects had been quite simple, but in this case the Hongō ridge lay between Suidōbashi and the Sumida River. A slice was cut through this ridge, and for once the extent and nature of the work involved can still be appreciated. The Kanda River, as Hirakawa's second artificial mouth was called, flows far down beneath its banks at Ochanomizu. Again the earth was put to good purpose, to fill in Hibiya Inlet and more of the tidal flats to the south and east, Ginza and Shimbashi, and such places.

Not only was the lay of the land beginning to take on an appearance with which we would be familiar today, but names were materializing that conform to modern Tokyo nomenclature. Shibasaki had vanished, and, even if Ōtemachi had to wait until the Meiji era to make its bow, Ōte Gate now existed. Marunouchi means roughly "within the castle walls," and the land that now bears this name stood within the castle's outermost fortifications by 1608. One of the first lordly residents of Ieyasu's new castle was the tea master Oda Urakusai, younger brother of the man who had once been Ieyasu's commander, Oda Nobunaga. Urakusai's Edo townhouse was built on land that had stood to the east of Hibiya Inlet. That Urakusai spent long there is much to be doubted, as, certainly in the first few years of the seventeenth century, there was still much reclamation work being undertaken in the area around his house, and all the noise would surely have distracted him during his contemplation of the Way of Tea. Urakusai spent his last years in Kyoto, where he died in 1621, thirty years after his teacher, Sen no Rikyū. He did, however, leave something behind in Edo, and that was his name. The "*sai*" has dropped off, and Uraku has become Yūraku, which, with the customary "*chō*" suffix, gives the familiar Yūrakuchō, the Quarter (*chō*) where Pleasure (*raku*) can be Had (*yū*); in fairness to the tea master, it should perhaps be said that the original meaning of *raku* is something like "spiritual ease," which is probably what Urakusai had in mind when he took this as his priest's name. Later, as we shall see, less subtle, more carnal nuances crept into the name.

Urakusai, it is said, built a teahouse in the *sukiya* style in the grounds of his residence. The name stuck, perhaps because all around was still semiwilderness, and the bridge across the newly constructed moat by Urakusai's house came to be called Sukiya Bridge, and the gate that led through the walls, Sukiya Bridge Gate. It seems extraordinary that a man who spent so little time here so long ago should have been such a successful bequeather of names, but that is the way it is. The bridge is still called Sukiya Bridge, even though it ceased to be a bridge sometime in the early 1960s when the former moat was filled in and an expressway built unceremoniously on top of it. Sukiya Bridge, in Edo days, led from within the walls, Marunouchi, to the southern limb of townspeople's Tokyo, to Owarichō, Izumochō, Shimbashi, and the site of the official silver mint, Ginza. Immediately across the bridge, on the townspeople's side, was the residence of the officials who superintended the shogun's utensils and fulfilled other sundry duties connected with the Way of Tea in all its ramifications. These officials came to be known as *sukiya-bōsu* because of their proximity to Sukiya Bridge. The district they lived in was known until not so long ago as

Sukiyachō, and, like a similar district in Ueno known as Sukiyamachi, Sukiyachō became a geisha district in the Meiji era.

Almost a hundred years after Urakusai had lived here, the site of the house became the official residence of one of the city's two magistrates. The structure of Edo, with its large areas of land occupied by the mansions of the military ruling class and its wretchedly overcrowded townspeople's districts, so alien to anything with which we today are familiar, required a very particular sort of administration. There was at root a dichotomy caused by the Tokugawa inability to back up its military power with direct administrative control over the provincial barons. What this meant for Edo was that the two city magistrates, officers appointed by the shogun and accountable to him, administered the whole of the geographical compass of the city (which itself was sometimes indistinctly defined) but had jurisdiction only over the townspeople, most of whom lived in a wide swath of land that ran north from Shiba through Shimbashi, Kyōbashi, and Nihombashi to Kanda. But there were pockets of land inhabited by townspeople all over the city. One of the most delicate of the problems that faced the magistrates and their deputies was presented by the military retainers, who had a high-handed way of kicking up trouble with the townspeople. These situations called for extreme diplomacy on the part of the city magistrates' deputies, who had no jurisdiction over the samurai, but, if all was handled well, the result would be the gift of a robe to the deputy or one of his assistants bearing the crest of the lord's family (no need for a cover-up—on the contrary, the official would be expected to wear the robe when he next visited the lord's residence). It was a peculiar system, but it seems to have worked after its own fashion.

The two city magistrates were known as the "southern town commissioner" (*minami machi bugyō*) and "northern town commissioner" (*kita machi bugyō*). For most of the time between their establishment and their demise in 1868 (but, in typical Edo fashion, not all of it), the South Magistrate occupied an official residence to the south of that of the North Magistrate. The South Magistrate eventually settled down within the walls by Sukiya Bridge Gate. As for the North Magistrate, his residence originally stood within the walls at Tokiwa Bridge Gate but was later moved to Kaji Bridge Gate and finally to Gofuku Bridge Gate, to a site in 1–8 Marunouchi where the Hotel

Kokusai Kankō now stands. Each of these sites was strategically placed within the outer moats but next door to one of the gates and bridges that led directly to the townspeople's quarters.

The titles "south" and "north" referred not to geographical divisions of jurisdiction but simply, more or less, to the location of the offices. The duties of the two magistrates were identical, but they took turns exercising these duties, one month north and the next month south. By all accounts they needed their month off to catch up with paperwork and recover from the long hours of the previous turn of duty. Each magistrate had twenty-five deputies, and many more junior officers; nevertheless, two magistrates was not many for a city of over a million inhabitants, about half of whom fell within their jurisdiction. Nor were the magistrates merely judicial officers. They were responsible for the maintenance of order, as well as for the punishment of offenders, for the financial conduct of merchants and traders and the justness of their prices, for the publication of posters, pamphlets, and the like, and for general observance of codes affecting public morality—from the propriety or otherwise of the women superintendents of archery ranges to the prosecution of illegal prostitutes.

The city magistrates adjudicated most criminal cases, but more serious affairs were dealt with by the shogunate's high court, which was situated within the walls, in 1–3 and 1–4 Marunouchi. This august body met three times a month and consisted of the commissioners for temples and shrines, the commissioners for accounts and audits, the shogunal censors (who superintended the city's military residents), and sometimes the councillors of state. They passed judgment on succession and territorial squabbles involving the feudal lords and on incidents of a political nature.

Another busy department of the shogun's government was the Kanjōsho, a sort of grand ministry of accounts and audits. The main offices of the Kanjōsho were within the walls of Hon Maru, the castle's central fortress, but much of the department's business was conducted in a building on the inside of Ōte Gate. All the commercial and financial affairs of the shogun—and much that would now come under the heading of personnel—were handled by this department. The shogun's retainers had their territory delineated and their rice stipend decided by the department's clerks. The affairs of the purveyors of goods to the shogun were examined here, and the stewards who administered shogunal estates were accountable to the Kanjōsho. Above all, there was the collection of taxes to superintend. So much work required a small army of bureaucrats. The clerks working in this and other shogunate departments—such as the construction office (across Dosambori from the Kanjōsho) in charge of the construction of waterways and upkeep of gates, bridges, walls, and so forth—were drawn from among the shogun's retainers.

South of the shogun's supreme court and the construction department ran a moat, Babasakibori ("Moat in Front of the Horse Ground"), named after a gate where in 1635 emissaries from Korea put on a display of horsemanship for the shogun. Halfway down the moat was the residence of Hayashi, the shogun's court pontificator on matters moral and academic. He held the title of Daigaku no Kami ("College Lord"), was the principal of the Confucian college in Yushima, and acted as censor for the shogunate. Two houses down from the Hayashi residence, on the site where the Meiji Life Insurance building now stands, was the compound in which the shogunate's fire fighters lived. The shogunate's fire brigade was founded after the Long-Sleeves Fire of 1657. Its duties were strictly limited to fighting fires in the castle and in the residences of the feudal lords. However, many of the lords themselves had fire brigades, while the townspeople organized their own brave bands of fire fighters, so that as the years passed the shogun's brigade saw less and less of the action. Here among the great mansions of the lords was born a man who should have followed in his father's footsteps and spent his life fighting fires, but instead became one of the greatest of *ukiyo-e* artists and a master portrayer of the life of the common people as well as the city they lived in: Andō Hiroshige.

Marunouchi, the area "Within the Walls," was known (another example, perhaps, of puckish Edo humor) as Daimyō Kōji, the "Little Lanes of the Great Lords." This had been one of the first areas to be filled up with the residences of the feudal lords after the establishment of the Tokugawa shogunate at the start of the seventeenth century. These sprawling mansions, some of them two or three hectares in expanse, were concealed from view. It was only the gates that could impress a passer-by with the rank of the occupant. The mightiest feudal lords—those whose fiefdoms encompassed a whole province, like the Maeda of Kaga or the Nabeshima of Saga or the Ikeda of

Inaba—boasted gates that were detached from the walls on either side. These were impressive structures with hip-gable roofs and a guardhouse on either side crowned by—most elevated of all status symbols—a Chinese gable, *karahafu*. An excellent example of a late Edo-period gate of this type can be seen on Ueno hill in front of the Tokyo National Museum. This gate belonged to the mansion of the Ikeda lords of Inaba in 3–1 Marunouchi, where the International Building and Tokyo Kaikan now stand. Feudal lords of lesser rank had to settle for gates that formed a continuum with the adjacent walls and smaller guardhouses of varying shape, but none of them with the distinctive Chinese gable.

The Little Lanes of the Great Lords presented an eerily unpeopled, desolate spectacle. The contrast with the teeming streets of the townspeople's quarters was commented on by several Western intruders into the shogun's city. Among them was Laurence Oliphant. Oliphant first visited Edo in 1858, ten years before the shogun's fall, as personal secretary to Lord Elgin, who was on a treaty-signing mission. Oliphant writes this of the district Within the Walls, "the Princes' or aristocratic quarter": "We were amazed at the different aspect which the streets here presented from those we had just left. On each side of the street, which was twenty or thirty yards wide, was an open paved drain, about four feet in depth and as many in breadth.... The lower parts of [the] walls were built of huge blocks of rough stone, above which they were raised to a height of about twenty feet, constructed of masonry, but carefully white-washed, and ornamented with raised groinings. In the centre was a gateway painted red or some bright color, with a pent roof, and ornaments in lacquer upon it. Beyond this there was no sort of architectural pretension about these palaces. They evidently covered a large area of ground, as four or five were sufficient to compose a whole street, the walls of one residence extending for two or three hundred yards, and here and there perforated with windows, from between the bars of which peered female faces."[4]

The foreigners presaged change, and change came to the country with remarkable alacrity and thoroughness. And to nowhere more so than to Marunouchi, the district that soon ceased to stand within walls. The gates at Sukiya, Kaji, and Gofuku bridges were knocked down in 1873, only five years after the installation of the Meiji government. A little later the wall that linked these gates along the former castle's outer moats was deemed dispensable and was dismantled.

The Meiji government's first concern was just the same as that of the Tokugawa shogunate: to protect the ruler in his castle/palace from outside attack. The shogun had surrounded himself with his allies among the lords. But with the fall of the shogunate, the lords had returned to their homes in the provinces and their vast mansions in Edo were unoccupied. The new government appropriated the land on which they stood and there built its ministries and barracks and parade grounds. In Ōtemachi, the new Home Ministry and Treasury were erected in the grounds of the former residence of the Sakai family, lords of Himeji Castle. In Yūrakuchō was built the War Ministry. The land that comprises modern Hibiya Park and the south of Kasumigaseki was turned into a huge military parade ground. Many of these early Meiji ministry offices were built in a hybrid style similar to the former main hall of the Tokyo Imperial University's medical faculty, built in 1876 and still standing in Koishikawa Botanical Garden.

Despite doubts about their ability to withstand earthquakes, brick and stone made an early appearance in the emperor's new capital—at Ginza, Shimbashi Station, the barracks of the Life Guard in Takebashi, and at a host of other places. There soon developed that strangely indefinable style of architecture that we now think of as typical of Meiji and that meant so much in cultural terms to the people of the time. It was a sort of domesticated neoclassicism with northern European tendencies combined with colonialist touches that conformed better with Tokyo's generally equitable climate. The area that had once stood Within the Walls became a testing ground for various architectural and cultural experiments. These experiments began in Hibiya, at the Rokumeikan, the "Hall of the Cry of the Stag" (a reference to a poem in the ancient Chinese anthology, *The Book of Songs*).

The main thrust of the policy of all the Meiji governments until the end of the century was revocation of the humiliating extraterritoriality treaties. To attain this end involved demonstrating to the Westerners that Japan had reached cultural parity, that it operated on the same rarified levels of enlightened civilization. The foreign minister of the day, Inoue Kaoru, decided that nothing would more impress the representatives of the foreign powers than a building where the upper crust of Japanese society could mingle with chancellors, consuls, and attachés, a building that would house a ballroom, a billiard lounge, and a music room. In 1883 just such a building was completed. The Rokumeikan stood on the south side of the modern Imperial Hotel, in front of the offices of the Yamato Life Insurance Company.

For a few brief years the Rokumeikan flourished. Distinguished Japanese gentlemen found themselves being invited to attend balls along with their honorable wives, and together husband and wife twirled in a flurry of lace around the dance floor in the close embrace of a waltz, a dance form which had shocked most of the aristocracy of Europe only half a century earlier. There were charity garden parties organized by imperial princesses, and galas, and it was all very splendid and highly enlightened. But it seems to have done little good in pursuing the aim of legal equality with the West. In 1889, the building was handed over to the Peers Club, and later on it housed a bank before being pulled down at the outset of the Pacific War (leaving us to wonder whether it might have survived the air raids of 1945).

The Rokumeikan was a two-story stuccoed brick building with Mediterranean arcades on both floors. Tuscan on the ground floor, vaguely Moorish on the second floor, but with a roof that was definitely French. It cost the exorbitant sum of ¥180,000 to build and was the work of Josiah Conder. Conder was a British architect who came to Japan on government contract in 1877. He was extremely active both as an architect and as a teacher. His style might best be termed eclectic, as can be seen in those few of his many buildings that still stand, such as the Mitsui Club (2–3 Mita, Minato Ward), the house he built for the Iwasaki family in Yushima, and the Nikolai Cathedral. Whatever his talents as an architect, Conder's influence among his students was seminal. One of these students designed the first Imperial Hotel, which was completed in 1890, on land adjacent to the Rokumeikan on its east. It was very similar to the master's Rokumeikan, with an extra floor whose windows were dormers in another Gallic roof. The Imperial Hotel became host to the same sort of clientele that had gathered in the Rokumeikan, but for the first year of its existence it had to cope with an added influx of guests, politicians seeking refuge from the Imperial Debating Hall.

This was the Diet, and it had only just been completed (in

Uchisaiwaichō 2-chōme, across the road from the Hibiya Public Hall) when it was burnt down. Within a year a new building had taken its place, and the Imperial Hotel was able to settle down to a prosperous existence, until in 1923 fire finally claimed it. But by then it was already about to make way for a more illustrious replacement, a building that became one of the most celebrated in the world. The architect was Frank Lloyd Wright, and the hotel he created (quite unlike anything else in Japan) was the height of architectural daring, tactile and cool and with a strong hint of ancient Mexico in the decoration of stone and tile and brickwork. It survived the great earthquake that sent so many other brick buildings crashing to the ground but fell victim to the developers, meeting its destroyer in 1967.

Opposite the hotel was another of the city's earlier Western accouterments, Japan's first proper park. Hibiya Park was opened in 1903, when the army's exercise ground was moved out to Aoyama. Like many a park in Western cities, Hibiya Park became a venue for rallies and demonstrations.

Tokyo's municipal tram network came into operation at about the same time that the park was opened, and this made it easier for large crowds to gather. At least thirty thousand people gathered around the park on 5 September 1905, the day of the signing of the Treaty of Portsmouth, which formally ended the Russo-Japanese War. There had been terrible loss of life in the war, and the Japanese had won some famous victories, but the financial toll was heavy and the country was on the brink of bankruptcy. The crowds that gathered to protest against the terms of the treaty felt they had been cheated by their government. Worse, they found that barricades manned by police had been slung across the entrances to the park. They broke through the barricades, entered the park, and listened to the speeches. From there most of the protesters joined a procession to the Shintomiza theater in Tsukiji. Some of them were not satisfied, however, with the perfunctory way events were unfolding. They split off from the rally and headed instead for the offices of the progovernment, protreaty newspaper, *Kokumin Shimbun,* in Izumochō (Ginza). They set the building alight, and then moved back to Hibiya, to the official residence of the minister for home affairs, which received similar treatment. From there on, things began to get out of hand. Mobs spent a night on the rampage, attacking police stations and churches all over the city but especially in the older, poorer districts of Nihombashi, Kanda, and Asakusa. The next morning, the cabinet of Prime Minister Katsura Tarō put the capital under martial law, and over the next few days the disturbances subsided. Not many years later the park was the scene of further rallies, against rises in the price of tram tickets and against the public order act, and then in 1918 against the exorbitant price of rice.

From Hibiya, we move back north to Marunouchi. By the 1880s the government had begun to realize that there was no longer any need to protect the emperor with barracks and parade grounds. One by one the military facilities moved away to less cramped quarters. Much of Marunouchi was now wasteland, and a slump in the property market impeded the army from being able to finance its new construction projects through the sale of its land in Marunouchi. No one would buy. Eventually, with the market price at ¥1.25 million, a buyer was found, although the obliging man in question was heard to say, when asked what he would do with the land, that he would plant bamboo or maybe keep some tigers there. But he must have known he was making a shrewd purchase. Who was this cavalier buyer? Clearly, not a pauper. He was Iwasaki Yanosuke, younger brother of Yatarō, who in turn was the founder of Mitsubishi and a Midas of a man whose fortune was made largely by acting as transporter and sutler on a grand scale to the Meiji army in its early escapades in Kyushu and Taiwan. This fortune was invested partly in property, and the Iwasaki family already owned vast acreages in Tokyo—in Hongō, in Komagome, in Fukagawa, and now, most strategic of all, in the empty heart of the city, Marunouchi.

Yanosuke decided to have the headquarters of his family's company, Mitsubishi, built here, and he commissioned the same Josiah Conder who was responsible for the Rokumeikan to design a building in the style then current in London. In 1894, Mitsubishi Hall No. 1 was finished, the first building of Tokyo's "London Block," Itchō Rondon. Over the next couple of decades, the London Block extended over several blocks west along the road on which stands the headquarters of the Tokyo Metropolitan Government toward Babasaki Gate and the Imperial Palace and then north toward the newly built Tokyo Station and south toward Yūrakuchō. Construction work does not seem to have been prosecuted with the speed that we now expect in Tokyo, and much of the area was still a wasteland, or at best a construction site, until well into the twentieth century. Indeed, it was known as Mitsubishigahara, the Mitsubishi Wasteland. The buildings themselves— four story, red brick—have that late-Victorian London air of Marylebone High Street or parts of Kensington, but without the architectural conviction and spontaneity that grows out of native soil. Photographs of the London Block in its early days reveal a pronounced sense of unease. The buildings need carriages and trolleys and the bustle of late-Victorian and Edwardian London. Instead, all they have to look out on is a few rickshaws and the occasional disoriented passer-by.

Eventually, this strange experiment—the architectural transplant that the London Block represented—succeeded. It was helped in no small measure by the completion of Tokyo Station in 1914. Until that time the Tōkaidō railway line from Kyoto, Osaka, and the west had finished at Shimbashi, and Ginza had been the entrance to the city, the door that opened onto the city's main "hall," Nihombashi. Tokyo Station was the new terminus. But instead of having its main entrance on the east side opening up to Nihombashi and the city's central trading district, the facade looked in the opposite direction. The pretext given was that it faced toward the Imperial Palace, but it has been suggested that Mitsubishi may have had more than a little to do with the affair. Certainly they had nothing to quibble about in the choice of a west entrance for Tokyo Station. Some years later, Nihombashi got its east entrance, but that was after the 1923 earthquake, and much had changed by then.

Tokyo Station is the work of Tatsuno Kingo, the first of the great modern Japanese architects, along with Katayama Tokuma (designer of the Akasaka Detached Palace and the Hyōkeikan of the Tokyo National Museum). Like Katayama, Tatsuno was a student of Josiah Conder. Of his two prominent works still standing in Tokyo, the earlier is the Bank of Japan, a formal, neoclassic structure. Tokyo Station is something rather different, a mixture of styles that has been described as "free classic" and that owes its inspiration to the architectural styles of north Europe. In its original form, it was a four-story building with domes capping the north and south wings. However, it lost its top two stories and its domes in the 1945 air raids. It needed them; it now looks too long for its height, and it suffers from having to face the wrong way. Not that this should be used as a pretext to knock the old building down.

Tokyo Station peers out toward the bleak facade of the famous Maru Biru, one of the first *biru* buildings, whose rounded (*marui*) corners enabled a little play on the Maru of Marunouchi to creep into its name. But play stopped there. Maru Biru is a bulk of a building, all mass and no air. So much so that, until the completion in 1968 of the Kasumigaseki Building, volume—of beer drunk in a year, for example—was expressed by the newspapers in terms of "so many Maru Birus-full." In its uniformity and its lack of frivolity Maru Biru seems to presage the years of militarism that lay ahead. It survived the 1923 earthquake, and so it, too, became a cause of gravitational pull toward Marunouchi, and it gave birth to a clone, the New Maru Biru, which still stands opposite Maru Biru at the western approach to Tokyo Station.

Not all Marunouchi's prewar buildings are quite so stern. There stands along Babasakibori, overlooking the great esplanade that is one of the wonders of Tokyo, the offices of the Meiji Life Insurance Company (2–1 Marunouchi). Here at last is a building by an architect who felt completely at home both with his material and with the nature of the business of his clients. This is not only a monument to neoclassicism but also to financial rectitude. The very stones seem to breathe fiscal propriety and sound bookkeeping, and the ten huge fluted columns that adorn the facade flout their Corinthian capitals with utter confidence. The architect was Okada Shin'ichirō, whose other famous work still standing in Tokyo is the Kabukiza in Ginza.

Four years after the completion, in 1934, of this building, another insurance company moved into a new head office along the palace moat. The Daiichi Mutual Life Insurance Company building is much more a child of its time, of the oppressive days of military rule. It too has ten huge columns supporting two top stories, but despite this structural resemblance, the two buildings could not be further apart in terms of mood and spirit. The Daiichi building, severely angular and austere, supremely cold and functional, was taken over as the general headquarters of the Supreme Command of the Allied Powers at the end of the Second World War. From its fortresslike windows the blue-eyed shogun, General MacArthur, could look across to the defeated emperor in his palace discreetly concealed behind Fushimi Tower.

The air raids of 1945 destroyed most of Tokyo, but the fires started by the bombs left many of Marunouchi and Yūrakuchō's sturdier buildings relatively unharmed. It was only natural, therefore, that the Allied powers would requisition these buildings and base much of their activity here. Yūrakuchō and the streets behind the fine buildings that looked out toward the palace became the stage for the seamier side of life under the occupying forces. The special circumstances of Japan's defeat and the occupation gave rise to the *pam-pam* phenomenon. The *pam-pam* catered to the need of the GIs for female company, and in doing so they adopted some of the more conspicuous traits and mannerisms of their conquerors: "the shameless *pam-pam*, painted like harridans, with huge heels and misshapen legs, who shout, smoke, spit, chew gum, and call out 'Hey, Johnnie!' at passers-by."[5] These harridans of Yūrakuchō were regarded with opprobrium by most but with barely concealed envy by a few. They had their own patches, their *nawabari*, which they defended fiercely. One of their distinctive characteristics was the way they tied their kerchiefs at the front. Thanks to the GIs and the *pam-pam* girls, Yūrakuchō became simple Rakuchō, and any nuances of spirituality that might once have been attached to the word *raku* disappeared.

The *pam-pam* were a local phenomenon. Not so the black markets. They sprang up under the arches of the Yamanote Line in Ueno and Shinjuku, Akihabara and Shimbashi, and other places, too. They had their own argot, one of many secret languages that litter the history of Japan. Ueno became Nogami; Kanda, Dagan; and Asakusa, Enkō, after its *kōen*, "park." As for Rakuchō, its black market was one of the biggest, the result in part of the proximity of the American army's post exchange in Ginza. When food and other goods came back into general circulation, there was no more need for black markets. But the *gādoshita*, the area under (*shita*) the girder bridge (*gādo*), continued to play an important part in the life of the city. Indeed, if there were any one word that might be taken to symbolize the Tokyo of the fifties and sixties before Japan entered its high-growth orbit, this suspect coinage, *gādoshita*, would be it. All over the city, people lived and worked, ate and drank under the railway lines.

From Ueno all the way to Yūrakuchō and beyond there were markets, workshops, and cheap restaurants under the railway line. At Yūrakuchō there was a preponderance of the kind of popular restaurants—most of them no more than a stall and benches and lantern—specializing in *kushiyaki* and *motsuyaki* and all the other kebabs that find their way into the generic word *yakitori*. *Yakitori* and beer and camaraderie were the order of every evening in Yūrakuchō's *gādoshita* and in the back streets on either side of the railway line. The atmosphere of lively banter and plentiful beer was enhanced by the number of journalists, from the *Mainichi Shimbun* offices on the west of the tracks and the *Asahi* on the east and the *Yomiuri* not far away in Ginza. But then the *Yomiuri* moved to Ōtemachi, the *Mainichi* to Takebashi, and finally the *Asahi* to Tsukiji. The metropolitan government supervised the construction of Kōtsū Kaikan, a building which houses shops, restaurants, and municipal offices. This dealt a telling blow to the Yūrakuchō of lanterns and roadside stalls, and more recent developments, including the construction of Seibu and Hankyū department stores, have changed Yūrakuchō beyond recognition. The remaining *yakitori* stalls have become relics of a past era.

There was a time after the war—several decades, in fact—when some of the original buildings of Mitsubishi's London Block still stood in the streets around the metropolitan office. They have all now gone, to be replaced, for the most part, by structures of unexceptional appearance.

But despite the architectural transformation of the area Within the Walls since the fall of the shoguns in 1868, it is remarkable, in a way, how little things have changed. The atmosphere is still formal and official, quite different from Nihombashi and Ginza beyond the walls. The Mitsui and Mitsubishi headquarters, the banks, and the insurance companies are the modern inheritors of the tradition of the feudal lords whose mansions once stood guard around the shogun's castle.

# # #

Kasumigaseki and Nagatachō

Subtle shifts in allegiance punctuated by sudden surges of murderous rage characterize the history of the districts to the south of the Imperial

Palace. Politicians and bureaucrats now rule the roost, but the story of the districts known as Kasumigaseki and Nagatachō has far older and perhaps more abiding links with soldiers and military power. Kasumigaseki once stood on the road from Kyoto to the north of the country. Japan's first warrior, the Mars of Japanese mythology, Yamato Takeru no Mikoto, established a barrier here during his campaigns against the Ezo barbarians of the wild east. Saved from stormy waters in Sagami Bay by the suicide of his newly wed wife, he reached a tract of high land overlooking the bay with a view so commanding that it pierced the clouds and mists. Here he set up his barrier, and he called it Kasumigaseki, the "Barrier of Mist."

We turn over the pages of the history books, many pages, and arrive finally at the year 1590, at the Eighth Month of that year, when Tokugawa Ieyasu first arrived at the site of his future castle and capital city. Ieyasu was so struck by the cherry trees—there are said to have been thousands of them—lining the paddy fields between Atago Hill and the hill on which he built his castle that he had them all moved within the walls of his fortress. The villagers had lost their cherry trees, and before long they lost their paddy fields, too, as the new city expanded south. Eventually, even the name of their old village disappeared. Sakurada, "Fields of Cherry Trees," had been the northernmost village in Ebara County. It had comprised several settlements of farmers and fishermen along the swampy banks of the bay. Two gates of the castle Ōta Dōkan built here were named after the cherry trees, Outer Sakurada Gate (now known simply as Sakurada Gate) and Inner Sakurada Gate (the present-day Kikyō Gate), where Dōkan and his Hōjō successors moored their boats and entered straight into the castle.

After having purloined the cherry trees for his own enjoyment, Ieyasu converted those parts of the cherry-tree fields nearest his castle into land for the houses of the most powerful outside lords. The Nabeshima of Saga in Kyushu and the Mōri of Chōshū in the far west of Honshu had their Edo mansions on land that is now Hibiya Park. Behind them, in what is now Uchisaiwaichō, was the main residence of the Nambu clan of Mutsu in north Japan. Where the Justice and Agriculture ministries now stand, two other outside clans from the north had their Edo houses, the Uesugi of Yonezawa and the Soma of Nakamura. The Foreign Ministry stands on land that contained the residence of the Kuroda lords of Chikuzen in the north of Kyushu. One of the gates of the Kuroda residence survived among the modern ministries until 1945, when it was burnt down in an air raid. Next door to the Kuroda were the Asano of Hiroshima, another family of great outside lords from the west of Japan. The site of the Asano residence has now become home for the crowded block containing the Ministry of Home Affairs, the Transport Ministry, and the Construction Ministry. The road that ran down the hill between the compounds of the Kuroda and the Asano residences was known as Kasumigasekizaka, "Slope of the Barrier of Mist."

At the top of this slope, behind another compound belonging to the Asano clan, was a more modest establishment, the house of a retainer of the shogun by the name of Nagata. Why it should be is not entirely clear from the old gazetteers, but the road that passed outside the Nagata house came to be known as Nagata Baba, the "Nagata Horse Ground."

Horses hold an important position in the history of the east of Japan. Indeed, the eventual supremacy of the east can probably be attributed in part to the superior horsemanship of its leading warriors. There was no lack of *baba,* training grounds for horse and rider, in and around Edo, or at least that part of the city where the feudal lords and their samurai retainers had their residences. There were *baba* in Kohinata and Koishikawa, to the northwest of the city, and there was another one on a hill a little further out that has left its name behind, Takadanobaba. There was, however, a horse ground much nearer by, along the banks of Tameike, the lake at the southern foot of the hill whose history we are now examining. So it seems strange, and slightly unsatisfactory, that the road outside the Nagata house should have been called Nagata Baba when it was neither a horse ground nor the bearer of any especially close historical link with the Nagata family. More likely, surely, is the possibility that there had once been here a long field, which is what *nagata* written differently means, and that the field was used for exercising horses. Whatever the derivation of its name, the street itself ran roughly along the course now taken by the road behind the Diet building.

If one followed this road north past the contentious Nagata house, one reached the walls of the residence of the Hosokawa lords of Kumamoto Castle and masters of the province of Higo in Kyushu. The

Hosokawa were outside lords, but they were regarded by the shogun as being more trustworthy than the Katō lords who had held the same fief before them. Katō Kiyomasa was one of the most important figures in the turbulent decades either side of the year 1600. The Tokugawa were always suspicious of him, and finally they dredged up a pretext to dispossess his son. Katō Kiyomasa had owned one of the largest compounds in Edo, next door, ironically, to that of the Hosokawa. It now passed into the hands of the Ii clan, compatriots of the Tokugawa, who had been made lords of Hikone Castle and Ōmi province on the banks of Lake Biwa. One of their rewards for long and faithful service was this compound on the hill overlooking Sakurada Moat, where the Parliamentary Museum now stands.

This change of occupants was one of the few in the Edo period. For the most part, neighbors in Kasumigaseki and Nagatachō at the beginning of the Edo period were neighbors 250 years later at the end. Then the foreigners arrived to pry Japan open and give rise to a series of events, many of which had Kasumigaseki and Nagatachō as their stage. The first of these, one of the most famous, had as its central character the last and most illustrious of the lords of Hikone, Ii Naosuke, grand councillor of state and architect of a policy of conciliation to the demands of the foreigners for trading facilities. What Ii regarded as conciliation others saw as capitulation, and this most influential and able of the shogun's advisers was slain outside Sakurada Gate.

This is how the deed was done. It was already spring, the third day of the Third Month of 1860 (24 March in the solar calendar), but all the previous night it had been snowing. The assassins had left the domains of their lord, in Mito, so as not to implicate him in their scheme. Nariaki, lord of Mito, was a kinsman of the shogun, but he had been among the fiercest of critics of the shogunate's handling of relations with the foreign powers. Ii had acted firmly against his opponents the year before and had had many arrested and some executed. Among those punished was the firebrand Nariaki. Ii knew, therefore, that he must expect a reprisal, but he little thought it would happen here at the castle gates. His guards, who had their swords encased in leather sheaths to keep off the snow, were caught completely unawares. Eight of them were slain along with their lord that snowy morning outside the Gate of the Fields of Cherry Trees.

The assassination, which came to be known as the "Incident Outside Sakurada Gate," deprived the shogunate of its strongest and ablest servant and so contributed substantially to the eventual victory of the imperial forces.

The very men who had been most rabid in their cry of "venerate the emperor and repulse the barbarians" (*sonnō jōi*)—lower- and middle-ranking samurai from the domains of the outer lords of Satsuma and Chōshū and from the fief of the "poor cousin" of the shogun, the lord of Mito—became the holders and dispensers of power in the armed forces and the ministries of the new Meiji government. And most of them had their new offices in Kasumigaseki and Nagatachō. The Foreign Ministry and the War Ministry and the headquarters of the Chief of Staff were here from the start, these last two buildings being situated on the former residence of the Ii of Hikone. Other ministries arrived not so long after, including the Justice Ministry, which came here from Marunouchi. The Justice Ministry, prime mover in the Meiji government's struggles to right the wrongs of the extraterritoriality treaties—the unequal treaties first signed by Ii Naosuke—moved in 1896 to a building designed, ironically, by two foreigners and still standing. This is the only one of the early ministry buildings that remains today, and the only one of several government buildings designed by German architects. With its upper-story collonade, its porticos to right and left, and its contrast of brick and stone, it is a notable landmark in the architectural wilderness of Kasumigaseki.

The most energetic, dynamic, and impatient prosecutor of the early Meiji policies to make of Japan a modern nation along Western lines was Ōkubo Toshimichi, son of a lower-ranking samurai from Satsuma in the south of Kyushu. His hand can be seen in nearly all the bold innovations of the early Meiji years that so radically altered Japan's course. Son of a samurai himself, he helped to disarm and dispossess the samurai and to decree them out of existence. And it was at the hands of a former samurai that he met his death, but a stone's throw from Nagatachō, in Kioichō, on his way from his residence to the emperor's temporary palace in Akasaka. Clara Whitney recorded the events in her diary entry for 16 May 1878: "As [Ōkubo] was passing through a secluded place, a young man in light blue or green dress approached, bearing a pink and singing. When he drew near the carriage he threw away his flower and drawing a dirk wounded the nearest horse and fired a pistol, at which five other young men sprang out of ambush and attacked His Excellency the Home Minister, killing both him and his coachman."[6]

Ōkubo's was the first of many assassinations in the Meiji era, culminating in the treason affair of 1910, in which Kōtoku Shūsui and twenty-three other socialists and anarchists were accused of plotting to assassinate the emperor. Twelve of them, including Kōtoku, were executed. The government was not prepared to tolerate the existence of left-wing radicals. Thereafter assassinations increased in frequency, but they were all the work of right-wing extremists or disaffected individuals without clear political allegiance—except one, the anarchist Tamba Daisuke, who took aim at the crown prince, the future emperor Hirohito, and shattered the windscreen of his carriage. This was in December of 1923, in the confused period after the Great Kantō Earthquake, and the attempt, staged in Kasumigaseki near the present entrance to the station of the Chiyoda subway line, led to the resignation of the government.

Emperors and emperors-to-be might have been the target of anarchists, but politicians were fair game for the self-appointed patriots who took the country down the road to war and almost to obliteration in the 1930s. First in a long line of prewar assassinations was that of Hamaguchi Osachi, one of the most popular, honest, and determined of Japanese prime ministers. His decision to ratify the treaty passed at the London Disarmament Conference in 1930 was seen by the military as a challenge to its prerogatives. An attempt was made on Hamaguchi's life in 1930 on the platform of Tokyo Station, the second assassination of a premier in Tokyo Station in the space of nine years. Hamaguchi struggled on, dying of his wounds several months later after a courageous battle. His assassin was soon released. This was a bad time for prime ministers. Another popular prime minister, friend of Chandra Bose and other leading Asian anticolonialists, was assassinated only a year and a half after the attempt on Hamaguchi's life. This was Inukai Tsuyoki, who was killed in his official residence in Nagatachō by young naval officers involved in a hamfisted attempt at a *coup d'état,* the so-called May 15 Incident.

The February 26 Incident of four years later was much less amateurish and far more murderous. The great and tragic events of the city seem to have had a way of occurring during the coldest days of winter when snow lay thick on the ground. The Long-Sleeves Fire was followed by snowstorms, the forty-seven loyal retainers of Asano, lord of Akō, made their way through the snow to avenge their master's death, and Ii Naosuke met his bloody end on that snowy morning at Sakurada Gate. But the snow that fell almost continuously from 23 February 1936 was well beyond the city's light winter carpeting. The like of it had not been seen for half a century. No doubt these historical precedents were not uppermost in the minds of the fourteen hundred soldiers from the first and third regiments of the First Division as they set out early in the morning of the twenty-sixth from barracks in Roppongi on their fanatical mission. Their aims were hazy: the "restoration" of power to the emperor and wealth to the people. Their means were savage. They executed the prime minister's brother-in-law (mistaking him for the prime minister, Okada Keisuke), two former premiers (Saitō Makoto and Takahashi Korekiyo), and the inspector-general of military training (Watanabe Jōtarō). They set up their headquarters under the Hie Shrine, and occupied strategic government buildings in the area. They held nearly all of Nagatachō, Kasumigaseki, and Hibiya, but they had no next move. Martial law was declared, sentimental appeals were made to the young soldiers to remember their beloved parents, and eventually the rebels submitted and surrendered in the snow of that unusually cold Tokyo winter. Their defeat led to the triumph of the faction they had been opposing in the military.

It was not so many months later that the edifice that still houses the Diet was built. At that time, in the mid 1930s, it had not been imagined that the Diet building would be as exposed to the eyes of the world as it is today. It had stood in the shade of the headquarters of the Chief of Staff. The war deprived the hill on which both buildings stood of its military outcrop. That left the Diet building, with its ponderous pyramid of a cone, to face the world on its own. In 1960, it had suddenly to face the world in earnest, for half the world, or at least half the Japanese part of it, was banging and shouting at its door. The occasion was the revision of the Security Treaty with the United States, which President Eisenhower was to come to Japan to formally conclude. In the highly charged atmosphere of the day, the treaty was seen by many as an instrument to reaffirm American suzerainty over

Japan. Massive numbers of people demonstrated outside the Diet—100,000 on the night of 20 May and another 30,000 the next day outside the prime minister's official residence. On 26 May, the Diet was surrounded by 150,000 protesters, and the culmination of the protests came on 15 June with nationwide strikes and rallies. In the meantime, however, the treaty had been automatically passed through the two houses of the Diet, the opposition having called a boycott of the sessions. Nevertheless, the demonstrations, in which the daughter of a professor at Tokyo University was killed, brought about the cancellation of Eisenhower's visit and the resignation of the mistrusted prime minister of the day, Kishi Nobusuke. Not long after, Kishi's successor, Ikeda Hayato, called general elections. The elections, however, had an unfortunate prelude when Asanuma Inejirō, one of the best-loved socialist leaders, was stabbed to death by a young right-wing fanatic while delivering a speech in Hibiya Public Hall in Hibiya Park, just east of Kasumigaseki. "Numa-san" was something of a folk hero, and in those days before the arrival of television as a force in politics, he had that invaluable asset, an unmistakable and highly attractive voice, which he used to good advantage both as a speaker and as the voice-over for the bulldog of a Walt Disney cartoon. The Socialists did well in the elections, but this had been expected, and it is doubtful whether Asanuma's assassination made a lot of difference.

Since the end of the Second World War, Kasumigaseki and Nagatachō have lost their military complexion, but Japan's history being what it is, who knows how long this state of affairs will last?

# # #

Kōjimachi

One of Japan's major archaeological discoveries was made in a railway carriage, in a train on its way from Yokohama to Shimbashi, not many years after the line had opened. Among the passengers was a new arrival in Japan, an American zoologist called Edward S. Morse. He was admiring the scenery from the window when he saw a rise in the ground, of a sort he immediately recognized. It was a shell mound, a midden, a rubbish heap where pre-Bronze Age people threw away shells and the other detritus of daily meals and daily life. Since that discovery, the Ōmori Kaizuka (Ōmori "Shell Mound") has become a *locus classicus*. After 1877, when Morse made his discovery, many other shell mounds came to light in Tokyo, in the grounds of Kan'eiji on Ueno hill, in Ochanomizu, and on the eastward-stretching limb of land once known as Momijiyama ("Autumn-Leaf Hill") on which the Imperial Palace now stands.

This ridge, the central one of Tokyo's five ridges that reach out finger-like for the sea, was known as Kaizuka Ridge, a name that was used at least from the fifteenth century, suggesting (but not, because of the usual uncertainty about derivation, proving conclusively) that the inhabitants of the area had been aware long ago of the existence of shell mounds here. It was in the early millennia of the Jōmon period, sometime around 6,000 B.C., that the sea made its deepest encroachments into the plains and valleys, forcing the inhabitants onto the ridges but giving them a plentiful supply of shellfish and fish to eat. After that, the sea gradually retreated, and later remains of Jōmon man have been found in the flat, low-lying areas of east Tokyo, in the grounds of the Asakusa Kannon temple, in Azumamori (Sumida Ward), and in Hanahatamachi in Adachi Ward. As it retreated, however, the sea left behind brackish swamps between the ridges, at Tameike by Toranomon, at Koishikawa near Suidōbashi, and at Shinobazu Pond beneath Ueno hill.

Of the five ridges, the Kaizuka Ridge had perhaps the most distinctive shape, which is no doubt one reason why it was chosen by Ōta Dōkan and later by Tokugawa Ieyasu as the site of their castles. It was a finger with a very narrow joint at the spot where it was connected to the rest of the hand, at Yotsuya. Along this ridge that opened out at its eastern extremity to form Momijiyama, there had from early times been a road and houses. This was the road that led to Kokufu (the modern Fuchū City) near the banks of the Tama River to the west, a town that had been an outpost of the central government almost since the foundation of the Japanese state in the seventh century. The name that came to be given to the settlements along the ridge was Kōjimachi, and it has been suggested that the "*kōji*" part of the name is a contraction of Kokufu-ji, the Kokufu Road. An alternative theory, however, claims that there was a collection of houses here making and selling the special strain of mold (*kōji*) with which beans are fermented to make bean paste.

There were temples, too, along the road to Kokufu, and among them a temple that was destined to be counted one of the greatest ecclesiastical establishments in the country, Zōjōji. A chance meeting gave rise to an abiding friendship between the temple priest and Tokugawa Ieyasu (at least, so goes the story), and the new shogun had the temple moved to more spacious quarters in Shiba, to the south of the city, where it became one of the two Tokugawa family temples. A temple left Kōjimachi, but a shrine arrived to take its place. The Hirakawa Temmangu had been founded in the walls of his castle by Ōta Dōkan as a subsidiary to the mother shrine in Kawagoe. Ieyasu's grand plans for his castle left no room for this shrine, and so in 1606 it was moved here to Kōjimachi, where it has remained. A market was held at the shrine's gates in the evening, one of the city's few evening markets.

One of the regular customers at the market in its later days must surely have been Takano Chōei, a farsighted and brave man, who ran a school a couple of blocks away. At the age of twenty-one, Chōei had traveled from his native Mutsu in the north all the way to Nagasaki to study medicine under the German doctor Philip von Siebold, who was attached to the Dutch trading office. In 1828, Siebold was accused of spying, and his students fell under suspicion of conspiracy. It was then that Chōei escaped and made his way to Edo, to Kōjimachi, where he set up his school near the residence of his friend, the painter and scholar Watanabe Kazan. There he taught Western medicine and translated, wrote, and campaigned for an end to the shogunate's ostrich approach to the world around it. Later he was imprisoned, escaped, fled, and then returned to Edo in disguise. Finally, in 1850, he was caught and forced to kill himself.

If Chōei had not taken his own life, he would most likely have met one of his neighbors, Yamada Kubikiri ("Head-Chop") Asaemon, eighth and last of a family line of executioners. Asaemon's last victim, whom he dispatched at the Ichigaya Prison in Ichigaya Tomihisachō, was Takahashi Oden. The date was 30 January 1879, Oden was twenty-nine years old, and she had left behind her (so it was later said, with scant regard for the truth) a trail of murdered husbands and lovers.

Head-Chop Asaemon was struck by her wantonness and her abandon, and he described his encounter with Oden thus: "Here before me was the wickedest scoundrel with whom I had ever had to deal, and I was astonished by her effrontery. As I was about to carry out the sentence, she cried, 'Wait! I want one more look at my man.' Since this was hardly a message I could pass on to someone, I grasped my sword in readiness. At this she went wild and started screaming. I tried to talk sense into her and then took a swing with my sword. But it wasn't a clean swing, and she became even more of a wretched nuisance, calling out again and again the name of her lover, until she was at death's very door."

Two years later, Head-Chop Asaemon put his skill with swords to less brutal use and became a sword inspector. The Yamada family were fishmongers here in Kōjimachi, one of several. All along this stretch of the Kokufu Road were shops, most of them selling and delivering food to the houses of the shogun's retainers, which lay to north and south. The shogun had seven thousand *hatamoto* retainers, vassals from the shogunal domains, and beneath them were thirteen hundred *gokenin* retainers, who lived in specially assigned quarters in various parts of town. Together they made up the shogun's own fighting force. Nowadays they are remembered for the miserably low stipends they received, which they were forced to supplement by taking on side jobs such as making straw flowers and fans. Furthermore, they were paid in bales of rice, which put them at the mercy of imponderables such as the weather and the unscrupulous merchants of Kuramae, whose manipulation of interest rates was referred to as "dances." The *hatamoto* retainers were divided into six *bangumi,* or regiments, and each one was allotted a district along the castle's western reaches back as far as Ichigaya, with the "male" odd-numbered districts on the outside protecting their "female" even-numbered counterparts. Later, this part of town rose in the world, and many members of the Meiji nobility built their mansions here. After the war, the six Banchō, as the districts of the regiments of the shogun's retainers had been called, became an area of halls, schools, and expensive apartment blocks.

One of the shops along the Kokufu Road that served the shogun's retainers was Yamakujira, "Mountain Whale," selling the meat of wild beasts from the mountains. There was a hunters' market a little further down the road in Yotsuya, where wild boar, deer, chamois, monkey, and other game was sold, some of it, presumably, to Yamakujira, to be resold to customers. But who were the customers? After all, for traditional Buddhist reasons, meat was not eaten in Japan. Not as a rule, that is. The eating of meat was countenanced, however, for its medicinal value, and especially as an elixir. A little further down the road was a shop where animals were treated in a different way. Kojimaya was one of the city's few veterinary institutions, highly regarded among the dog-owning members of the households of the feudal lords. Not far beyond, down the road to Kokufu, stood Yotsuya Gate.

Modern Kōjimachi still contains reminders of its history, especially in the roads between the main street and the Hirakawa Temmangu shrine. Here small shops and houses are to be found surviving precariously among the bigger, posher buildings of the center of the modern city, supplying goods and services to the government offices, publishers, schools, embassies, and halls to north and south, just as their ancestors supplied and delivered to the houses of the feudal lords and the shogun's retainers.

# # #

Kudan and Takebashi

Progress has had a leveling effect on a hill that was once so steep that nine steps, *ku dan,* were built to make it easier to negotiate. The occasion was taken after the earthquake of 1923 to flatten things out and make Kudan Hill a much gentler slope. The nine steps had been fitted to the road in 1709, when nine houses were built on either side to accommodate the shogunate's gardeners. Before then the slope had been known as Iidazaka, after the village that stood on the crown of the hill, a village whose existence is recalled by the present-day Iidabashi.

In those days castle turrets and trees provided the tallest obstacles to the view from the top of Kudan Hill, and the prospect of Kanda and Nihombashi, the townspeople's quarters, lay spread out before one. Beyond them, across the waters of the bay, were the hills of the Bōsō

Peninsula. Every year, on the twenty-sixth day of the First and Seventh months, tens of thousands of men and women would congregate on the top of Kudan Hill and pass the night in jollification and chanting to celebrate the appearance of the full moon. So high was this eminence, indeed, and so clear the view that a lighthouse was built here in 1871 as a navigational guide for boats in the bay. The lighthouse stood in the grounds of Yasukuni Shrine, another early Meiji addition to the scenery on Kudan Hill, but it has since been moved to the south side of the road.

At the top of the hill there remains one survivor from the Edo period, the Tayasu Gate—not only a beautiful gate in itself, but also one of the few remaining complete *masugata,* square gates so named because they were built in the shape of a *masu,* or cubic vessels for measuring volume. *Masugata* gates consisted of two portals. The first and smaller one was a "Korean gate," with two roofed, projecting support columns at the back. Raiders who managed to force their way in through this small portal would find themselves in exactly the same sort of courtyard that we can see today at Tayasu Gate, with guards poised to shoot at them from the embrasures in the second of the two portals, a fortified hulk of a gate that must have been hard indeed to penetrate. These gates stood at all the entrances to the castle.

Tayasu Gate, which was named after another of the little villages absorbed into the shogun's city, led not directly into the castle but into an outer fortress known as Kita no Maru, with the compound of a junior branch of the Tokugawa family on each side of the central road, the Tayasu on the right and the Shimizu on the left. In the Meiji era, the barracks of the first regiment of the infantry guards were built on the site of the Tayasu residence, and of the second regiment on the land opposite where the Shimizu compound had stood. The barracks were long, low buildings that were among the very first in the country to be built of red brick. On the night of 23 August 1878, at least two hundred guards rose in revolt. They were angered by what they saw as the unfair distribution of rewards after the successful operation to put down Saigō Takamori's Seinan insurrection; they claimed that the officers had received all and the privates nothing. After killing several of their commanding officers, they marched on the emperor's temporary accommodation at the Akasaka Detached Palace to present him directly with their petition. Loyal troops were waiting for them. Their mutiny was quickly quelled, and forty-nine of their number were executed. This is one of the very rare occasions in modern Japanese history when Japanese privates have rebelled against their commanding officers. It is known as the Takebashi Incident, after the bridge that stands just east of the site of the barracks.

Under Tayasu Gate, at the beginning of Kudan Hill, is a part of the moat that testifies to the former steepness of the slope here. This stretch of moat is called Ushigafuchi, the "Ox Depths." It got its name from an accident that befell one of the floats in the procession of the Kanda Myōjin festival. The float was about to make its way into the castle grounds at Tayasu Gate when the ox that was drawing it lost control on the steep slope and cascaded with its float into the moat. Neither ox nor float were ever seen again, but the citizens of Edo were not about to pass up such an excellent opportunity for coining a new name. On the outside of the moat stands the Chiyoda Ward Office and Shimizu Gate, another of the better-preserved of the castle's old gates.

At the bottom of Kudan Hill, there was—and still is—a bridge called Manaitabashi, "Chopping Board Bridge," straddling the Nihombashi River. What is a Chopping Board Bridge? A bridge, so one theory goes, that leads to the Kitchen Quarter. Odaidokorochō, the "Kitchen Quarter," was just down the road from the bridge. If you cross the bridge going east and turn right (south), you will reach, after a ten-minute walk, Kanda Nishikichō. It would be hard to believe now, but this was once an open space, a firebreak created in 1717 after a temple and other buildings that occupied the land here had gone up in flames. The temple, Gojiin, was rebuilt to the northwest, in Otowa (Bunkyō Ward), and the land left open was called Gojiingahara, the Gojiin Field. The Gojiin Field lay directly to the northeast of the castle. In winter the cold, dry winds blow down on the city from the north, and indeed many of the most ruinous fires of the Edo period were started in the temples in the north of the city, chief among them the Long-Sleeves Fire. It was after that fire that the first firebreak had been created to the north of the castle. The addition of the Gojiin Field offered the shogun another advantage. Yoshimune, most falcon-crazy of all the falcon-crazy shoguns, could now take time off to go hunting next door to his castle in the Gojiin Field. But Yoshimune was concerned, too, for the well-being of his citizens. In winter and spring, he kept the field closed for his own falconing. For the rest of the year, however, the gates were opened and anyone who chose to could enter the Gojiin Field and enjoy its pines and cedars and sit down at one of its teahouses and have a drink.

A short walk under the shady pines and cedars would have taken the citizen of Edo to the gates of the castle itself, and, in particular, to one gate that still stands, the Hirakawa Gate. This was the gate used by the women of the inner chambers, for which reason it became known as the Honorable Gate of the Tsubone, *tsubone* being the title given to the higher ranks of the shogun's ladies. However, it was only on a very few carefully vetted occasions that the ladies were allowed to use it and leave the castle grounds. Or so it was supposed to be. In 1714, Gekkōin, a favorite of the recently deceased shogun, Ienobu, and mother of the then shogun, Ietsugu, who was still a child, was to pay a New Year visit of respect to the late shogun's mausoleum. However, she sent in her place one of her senior attendants, a lady known as Ejima. On her way back from the grave at Zōjōji in Shiba, Ejima was lured to the theater by a group of shogunate officials with whom she was friendly and merchants in search of lucrative contracts. There at the theater she was entertained by Ikushima Shingorō, leading actor of the celebrated Yamamura troupe.

How exactly was she "entertained"? In the light of the politically motivated charges that were made against her and of the dramatized versions of the affair that appeared on the Kabuki stage, it is hard to gauge the extent of the conviviality enjoyed by the couple. If we abide by the more fanciful versions, then we must believe that a passionate liaison developed, in which were implicated and embroiled a host of officials, guards, and ladies of the inner chambers. It could be, however, that the two simple enjoyed a drink of tea together, and that the storm, true to proverbial promptings, brewed among the tea leaves. It does seem likely that a brief flirtation ensued, since this became the focus of the accusations hurled at the unfortunate woman and her accomplices by the enemies of her mistress, Gekkōin. The affair was seized upon with glee by the faction that resented the power gained by the young shogun's mother and her coterie of advisers. Ejima was banished to the mountains, where she was forbidden contact with the outside world. Ikushima was packed off to the penal colony on Miyake Island, where he was to spend all but the last of his remaining years. Ejima's elder brother, as head of the family, bore responsibility and was executed. The Yamamura troupe was disbanded, and banishments were dished out generously. In such carnage ended the teacup incident known to the Japanese as the Ejima-Ikushima affair.

# # #

Kanda

Kanda incorporates the great historical dichotomy of this city: half of it is official, national, imposed from the outside; the other half, although alien in the first place, sprang local roots and nourished a local culture. The two institutions that perhaps more than any other represent these two traditions stand together on Kanda's hill. On the one hand there is Yushima Seidō—cold, gray, austere, a monument to official dogma—and on the other, Kanda Myōjin, the shrine overlooking the townspeople's quarters, whose festival is the very stuff of the city's popular culture.

Kanda Myōjin is said to have been founded in 730 in the village of Shibasaki (in present-day Ōtemachi). Its early history is connected with an eastern warlord called Taira no Masakado, who led one of the first revolts against the emperor in Kyoto and paid for it with his life in 940. Masakado's career was a stormy one. He killed his uncles, alienated the members of his clan, and, after seizing control of the eastern provinces, declared himself emperor. He became over the centuries a deity himself, and when his shrine was moved to its present site in 1616, he was adopted by the townspeople of the new city as a sort of patron saint. They appreciated his rebelliousness, his intractability, his irrationality. He challenged established authority, which is what they might have liked to have done. He had lost his head on their behalf, and they knew that the same fate would befall them if they were to challenge the status quo. Taira no Masakado came to be regarded as an avatar of Okuninushi no Mikoto, one of the divine pacifiers of the archipelago. Later, when the emperor Meiji wanted to pay his respects at the shrine, concerned officials of the imperial household decided it would not be good for him to offer prayers at a shrine to a rebel, and they prevailed on the shrine priests to have Masakado's spirit transferred to a separate building.

Kanda's cultural schizophrenia, part townspeople and part samurai, derives from its position both on the bluff that extends south from Yushima and in the flatlands east and south of this bluff. Kanda was not an old village like Shibasaki to the south; its name appears in the records no earlier than 1559. Much of the southern tip of the Kanda bluff was cut away in one of the early engineering works conducted by Tokugawa Ieyasu to fill in the marshlands directly east of the castle and create firm land on which to build the districts for his merchants and craftsmen. Some years later, further indentations were made on the topology of the area when a water channel was dug through the Kanda hill from Iidamachi to the Sumida River. The aim of this massive undertaking was threefold: to stop the flow of silt down the Hirakawa and into the port, to complete the outer ring of moats that surrounded the castle and much of the city, and to protect the castle, Nihombashi, and other central areas from floods. The predictable result was to make Kanda particularly flood prone.

Kanda was now divided by this river, which itself was called the Kandagawa. It was divided into an outer and inner district, a division that is still respected. Soto Kanda is the area north, outside, the Kanda River and Uchi Kanda the area south, inside it. Kanda's boundaries were now drawn: on its west they were marked by the Nihombashi River and the course of the old Hirakawa; on the south, by a waterway that flowed east from a point on the Hirakawa behind the international post office in Ōtemachi; on the east, by the Sumida River; and on the north, in part by the Kanda River and in part, to the east, by a line drawn a few blocks north of the river, thus including Soto Kanda.

It was for many centuries one of the features of this city that what had become its local culture, the Shitamachi element, although assailed by new waves from the outside, was always stronger than other cultural veins. Shitamachi was the belt of land stretching from Ginza in the south to Kanda in the north, but it came to represent in people's consciousness all of Edo, so much so that people talked in Yamanote areas about "going to Edo" when what they meant was going to the townspeople's district, Shitamachi. And no one would have thought of an Edokko being born in the Yamanote hills, where the dominant cultural force was represented by the military class. The term

"Shitamachi" itself probably derives from the position of these districts (*machi*) under (*shita*) the shogun's castle. Its first use in distinction to Yamanote has been traced back to 1662. Despite its ambiguous position encompassing both one of the extended fingers of hill and the low-lying land under it, Kanda came in the folklore of the city to stand for Shitamachi, almost as Shitamachi stood for the city itself. The Edokko was said to have been born in Shiba, outside the city, but raised in Kanda, "*Shiba de umarete, Kanda de sodate.*" Nihombashi, the center of Shitamachi, lost its qualifications as base for the Edokko as perceptions of the Edokko himself shifted. He ceased during the passage of the years to be the wastrel son of a great merchant and became a more appealing figure, the happy-go-lucky shop clerk with few social pretensions. This was the Edokko who lived in Kanda.

The Edokko had to share his Kanda. In the early years of the city, he had to share it principally with temples. There were sixty-nine temples built in the first four decades of the seventeenth century along the south bank of the new Kanda River. Some of them, like Kichijōji, had been moved there from land now occupied by Edo Castle. Others had opened branches in Edo, just like the shops of Nihombashi. They had all been placed in the district called Kanda Kita Teramachi because it was far from the city center, and so there was less danger of a temple fire, started perhaps in a crematorium, spreading to the castle. Soon, however, the city had grown beyond these original limits. The temples were a source of congestion. They took up too much room, and so were moved further out of the city. The Long-Sleeves Fire of 1657, which was started in a temple, hastened this process, and before too long there were no more temples left in Kanda.

The Edokko also had to share his Kanda with the military classes. Only a few feudal lords had their Edo estates in the low-lying parts of Kanda, but the situation was different on Kanda hill. When Ieyasu died in 1616, his personal retainers moved to Edo from the old man's base in Suruga province (Shizuoka Prefecture). They were given land on the chiseled slopes of Kanda hill, which henceforth came to be known as Suruga Shū no Dai, the "Hill of the Band from Suruga," or more simply, Surugadai, the name it bears to this day.

For all the temples and for all the men from Suruga, Kanda was from its very earliest days best known for its market, the central point of exchange for almost all important daily commodities. Roads and rivers converged on Kanda. The Nakasendō, "Central Mountain Road," and the Nikkō Kaidō, the road to Nikkō and the north, met at Sujikai Gate, at the north entrance to Kanda. The Kanda River, on which Sujikai Gate stood, opened out onto the Sumida River with its busy traffic of boats from all parts of the eight provinces of the east. And in the south of Kanda, along the banks of the Nihombashi River (the old Hirakawa) was the busiest unloading stage of them all, the Kamakura Quay (between Kamakurabashi and Kandabashi). Vegetables, firewood, and bamboo were all unloaded here. The vegetables came from the provinces of Kazusa, Shimōsa, and Awa east of the city. Fish was traded here, too, although not in the same quantities as at Nihombashi, the great fish market in the heart of the city. Vegetables from Kasai, in the swampy districts just east of Edo, were unloaded at Inari Quay in Soto Kanda Hanafusamachi, close by the Sujikai Gate. Radishes and cabbages were brought there by horse from Nerima, Mikawashima, and other villages just north of the city. In the next block east, Sakumachō 1-chōme, timber merchants had their stores, and along with them rice dealers, whose stores here were second in number only to those of Fukagawa.

At some early stage, but when is not quite clear, the various markets that had arisen around Kanda coalesced into one large market in a quarter called Tachō (one of the old names that have been mercifully left for us). This, the Kanda market, was where a runner from the castle kitchen came to buy supplies. It was situated just to the west of Kanda's, and Edo's, main street, which ran north from Nihombashi to Sujikai Gate and was known as the Torichō Suji. On either side of this main street were reminders of the early days of the city and of the attempts to have people of the same trade living in the same quarter. Thus, the metal casters were brought together in Nabechō, the blacksmiths in Kajichō, the porters in Norimonochō, the silver smiths in Shiroganechō, the dyers in Kon'yachō, the plasterers in Shirakabechō, the carpenters in Daikuchō, the lacquerers in Nushichō, the sword polishers in Saegichō, and so on. The administration of each of these quarters was given over to one family, normally compatriots of the Tokugawa from Mikawa and the provinces along the East Sea Road. Kon'yachō, for example, was a grant from Ieyasu to a retainer called Tsuchiya, who had been wounded in battle. This man was given the task of administering six dyers' quarters, three in Kanda and three in

Kyōbashi. When the shogunate wanted material dyed, he was given the order to farm out to the craftsmen of the quarter. Another of these families was the Shiina, hereditary heads of Nabechō. The metal caps that can still be seen on the railings of the wooden bridge at Hirakawa Gate are their work.

This system of congregation according to craft broke down quite quickly, mainly as a result of population pressure in the fast-expanding city. But it has been preserved to this day in the names of the quarters. Tokyo still has its Kajichō and its Kon'yachō, into the middle of which a Norimonochō has been sandwiched. The idea of grouping people of similar occupation and then naming the district after them gave rise to the curious phenomenon of the moving quarter. For example, when Renjakuchō, the quarter south of Sujikai Gate, was cleared after the Long-Sleeves Fire to form a firebreak, the inhabitants were moved to the wilds of the Musashi Plain, taking the name of their quarter with them. Even now, Mitaka has its Kami and Shimo Renjaku. One of the smallest quarters in Kanda, occupying a slit of land above Akihabara Station on the Hibiya Line, is called Kanda Hirakawachō. This is a quarter and a name that has moved many times. It was moved first from its original site, by the mouth of the Hirakawa on the site of Edo Castle, to Kōjimachi when the castle was built, and there most of it remains, with its shrine, just behind the Supreme Court. But later, a section became part of the estate of a feudal lord, and so the townspeople inhabitants were moved, together with their quarter's name, here to Kanda. There are many other examples, too, including one quarter whose name no longer exists that was moved three times between Kanda and Fukagawa.

Among this patchwork of moving names stood a building that itself had moved from Ueno in 1691. The Confucian academy, spiritual precursor of the modern Yushima Seidō ("Sacred Hall"), had been built exactly sixty years before that on Ueno hill near where the statue of Saigō Takamori now stands. Tokugawa Yoshinao, lord of Owari and ninth son of Ieyasu, had been granted the land to build a hall for the study and propagation of the Confucian classics under the direction of Hayashi Razan, Ieyasu's court Confucianist. Between them, the Hayashi family—Razan, his son, and grandson—and the Tokugawa—with Ieyasu, his sons Yoshinao and Mitsukuni, and great-grandson Tsunayoshi foremost among them—established and cemented the position of Confucianism as the dominant state doctrine. The Tokugawa were the supreme patrons, while the Hayashi were the high priests. The Confucianism they espoused was the modified variety that developed in China from the tenth to the twelfth centuries and whose greatest champion was Zhu Xi. As with all their cultural borrowings, the Japanese were carefully selective in what they chose to absorb, and what they did absorb they transformed to their liking. The Confucianism of the Edo period was strictly empirical and oriented toward man and society, eschewing most of the metaphysical theorizing that had been a characteristic of this modified Confucianist thought in China. There was a tendency in Japan to use Zhu Xi's ideas, especially that of the primacy of the five great human relationships (between father and son, ruler and subject, etc.), as a tool to enforce obedience to Tokugawa rule and the feudal system. In the establishment of this orthodox, "official" brand of Confucianism, the Hayashi family and their educational institute played a leading role.

The most fervent Tokugawa advocate of Confucian ideals was the fifth shogun, Tsunayoshi. He it was who had the college moved from Ueno to Yushima, where it stood on ground now occupied by Yushima Seidō and by the Tokyo University School of Medicine. The college, conveniently situated for the purpose, became a sort of state academy with the sons of Tokugawa retainers, who lived on the slopes of Surugadai just south of the academy, and many of the feudal nobility attending. Hayashi Razan's grandson was appointed principal, a post which became hereditary in the family. The institute was renamed the Shōheikō, Changping Academy, after Confucius's birthplace in the ancient Chinese state of Lu. It continued to flourish throughout the Edo period, despite the gradual degeneration of Confucianism as a political philosophy. As well as the academy, there was a hall where ceremonies to Confucius and his disciples were held twice a year, in spring and autumn, when the shogun and lords presented offerings and listened to a lecture delivered by the academy's principal.

Today in Tokyo the cramming schools and publishing houses tend to cluster round the important universities. In Edo it was much the same. In the streets of Kanda there was a large number of private academies and print shops. The ground was thick with Confucianists, especially in Soto Kanda north of Sujikai Gate and near the site of a pond called Otamagaike in what is now Iwamotochō in the east of

Kanda. The pond seems to have been named after a beautiful woman called Otama who served tea in a nearby stall. According to some stories, she took her own life, throwing herself into the pond, distressed that she had been the cause of a fight for her hand. The pond itself disappeared after a while, victim to the excessive numbers of people who lived in Kanda. But its memory, kindled by the spirit of Otama, lived on. There were poets and painters living near the site of the pond. The great eccentric Hiraga Gennai lived nearby for a while, and later the writers Tamenaga Shunsui and Ryūtei Tanehiko lived there, too. The swordmaster Chiba Shūsaku had his academy there. Itō Gemboku set up the first smallpox vaccination clinic by the site of the pond in 1857, only for it to be burnt down six months later. It was moved elsewhere and became the direct precursor of the medical school of Tokyo University. In Soto Kanda Sakumachō a medical school of a more conservative nature had existed for many decades before. Founded by the shogun's doctor in 1757, it later became the official shogunate medical college. On the other side of the Kanda River was Kijichō, once famous for its bathhouses where compliant women of renowned beauty did more than scratch the dust off the backs of weary customers. Kijichō, now a part of Kanda Tsukasachō, had a most remarkable family as its hereditary chiefs, the Saitō family, who over three generations compiled the greatest book about the city, the *Illustrated Gazetteer of Famous Places in Edo*.

In the west of Kanda was another district with a distinguished literary pedigree, Iidamachi. Here in this townspeople's enclave, townsmen and members of the military class, including retainers of the shogun like Ōta Nampo, used to meet in associations called *ren* to compose comic poetry. Here, too, lived a widow called Oyaku who ran a shoe shop ("between the charcoal seller and the greengrocer on the south side of the street"[7]). She married again in 1793 and took into her home her new husband. It was a strange match. Her husband, born in Fukagawa the son of a low-ranking samurai, was very conscious of class distinctions and of the need to uphold the dignity and moral qualities of his rank. He was a writer of *yomihon,* "reading books" (as opposed to the more heavily illustrated forms of fiction such as those of which Santō Kyōden was the master). He was a protege of Kyōden and his name was Takizawa Bakin. For the next thirty-one years, Bakin lived in this house, with its little garden of fruit trees, an appallingly bad seller of clogs but an increasingly successful writer. His greatest work, *The Saga of Eight Dogs of Satomi,* occupied him for twenty-seven years from 1814 onward and ran to 106 volumes. It is a stirring romance that tells the story of eight heroes born of a mystical union between a valiant dog and the daughter of the first Satomi lord of the province of Awa, whose eight descendants fought courageously and stubbornly against the Hōjō rulers of the eastern provinces in the sixteenth century.

When the statesmen and generals of the emperor Meiji took over from the retainers of the Tokugawa shoguns, Kanda maintained its split identity. In the large open spaces left by the departed retainers, schools and universities found fertile ground. In the 1880s the forerunners of several of the country's leading universities—Meiji, Chūō, Nihon, Hōsei, and Senshū—settled here. Across the Kanda River, Japan's first teachers' training school was built in 1872 on the site of the Shōhei Confucian academy. The country's first museum was built here too (it left for Ueno five years later) and the first official library, predecessor of the National Diet Library. The first official exhibition was held here, in 1872. Hospitals like Juntendō found the area attractive; the land was cheap and plots extensive. So too did Christian organizations, like the YMCA and the Salvation Army. Nikolai Cathedral, center of the Russian Orthodox Church in Japan, was built on Surugadai by the British architect Josiah Conder in 1884. Like Tokyo Station, it lost its top in the earthquake of 1923, and, although it has been restored, it looks squatter than it should. Political organizations came to Kanda. The Japan Socialist Party held its first meetings in Kanda, and a different organization with a name pronounced the same way, Shakaitō, had its offices here. This was the rickshaw pullers' association.

And then there were the bookshops. They have been in Kanda as long as the colleges, from around the 1880s. They include among their number both shops selling new books and antiquarian bookshops. Some are specialist shops, but most are general. The heyday of the seller of old books came just after the war, when the publishing industry lay in ruins and few new books were appearing. Books require printers and publishers, and these were drawn to Kanda. Most of the early printers of government material established themselves in Kyōbashi, but in Kanda, and in particular in Misakichō, Nishi Kanda, and Iidabashi, many of the printers who worked for the publishers set up shop. Of the publishers, some of the most famous in the country, including Iwanami Shoten and Shufunotomo, have long had their offices here, near the bookshops, in that part of Kanda known as Jimbōchō.

Kanda was one of the first fifteen wards created in 1878, and it remained a local government entity until 1947, when it was merged with Kōjimachi to form Chiyoda Ward. For a while, the center of Kanda Ward—indeed, one of the centers of Tokyo—was Sudachō. In 1912, the Chūō Line was extended from Iidamachi to Manseibashi, which thus became one of the three big terminus stations, along with Ueno and, in 1914, Tokyo. The remains of the station can still be seen, just to the west of Mansei Bridge over the Kanda River. The Kanda market was still here in Tachō, just south of Sudachō. And to add to the clatter and congestion of the place, many of the city's tram lines passed through, among them the Number Twelve from Shinjuku to Ryōgoku and the Nineteen from Asukayama to Shimbashi. But Sudachō's day was short-lived. In 1919, the Chūō Line was extended to Tokyo Station, and in 1928 the market was moved from Tachō north to its present site in Soto Kanda. Nowadays, Sudachō is a bit of a backwater. It remains the capital's main wholesale district for fabric for tailoring into suits, with some fifty shops within its boundaries, and it retains, like Ogawamachi down the Yasukuni Road, some old, prewar buildings with copper tiles and art-deco motifs, houses that nowadays fall easy prey to the that very insidious sort of gangster, the "land grabber," or *jiageya*.

Some years before the Kanda market was moved north across the Kanda River, a railway line for cargo trains was built from Ueno down to Akihabara. This was the start for a new transport center in Tokyo, one that was soon to eclipse the others around it. Neither Akihabara nor any of its several variants—Akibahara, Akibappara, Akiba no Hara—is an old name. It dates back only as far as December of 1870, when the area was denuded by flames and left bare as a firebreak. A shrine called Akiba Jinja, consecrated to the deity who subdues fire, was built here (it has since been moved to Matsugaya in Taitō Ward), and the area came to be known as Akiba no Hara. To this tract of open land came Japan's first bicycles and the men who hired them out. Horses were to be had for hire here too. The open space was a venue for acrobatic acts, performances of sumo wrestling, and a visiting Italian circus. Nowadays, it is hard to think of a name more outrageously inappropriate for the area than Akihabara, "Field of Autumn Leaves."

The electronically propelled juggernaut of a market that is today's Akihabara has its origins in the years of scarcity after the war, when a black market sprouted in the environs of the station, which by this time had become an important railway junction where the Yamanote and Sobu lines crossed. There had been a steady increase in the number of stalls selling spare parts for radios, and in 1951 provision was made for them under the tracks of the Sōbu Line. This little market went on growing, and growing and growing, until now it has a turnover of ¥30 trillion, which represents very nearly 10 percent of the total national turnover in domestic electrical products. In this land of mini Ginzas, Akihabara has the distinction of admitting to only one rival, a very mini Akihabara in Osaka. With its thousand shops crammed into a few acres of land, Tokyo's Akihabara can safely claim to be the only place of its kind in the world. But at the same time it is unmistakably Japanese—in its single-mindedness, in its commercial gregariousness, and not least in its concentration on homemade products. It is a monument to Japanese love for, faith in, and mastery of electrical gadgetry, a giant temple in which are worshiped the modern idols of power and noise, material comfort, vicarious pleasure, microcosmic efficiency, and instant, unrelenting newness, as well as an older cult, that of cleanliness and neatness.

The gaudy bright lights of Akihabara nowadays throw much of the rest of Kanda into shade.

3

Central Tokyo:
Chūō Ward

Nihombashi

"We passed over several stately bridges laid over small rivers and muddy ditches," wrote the traveler and scholar Engelbert Kaempfer of his first visit to Edo in the 1690s, with the representatives of the Dutch trading mission. "Among the bridges, there is one 42 fathom in length, famous all over Japan.... It is called *Nihonbas,* that is, the bridge of Japan."[1]

Nihombashi, "Bridge of Japan," the most famous bridge in a city of bridges, was never a particularly impressive sight, but it made up for its lack of glamour by its geographical importance. When he had the bridge built in 1603, Ieyasu declared that it should be made the starting point for the five great roads leading out of the city. All distances were to be measured from Nihombashi, and at every league along these great roads, a mound was built and a hackberry planted on the mound to bind the earth together with its long roots. At intervals along the roads were stages or post houses offering lodging and a change of horse and runner. The official messages of the shogunal government were conveyed on foot rather than on horseback, the fifty-three stages of the Tōkaidō, the East Sea Road that linked Edo and Kyoto, being covered in but sixty hours in the case of the most urgent messages. Both horses and men were available for hire at the post houses at set prices. The center of this national relay system, known as the "post-horse system," was situated not far from Nihombashi, at Ōdemmachō ("Large Post-

Horse Quarter") to the north of the bridge, alternating with Minami Demmachō to the south. Nor is this all just a thing of the past. Distances along the national highways (but not the expressways) are still counted from the bridge, and at its northern foot stands a large stake marking the "zero leagues" spot.

Nihombashi, center of the nation's road network, claims for itself one of the most momentous transport innovations of Meiji years, the *jinrikisha* ("man-powered cart") or rickshaw. Although the discovery has been attributed to various people in Japan, not all of them Japanese, credence is generally given to the claim of Izumi Yōsuke, who had a workshop at the foot of the bridge where he embarked on his rickshaw business in 1869, a year after the arrival in the city of the emperor Meiji and the inauguration of the era of civilization and enlightenment. In four years' time, there were already over thirty-four thousand rickshaws in the city, and the quiet streets had become a cacophony of clattering iron wheels and yelping runners. Most rickshaws had one puller, but some had two, and there were extra men for hire to pull and push them up Tokyo's many slopes. The charge of ten sen (in 1875, less than ten U.S. cents) was enough to allow the authorities to levy taxes on the pullers, some of whom notched up 150 kilometers a day. In 1909 rubber wheels replaced the noisy iron ones, but by then the municipal tram service had been put into service, and the slow decline of the rickshaw had begun. By the time of the 1923 earthquake, there were fewer than twenty thousand of them. Nevertheless, rickshaws were a common sight on the streets of the city until the Pacific War, with doctors, in particular, being frequent users. During the war, the pullers were conscripted, but the decade after the war saw the appearance on the streets of Tokyo of the pedicab.

Pedicabs soon retreated before the advance of four-wheeled motor traffic. Not many years after the last of them had disappeared, the authorities were planning to build a system of expressways to relieve the city of its awesome traffic congestion. One of these expressways was routed smack over Nihombashi, as if the planners were taking a malicious satisfaction in obscuring the bridge that was the starting point for the great highways of the Edo period with one of their modern successors. There was, not unnaturally, opposition to the plan. Petitions were raised, alternatives suggested, but it all came to nothing. Alternative routings would cost too much, and besides, this was 1962, just before the Tokyo Olympics, when Japanese eyes were fixed firmly on the future. So Nihombashi fell into perpetual shade, a great shame for aesthetic as well as sentimental reasons. The present bridge, which was constructed in 1911, has four proud bronze Chinese lions guarding it at its feet and four unicorns seated like dogs waiting on their masters on either side of two bronze needles whose tops are lost in the ferroconcrete swirl of the expressway. The sidewalks are elegantly paved in granite.

With all the traffic both mechanized and human and the unwelcome presence overhead, there is little inducement to stop and admire Nihombashi. But it should not be thought that things were so different in the Edo period. Traffic congestion was a considerable problem, especially after 1716, when the authorities gave up their attempts to curb the number of basket-chair taxis. The parking of horse-drawn carts by the roadside was strictly forbidden, and banishment or worse was the punishment for causing an accident resulting in the death of a pedestrian. Nihombashi, at the center of the desperately overpopulated part of the city inhabited by the townspeople, must have been every bit as crowded as the sidewalks of modern Shibuya and Shinjuku. On one occasion at least, the weight of people was too great for the bridge's wooden legs to bear, and it collapsed, causing the death of about twelve hundred people who were fleeing one of the city's periodic fires.

This great little bridge, Nihombashi, stood—if not quite at the geographical center of the city—at the heart of the part of Edo which belonged to the townspeople and to the culture that made the city such an unusual and distinctive place. Immediately to the south and east of the bridge were the quays, as many as thirty or forty of them, where all the goods necessary for daily life—from bamboo poles to saké— were unloaded and stored in the markets before being sold to the retailers (see map on page 256). To the north were the main streets of the city, lined with the handsome black facades and the elegant awnings of the great dry goods stores. Because of Nihombashi's position at the hub of the city's activity, one of the largest official notice boards was situated at the foot of the bridge. This was not so much a notice board as a space set aside for the erection of any number of wooden plaques bearing notices. Supervision of these sites for official notices was normally the responsibility of barbers, whose shops tended to be strategically placed at the entrance to each quarter. Thus the barber's unofficial role of rumormonger and propagator of gossip was authorized and institutionalized. Also at the southern foot of the bridge was ground set aside by the city authorities, again for display and again chiefly for admonitory purposes. The objects of display here were of two kinds. First, there were people whose wicked deeds, it was felt, were of a sort to merit public exposure in fetters. The perpetrators of the following types of "crime" were regarded as suitable exhibits: priests caught indulging in the pleasures of the flesh and the parties to an unsuccessful double suicide. Culprits belonging to the other category of exhibit were in a less fortunate position. These were people who had murdered their master or one of their own relatives and who were therefore condemned to death by crucifixion. They were given a chance here at Nihombashi to avoid this end. They were placed in a hole with neck and head protruding. The victim's neck was placed in shackles, two saws were left on either side of the protruding head, and marks made on the neck. The saws were there in case a passer-by should decide to try his hand as executioner, and the marks were there to help him. Few people ever took up this grisly offer.

The priests and others who were put on public show at the foot of the bridge may at least have felt themselves lucky that they were not locked up in the city prison, which was situated near Nihombashi at Kodemmachō ("Small Post-Horse Quarter," serving the countryside around Edo). Kodemmachō prison covered one block of land. It was administered by officials working under the city magistrates and contained up to four hundred prisoners, not such a large figure when one considers that Edo's population grew to well over a million.

Edo-period Japan was a feudal society, and its ranks and hierarchies extended even into Kodemmachō prison. Indeed, the prison offered a parody of feudal society that at times rose to grotesque heights. Thus, high-ranked priests and samurai of sufficiently high status to be received in audience by the shogun were consigned to a prison building where they enjoyed the luxuries of space and their own personal attendant, chosen from among lower-raking prisoners with a good record. Lowly samurai, priests, and doctors were detained in one of two halls known as *agariya,* written with the same Chinese characters as *ageya,* the teahouses of the Yoshiwara licensed quarter. To one of the two *agariya* were sent those prisoners who were awaiting shipment to the islands for convicts in the Izu archipelago. In the other *agariya* were confined, in the prison's later years, three of its most famous inmates: Watanabe Kazan, Takano Chōei, and Yoshida Shōin. Kazan, scholar and painter, was thrown into jail in 1839 for his hostility to the shogunate and released six months later. Takano Chōei, a fierce critic, like Kazan, of the shogunate's xenophobic policies, became the first and only inmate to break an unwritten prison rule: he failed to return after he and his fellow prisoners had been released because of a fire that threatened the prison in 1844. The third celebrated inmate was Yoshida Shōin, whose zeal for moral, military, and political reform infected many of those who became the most influential statesmen of the Meiji era but whose impetuosity led to his execution at the prison in 1859 for his part in an assassination plot.

The lowest class of convict lived in utter squalor. Perhaps a prisoner's only chance of survival was to smuggle in some coins with which to bribe the prison officials. All offenders were searched when they entered the jail, but the search was never *too* thorough, and so it became something of a prison custom to treat coins temporarily as suppositories. The treatment normally worked, for the coins would then be handed over to the top-dog prisoners, who would hand them over to the jailers as they saw fit. The prisoners early in the Edo period had organized themselves, appointed a leader, and given each other duties. The attempt had been well meaning. But it was soon abused, and there developed a strict hierarchy—a straw-mat hierarchy, with the convict boss appropriating for himself as many as seven of the tatami mats that were spread on top of the cold wooden floorboards. On top of this mountain of seven mats he sat, and ruled. And he dispensed justice according to the size of the bribes he received and was able to pass on to the jailers. His assistants, too, purloined far more than their fair share of the only article the prisoners had with which to display their levels of power and status: the tatami mats.

As for the others, they had to squeeze themselves five, six, seven, and sometimes more onto the same 1 x 2-meter mat, and this they had to make do with by night and by day. Conditions often surpassed levels of physical tolerance, especially in the humid summer months. Death from disease was distressingly common, especially since sanitary conditions were appalling. There is some disagreement among scholars about the extent of torture. It was probably administered more frequently by the unofficial prisoners' boss than it was by the jailers.

One form of torture inflicted on their less fortunate fellows consisted of stripping the victim naked and plastering him with sweetened fermented bean paste. After a night passed in this state, the man was clothed again, upon which his body would swell grossly and he would in all likelihood die. However, this sort of treatment was normally reserved for the shogunate's unofficial spies and others against whom prisoners had a grudge to bear.

The prison was moved to Ichigaya in 1875. On its site now stands a primary school and a playground, some commemorative stones, and three temples built in remembrance of the horrors suffered in the prison.

Until as recently as the Great Kantō Earthquake of 1923, Nihombashi was best known for something quite different. Its smell gave the bridge away. At its feet, along the north bank of the waterway that flowed under it, was the city's fish market. Not only along the bank but also in the streets behind, there were thousands of shops, many of them no more than a meter broad. The Nihombashi fish market—this was the preserve par excellence of the Edokko, the sons of the city. Things were different, however, in the city's early days, when not only goods and services but skills and people too had to be imported from elsewhere. This applied even to something as basic as fishing, for the fishermen of the bay and its adjacent peninsulas had no experience— had never had any need—to fish on a larger scale. The origins of the market are obscure, but it is normally thought to have started as an outlet for the surplus catch of the fishermen of Tsukudajima, who had been moved from Osaka to Edo by the shogun and whose brief was to supply the castle with whitebait, keep a weather eye on shipping in the bay, and report any strange happenings. The Tsukudajima fishermen have a connection with the fish market that endures in the modern market at Tsujiki, where many of their descendants still work.

In 1628, a merchant from Nara who was already trading in fish in the new city of Edo arranged with fishermen from the province of Suruga that they should give him a regular supply. He is supposed to have introduced the large-scale use of corfs so that the sea bream caught hundreds of kilometers down the coast could be kept fresh and succulent for the table of the shogun and his ladies. The business that this merchant supervised soon developed into a *kumi,* a "gang" or—more properly—a trade association, the Hon Odawarachō

Association, named after the area in which it was situated. In rapid succession, other wharves for fish, each one under the umbrella of its own association and each one a part of Nihombashi market, opened in the immediate vicinity of Hon Odawarachō, along the banks of the waterways at the northern foot of the bridge. One of these wharves was situated in the part of Nihombashi known as Anjinchō, the quarter where a famous Englishman had lived in the city's earliest days, an Englishman by the name of William Adams, navigator of a Dutch ship shipwrecked on the Japanese coast and later adviser to Ieyasu and the possessor of his own fief and a Japanese name, Miura Anjin.

One of Adams's fellow officers aboard the Dutch ship that ran aground on the coast of Kyushu was a man called Jan Joosten van Lodensteijn, who like Adams was given a house in Edo where he lived with his Japanese wife, directing shogunate trade ships to Southeast Asia. Joosten's residence was situated near the castle by the stretch of moat known as Babasaki, and the quayside here became known in honor of the Dutchman as Yayosu, which was a valiant Japanese attempt to make something of Jan Joosten. Yayosu over the centuries has become Yaesu, but another transformation has occurred, a geographical one. Until 1929, Yaesu was situated where it should be, along the banks of the moat, but eventually Yaesu was subsumed into Marunouchi 2-chōme. In 1954, Yaesu reappeared, this time a little way to the east, on the other side of Tokyo Station, between the railway tracks and Nihombashi and Kyōbashi, and there it has remained.

The fishermen and wholesalers of Nihombashi were not allowed to forget that they were in business in order, first and foremost, to supply the castle. Only fish that was not chosen for the delectation of the shogun, his officials, and the ladies of the castle could be sold to whomsoever they wanted at whatever price they chose. Every morning, the dreaded visitation occurred. An official from the castle kitchens arrived with fifteen or so assistants. They went about their work vigorously and peremptorily. They brooked no opposition. When one of them saw a fish he thought looked good he unsheathed from inside his sleeve a large metal claw, uttered the magic word *goyō*, "official business," and appropriated the fish. Payment was made twice a year at prices much lower than market value. This was a considerable inconvenience for the traders, especially as there was no telling what kind of fish or how many fish the castle would be wanting.

Attempts were sometimes made to alert traders to the following day's likely order, but this normally led to the "disappearance" of the required fish. They would be unloaded and sold, for example, at Shinagawa down the coast, and so the castle cooks would have to trudge all the way down there. Another obvious ploy was to hide the best fish. This the traders did, in all sorts of places, including quite often the latrine. No measures were taken against traders caught trying to cheat officials in this way; it was all part of the game.

Sea bream, the fish of good fortune (the connection being based on a play on words), was perhaps the most prized of fish. Its sale was forbidden except at Nihombashi. Other white-fleshed fish were also regarded as being of a sufficiently high culinary class to be served on the shogun's table. But such fish as tuna, sardines, and mackerel, as well as other staples of our modern diet, were disdained—too oily perhaps for the delicate palates of the shogun's ladies. The high-handed nature of the arrangements for supplying the castle continued to cause friction and ended in 1815 with a fracas as a consequence of which five young fish traders who were adjudged to have caused the trouble were sent to nearby Kodemmachō prison, where they all died.

Despite the vagaries of the castle supply system, some of the larger wholesalers managed to accumulate fortunes. One of the more prosperous dealers in sea bream, Sugiyama Sampu, himself an accomplished poet, was several times host and benefactor to the master of haiku poetry, Matsuo Bashō. Bashō's disciple Takarai Kikaku lived only a stone's throw away from the Nihombashi fish market. And Bashō himself has left us the following uncanny reminder that a fishmonger's shop can have changed little over the centuries:

> And even the gums
> Of the salted bream on the
> Fish shop shelf look cold.

The market operated according to a complicated system of licenses, subcontracts, and rents, and life cannot have been so easy for the lessee of a meter-wide back-street wholesale shop or a barrow boy working for one of the delivery firms known then as now in the market as teahouses, *chaya*. But it is hard not to believe that the same spirit of comradeship and good health informed the Nihombashi market as it does the market's successor in Tsukiji.

The fish market was forced out of Nihombashi after the earthquake of 1923. The move to Tsukiji had already been in the cards. Nowadays there would not be the faintest whiff of fish at Nihombashi were it not for a shop called Yagichō, which has been selling dried bonito flakes in Nihombashi since 1737, and another shop round the corner also selling bonito flakes, Nimben, of even older ancestry. From both these premises issues the delicious aroma of dry fish. Almost next door to Yagichō is one of Tokyo's most famous shops selling the bay's most famous product, *nori,* or dried laver. The shop in question, founded in 1849, is Yamamoto Noriten. In addition to these shops, the market has left behind it, at the northeastern foot of the bridge, a commemorative statue of Otohime-sama, daughter of the Dragon King, whom Urashima Tarō followed to her seabed home and married and then left to return to his village, only to discover that underwater years had been centuries on earth and his family and friends had all died hundreds of years before.

The shops and statue are all that is left to remind the visitor of Nihombashi's fish market. The fish market itself, however, was but one of many markets in the area, and its wharves were several among scores of other wharves. For this was where Edo's port was situated. Edo had nothing when it was built. The inhabitants had to rely totally on goods delivered from elsewhere, normally from Osaka, Kyoto, and the more sophisticated regions in the west of the country. However, goods were seldom hauled long distances overland if it could be helped: too many ferries to board, too many barriers to cross. Whenever possible they were shipped by sea. But the coastline at Edo was marshy, full of tidal flats, and unsuitable for the construction of a harbor. Instead, a series of canals was built and lined with wharves. Ships carrying cargo from the west would moor off Shinagawa down the coast, and goods would be transferred onto smaller, flat-hulled boats and thus down the canals to the wharves. This led to great confusion of traffic on the city's waterways. Things were not made easier by the fact that each feudal lord possessed his own wharf and warehouse, and that the size of the port was restricted for defense reasons (military considerations were always paramount in the planning of Edo).

Rice and salt and dried goods were deposited in warehouses along the banks of the canals near Nihombashi's fish market. There were several vegetable markets, the largest to the northwest of Nihombashi at Kamakura Quay (see page 68). Opposite the fish market was another fruit and vegetable market, this one famous for its melons, tangerines, and radishes. Still another vegetable market was held further south at Kyōbashi. Here, too, radishes were at the top of the billing, and the market was known as Radish Quay. Nearby were the wharves for firewood and for bamboo poles.

Between Kyōbashi and Nihombashi was another central area of quays and warehouses called Hatchōbori, "Moat of the Eight Blocks," where the officials known as *yoriki* had their quarters. The *yoriki* were deputies of the city magistrates, and there were twenty-five of them to each of the two magistrates. They were themselves from the samurai class, but they received low stipends, which they were forced to supplement by receiving gifts. They were, indeed, famous for their capacity for accepting bribes. Unlike the *yoriki* who worked out of the public eye in others of the shogunate's departments, the deputies of the city magistrates kept their post in the family and so established a close-knit community with its own peculiarities, one of which was the unfailing and comic way in which they and their wives gave themselves airs. They left most of the actual patrolling of the streets to their assistants, the *dōshin,* low-ranking samurai who carried only one sword and who had teams of townsmen working under them armed with a truncheon known as a *jitte.* The *yoriki* only occasionally ventured out, riding a horse, high and mighty, carrying a lance and wearing chain mail under a fine new robe, the latest gift from a lord whose retainers had got drunk and disorderly and who had wanted the affair hushed up.

The compounds of the *yoriki* in Hatchōbori formed a samurai enclave among the lodgings of the townspeople. Hatchōbori was known until not so many years ago for its carpenters. They had remained behind when the timber wharves and warehouses had been moved east of the river in 1670. The timber merchants were among the earlier millionaires of Edo. Like the other rich merchants, they had their houses in the Nihombashi area. The east of the river was not for them, except as a site for their suburban villas. In Hatchōbori lived one of the wealthiest of the timber merchants, Kinokuniya Bunzaemon. In a city built of wood where a year without a major fire was a rarity, the timber merchants stood to make a handsome profit, and indeed many did. But few of them were in the same league as Kinokuniya Bun-zaemon, whose wealth was such that historians still have to sift facts from the abundance of legends that have accumulated like promissory notes around his name. Nowadays, it is thought unlikely that he started off his career, as some of the legends would have us believe, as a trader in tangerines. No one, however, would deny all of the stories of prodigal entertainment of the greatest courtesans of the day in Yoshiwara. A change in the political wind left the greatest spender of his day penniless.

Kinokuniya Bunzaemon had made his first million (in the inflationary terms of modern money-making) by selling the authorities the best cypress wood from the mountains of central Japan for the construction of the new main hall at the temple of Kan'eiji on Ueno hill. Kinokuniya Bunzaemon's great rival, Naraya Mozaemon, who lived almost next door on the island of Reiganjima, had also seen his fortune grow as a result of supplying good-quality timber for an official project. If he was in any way Kinokuniya Bunzaemon's inferior, it was only in his failure to lose all he earned in as spectacular a fashion. Mozaemon seems to have adhered to more orthodox family patterns and left it to his son and grandson, whose liaison with a Yoshiwara courtesan has found its way into the annals of the quarter, to squander all he earned. Neither of these two timber tycoons was born in Edo. Nor was Kawamura Zuiken, who died in 1699, just about the time when these two millionaire wastrels were reaching the summit of their lavish living. But Zuiken, who also lived on Reiganjima and made his fortune in timber (after a brief career selling pickled vegetables), contributed in several important ways to the administration of his adopted city. He pioneered two new routes for the transportation to Edo of rice from the shogunal domains in the north of the country and planned a course for a water conduit serving the area of Asakusa.

Reiganjima, "Island of Miracles," originally reclaimed out of a mud flat at the mouth of the Sumida River at the beginning of the seventeenth century, lost the temple after which it was named as a consequence of the new city plan prompted by the Long-Sleeves Fire of 1657. (The temple, Reiganji, was moved to Fukagawa.) The Island of Miracles seems to have undergone more reclamation work than was good for it. It suffered from a permanent structural wobble and hence earned itself the name of Konnyakujima, after the devil's-tongue jelly (*konnyaku*) that forms an unstable part of many Japanese meals. The island's prostitutes came to inherit the same name of *konnyaku*. Wobbly Reiganjima was the site of Edo's saké warehouses. Of these there must have been many: the average annual intake of each male townsman resident of the city (and men were always in the majority) was about twenty-five liters, no mean quantity. Most of the saké came from ports to the west of Osaka, where saké is still made, aboard ships known as *tarubune*, "barrel boats."

Other goods from the west were transported aboard ships with stoutly built bamboo bulwarks to prevent the cargo from rolling overboard in a storm. The merchants who organized the shipment of goods from Sakai and the other ports serving the great cities of the west, Osaka and Kyoto, formed an association to which they all subscribed and which became the prototype of the modern marine insurance company, handing out funds to traders who had lost ships and cargoes through mishaps at sea. Later, a similar association was formed by merchants dealing with goods from the north of the country. Another of these insurance cooperatives named itself the Sumiyoshi association as a token of its connection with Sumiyoshi Daijin, protector of sailors and travelers by sea, among whom the Sumiyoshi Jinja in Tsukudajima was a popular place of worship.

The saké warehouses and the radish quays left early, but the giant trading houses of modern Japan held on until recently to their giant warehouses in the area—Sumitomo and Mitsubishi on Shinkawa (the new name for wobbly old Reiganjima), and Mitsui across the Nihombashi River in Hakozaki. Now these are being transformed into a phalanx of skyscrapers, and the area at the mouth of the Sumida is being given a radical face lift. Next door to Reiganjima, Teppōsu ("Gun Sandbank"—in usual fashion, there is disagreement over whether an artillery range or the shape of the land gave rise to the name) was once a spit of land that marked the entrance to the port. The name lives on, although the land lost its distinctive form as a result of reclamation work after the Long-Sleeves Fire. It lives on in the name of a shrine, Teppōsu Inari Jinja, which once stood like a beacon at the mouth of the port's web of waterways and which still possesses in the back of its grounds, covered by lichen and enclosed within sacred straw ropes and paper festoons known as *shimenawa*, a miniature Mount Fuji, surrogate for the real mountain itself.

Modern Tokyo's port stands much further south at Ōi, off Shinagawa and Ōta wards. But there is no lack of reminders of the location of the old port. Take the Tokyo Grain Exchange, for example, not a minute's walk from where the rice storehouses once stood, their stern whitewashed earth-and-mortar facades lining both banks of the canals in identical rows. Surrounding the grain exchange are the offices of the leading Japanese companies dealing in corn and other grains. Immediately south of the grain exchange but cordoned off from it by the Nihombashi River and its attendant expressways is Tokyo's stock exchange, in Kabutochō. And around the stock exchange are clustered the offices of the country's leading securities companies. When the exchange first opened, in 1878, business was conducted on tatami mats, messages were sent by relays of boys stationed at street corners, and the day's business was over when a certain length of rope had smoldered into ashes. Little over a century later, business is conducted with computers, telephones, and a bewildering set of hand gestures.

Like most financial proceedings in Japan, the stock exchange's workings are in some important respects different from those of the exchanges of the West. They are also in certain respects more complicated. But financial transactions seem always to have been complicated in Japan. In the Edo period, there were no fewer than three currency systems, one in gold, one in silver, and the third in copper. The gold mint was set up in 1601 at the eastern foot of one of the city's oldest bridges, Tokiwabashi, only a few hundred meters west of Nihombashi. The employees of the mint were subjected to a rigorous body search every evening when they finished work. This included, so we learn from contemporary prints, stepping twice, naked, over a bamboo pole to ensure that none of the body's apertures contained any coins. The site of the mint is not hard to find, for on it now stands the Bank of Japan, a hundred years old in 1982. The bank's former main hall, a splendid old stone building in neoclassical style, one of the very few surviving Meiji-era Western buildings in Tokyo, was designed by the doyen of Meiji- and Taishō-era architects, Tatsuno Kingo, whose other famous landmark is Tokyo Station. The modern, fortresslike building immediately to the north is the new headquarters of the Bank of Japan.

A further financial complication in the Edo period arose from the fact that in the west of Japan, silver currency was predominant, while in the east gold was in wider use, with copper for everyday purchases. Each currency had its own set of coinage. There was, therefore, a great demand for exchange facilities. Indeed, what with frequent changes in the value of the currencies, the situation was a particularly favorable one for the furtive operator. Of these there seem to have been many, particularly in the district directly north of Nihombashi, where greengrocers and other retailers operated an under-the-counter exchange service. More capital and resources than these small-scale operators could ever muster was needed to provide a proper service. It was for this reason that the authorities appointed a number of merchant houses to superintend smaller exchanges and carry out money-handling activities for the shogunate. To this list was added the name of the most famous trading family in the city, the Mitsui.

The business of trading and money-making in Edo was virtually a monopoly of people from the provinces of Ise (round the coast from Nagoya) and Ōmi (on the banks of Lake Biwa near Kyoto). "Ōmi thieves and Ise beggars" was what the Edo citizenry thought of them. "Ise shops and Inari shrines—as common as dogs' muck," they sneered. One such merchant, from Matsuzaka in Ise, where his parents ran a successful saké shop and money-changing business, was Mitsui Hachirōbei Takatoshi. In the space of twenty years after opening his own dry goods shop in Edo in 1673, Takatoshi had built a business empire that is the direct forbear of the modern conglomerate. The shop in Edo was a branch of Takatoshi's main store in Kyoto. Before long the business was diversified to include various banking activities, including the transferral of taxes and other dues for the shogunal government from Osaka to Edo, which Takatoshi, like his fellow bankers, managed to incorporate into his own private lending activities to his immense benefit.

Takatoshi, astute and ambitious, acquired in Kyoto just the sort of brocade the people in Edo wanted to buy. It was at the Edo branch, called Echigoya and situated just to the north of Nihombashi very close to the site of its direct descendant, Mitsukoshi department store, that Takatoshi introduced a new sales system of such stunning simplicity and usefulness that it ensured the prosperity of his successors for generations to come. It had been the custom among dry goods shops to charge an arbitrary price depending on the customer and to receive payment twice a year. The writer Ihara Saikaku describes Takatoshi's innovation in his collection of tales of merchant life, *The Japanese Family Storehouse:* "Everything is decided in cash with no surcharges. There are over forty lively assistants at hand, each one responsible for one line of goods, one assistant for gilt brocade, for example, one for Gunnai silk from Hino, and one for *habutae* silk.... Even if you want nothing more than a square inch of velvet or damask for a pouch for your tweezers, they'll cut it to order and sell it to you. Moreover, if you suddenly find you need a ceremonial robe for an audience with the shogun or a formal coat, they will ask you to wait while a score or so of their tailors stitch the cloth together and in next-to-no-time hand you the finished product."[2] This was Takatoshi's commercial revolution.

Echigoya's customers came mainly from among the townspeople and lower-level samurai and retainers. Other dry goods stores were more expensive and conservative and preferred to cultivate a clientele among the wealthy families of the feudal lords. One such was Shirakiya, founded by an Ōmi merchant in 1662 on the site where Tōkyū department store, its modern incarnation, now stands, at the main Nihombashi intersection. Shirakiya's salesmen wrapped up their goods in a bundle and set off on their sales beats in the Yamanote hills, where the great military families had their suburban residences. The city's large dry goods stores had other peculiar features, two of which are noted by Clara Whitney in her diary of Meiji Tokyo. On one occasion just before Christmas of 1876, she visited Daimaru, a famous old Osaka dry goods store with a branch in Edo. "Many people of all classes were there buying, while the clerks and boys kept up a continual clatter, yelling and shouting to each other. The call of the house was a kind of dismal wolf wail, and when about a dozen would strike up with the various howls between, the effect was very interesting. A clerk would stop in the midst of a despairing howl or demoniac yell to give the price of a piece of goods or answer questions of the customer."[3] On another occasion a little over a year later when Clara visited Daimaru, she was offered a pipe and a brazier. "I took the pipe which was a long one used by ladies and the [clerk] offered me some tobacco and invited me to smoke."[4]

Fifty-six years earlier, when the Dutch warehouse master Fischer visited Edo on one of the quadrennial journeys of obeisance from the Netherlands' enclave off Nagasaki, he drew attention to another unusual aspect of Japanese shops: "We passed along wide streets, paved on both sides with stone, and, as in other towns, lined by uniformly built houses. We saw also very large edifices and shops, the latter protected by awnings. In front of these, and of every place where goods were exhibited for sale, stand a number of lads, who clamorously recommend the wares to draw the attention of passengers."[5] The Hollanders were given quarters a few blocks north of Nihombashi at an inn called the Nagasaki. Here they were supposed to be held incommunicado, but this does not seem to have deterred a steady stream of visitors, including a "silk-mercer...named Itsigoya [sic], who has shops in all the great towns throughout the empire. If you buy anything of him here and take it to another town, say to Nagasaki, and no longer like it, you may return it, if undamaged, to his shop there, and receive back the whole sum paid for it at Yedo."[6] These last comments are from the account of the president of the Dutch factory, Doeff. This was the spring of 1806, and Doeff relates how, not long after Echigoya [Mitsui]'s visit, a fire destroyed the Nagasakiya, an Echigoya shop and warehouse ("containing upward of a hundred thousand pounds' weight of spun silk"), and the surrounding area, including Nihombashi. It was on this occasion that the bridge collapsed, killing hundreds of panic-stricken citizens. "The second day after the conflagration [Echigoya] was already rebuilding his premises, paying every carpenter at the rate of about ten shillings (English) a day."[7]

The lavish amount of present giving (robes being the most popular choice) which has always been a characteristic of Japanese culture from the days of Genji onward—and never more so than in the Edo period—helps to explain the number and wealth of dry goods stores. The road that ran due east and north from near the Nagasakiya toward Asakusabashi passed through the district of Ōdemmachō, the starting point for the post-horse service. Here in Ōdemmachō were to be found many of the city's cotton textile emporiums, run for the main part by traders from Ise province. Shop after shop, each with the same austere facade but its own distinctive awning, sold nothing but cotton cloth.

The dry goods stores of Ōdemmachō have moved away, but Mitsukoshi, the new name for the old Echigoya, is still there. Like the other great old shops of Japan, but perhaps even more so, Mitsukoshi's continuing success is attributable to the speed with which it adapted to new commercial influences in the Meiji era. Instead of keeping its goods stored on shelves, Mitsukoshi took to displaying them. In 1903, it started using delivery vans, and shortly afterward it enrolled its first women shop assistants. In 1908 a new three-story Western-style building was completed in imitation of Harrods in London. In this new building, imported Western goods were displayed beside local wares. And then in 1914 came yet another building, this one five stories high with an escalator (first in the country and a great crowd-puller), two lions modeled after the beasts in Trafalgar Square guarding its main door, and a whole floor of stalls selling only food. The present building is roughly the same as the one that was constructed in 1935. Its early Meiji predecessor is invariably shown in prints with Mount Fuji in the background, and, because Mount Fuji was situated in the old province of Suruga, the district here on the north side of Nihombashi was until 1932 known as Surugachō. Thus the great little bridge was set in counterpoint with the country's greatest natural monument.

# # #

Ginza and Shimbashi

Ginza—to Japanese and foreigners alike the name suggests urban elegance, sartorial restraint, and a successful Eastern raid on the Western storehouses of sophistication. But there was little in Edo-period Ginza to suggest its later preeminence. If anything, it was something of a backwater. And Shimbashi, the "New Bridge," was thought so unglamorous that another bridge and gate, Shibaguchi Gomon, was built alongside it. However, fire claimed Shibaguchi Gate, and the New Bridge was reinstalled as the conveyor of travelers and transport out of the city proper and on the first stage of their journey westward.

The parts of town now known as Ginza and Shimbashi were in the Edo period sandwiched between the mansions of the feudal lords and the reclaimed land of Tsukiji, site of yet more military mansions. It formed the southern limb of the townspeople's Edo, on the great East Sea Road, the Tōkaidō, which led from Nihombashi all the way to Japan's imperial capital, Kyoto. The first bridge one crossed in setting off on the long journey from Nihombashi to Kyoto was named—in anticipation perhaps of a safe arrival—Kyōbashi, "Bridge of the

Capital." The second block of houses on the left after the bridge was occupied by the Tokugawa silver mint, the Ginza.

It occurred to Ieyasu to unify the country's coinage in 1598. He called on the services of an experienced silversmith and mint-master, Daikoku Jōze, and had him set up shop first in the Tokugawa home province of Suruga and then, from 1612, here in the district that soon came informally to be called Ginza (the place where silver, or *gin,* is minted). As well as minting silver coinage, Daikoku and his successors exchanged silver for copper coins and so coined the official name for their district, Shinryōgaichō, "New Exchange Quarter" ("new" in contrast to the older gold mint in Nihombashi). The Ginza was located in the same block as the district chief's residence. It can be imagined, therefore, that a close watch was kept on the mint, and when a misdemeanor (of what sort is not clear) was committed in 1800, the mint was moved to Kakigarachō, on the other side of Nihombashi. The name Ginza, however, remained behind.

Until 1930, Ginza comprised only four districts, half its present complement. The district on the south side of Ginza 4-chōme was known as Owarichō, south of which lay various other districts, each one named after the province of the feudal lord responsible for its reclamation. The southernmost of these, occupying part of the present Ginza 8-chōme, next door to Shimbashi, was commonly known as Komparuchō. This was where the Komparu family of Noh actors had their house. The Komparu troupe was the oldest of the four Noh troupes whose expenses were met by the shogunate and who performed regularly in Edo Castle. All four troupes lived in or near Ginza, but nowadays only the Komparu has its theater here. In the nineteenth century, the name Komparu was associated less with the Noh troupe than with the geisha whose houses of assignation transformed the district and neighboring Shimbashi into one of the city's unlicensed pleasure quarters.

The pleasure of the geishas' company was not only to be enjoyed on land. Strung along the waterways near Komparuchō were the boat-houses of Shimbashi, the most famous and numerous in the city after those of Yanagibashi upriver. Each boathouse administered not only the business of hiring out the boat but also the entertainment that was provided on board. Originally, the boats were used for idle pleasure trips up and down the river and for fishing expeditions in the bay.

Increasingly, however, the purpose of the trip became connected less with the waters of the river and more with the refreshments and the charms of the female attendants. The boats became floating houses of assignation, equipped with food supplied by restaurants on the banks of Shimbashi's canals and with girls from the local houses. How comfortable they look, these boats, with their handsome rooflike awnings. They and their elegantly clad and comfortably disposed occupants were a favorite subject of *ukiyo-e* artists—Torii Kiyonaga's tryptich *A Moored Pleasure Boat Beneath the Bridge* being a classic representation of this theme. In the Edo period, the number of geisha in this part of town was still quite small. But after the change of regime in 1868, Shimbashi became one of the most celebrated geisha quarters (*karyūkai,* "world of flowers and willows") in the new capital.

The new Meiji generation of Shimbashi geisha were landlubbers. They daubed on thick layers of powder and painted coarse black lines in place of their plucked eyebrows. Their professional qualifications were skimpy and their repartee of inferior quality. They were, in other words, well suited to the nation's new ruling class: the bureaucrats and businessmen from the far west of Japan who soon became regular patrons of the Shimbashi quarter. Itō Hirobumi and Katsura Tarō, two of the most prominent Japanese statesmen of the Meiji era, were known to frequent the geisha houses of Shimbashi. Katsura, who was prime minister of Japan three times in the early years of this century, paid ¥2,000, a substantial sum at the time, as a redemption fee for one of the most famous geisha of the day, Okoi.

Okoi had been born to a lacquerer in Yotsuya in 1880. When she was four her father went bankrupt, and she was taken in by a family who ran a geisha house in the Hamachō district by the river, where she became proficient in the arts of entertainment. Later, she was sent as a novice geisha to a house in Shimbashi. She possessed an unusually striking form of beauty: full lips, a pronounced chin, a slender nose. Hers was an intelligent, mature face, quite different from the other faces—childish, demure, or featureless—that peer out of the photographs of the geisha of her day. No doubt her employers were furious when she told them that she was going to marry the attractive young Kabuki actor Ichimura Uzaemon. The marriage was an unhappy one, bedeviled by a well-publicized rivalry for the actor's attention, and terminated four years later when Uzaemon was discovered in bed with the wife of a prominent banker. Okoi returned to Shimbashi, and it was then that she was redeemed by Katsura. Now she found herself at the center of Japanese politics. Indeed, on one occasion she was besieged in her house by angry mobs incensed by the terms of the treaty that ended the war with Russia in 1905. After Katsura's death, she became manager of one of those most fashionable of establishments, a Ginza cafe. Years later, she took the tonsure after becoming implicated in a political scandal, and during the war she traveled widely in China, offering prayers, it is said, for both Chinese and Japanese killed in action.

In the years when Okoi was a geisha there, the Shimbashi quarter grew in size and prestige. It encompassed within its geographical and cultural precincts the Kabukiza theater, which opened in 1889, and from 1925 the Shimbashi Embujō theater, which the geisha used until quite recently for spring and autumn performances of singing and dancing. The writer Nagai Kafū evokes the "world of flowers and willows," of swaggering rich businessmen, sought-after Kabuki actors, and the geisha themselves, calculating and insecure, in his novel *Rivalry*.

The latticed windows and narrow streets of the geisha quarter disappeared from Komparuchō at the end of the last war. They were replaced by the bars and clubs that were more congenial to the mood of the modern city—as well as being more profitable. But those houses that were situated a little further from fashionable Ginza, in the back streets of Shimbashi and Tsukiji, reopened after the war, and many of them have remained open to this day. There are still at least thirty houses in the area where "the box enters," the box being the samisen case carried in days gone by from geisha house to house of assignation by the geisha's servant, her *hakoya*——"boxman." Nowadays the box no longer literally enters, since the former trilateral arrangement of geisha house, restaurant supplying food, and house of assignation (*machiai*) is extinct, and the functions of the three houses have been amalgamated into the one building. It is still possible, however, to see both here and in Akasaka rickshaws conveying a geisha from one house to another— a journey often too short for a taxi and too long for a walk. And who, you might wonder, would want to spend their evenings pulling rickshaws around town? The answer, as often as not, is that most common of contemporary figures, the student doing *arubaito,* or part-time work.

Geisha belong more to Shimbashi than to Ginza. They belong to a purely Japanese tradition. Ginza's fame, on the other hand, stems from its place in the vanguard of the Japanese movement to absorb Western culture. Why did it fall to Ginza's lot to be chosen as the leader of the Western cultural invasion when, as we have seen, it was something of a backwater in the Edo period? The answer has a logic of its own: fire in the first place, and then steam. Ginza and surrounding areas were twice destroyed by fire in the space of three years. The second fire, in 1872, was particularly devastating, razing nearly three thousand houses and leaving nearly all of Ginza and Tsukiji a ruin (although it is interesting to note that only three people died in the blaze). At the prompting of several of the new Meiji government's leading politicians, the governor of Tokyo decided to replace wood with bricks and build Western avenues with trees and arcades. The second catalyst for this face-lift was the completion in 1872 of the railway line, the country's first, from Yokohama to Tokyo. On 13 September of that year the first train pulled in at Shimbashi Station. Ginza thus became, by virtue of its proximity to Shimbashi, the gateway to the city.

Over the next five to ten years, at the extravagant cost of nearly ¥2 million, the main street of Ginza as well as the transversal streets and some of the back streets, were transformed into a passable imitation of a Western city. On the main street, terraces of two-story brick houses with colonnades and balconies looked out over the country's first sidewalks and gaslights. The street was lined with maples, cherries, and willows, with pine trees in their traditional place at street corners. The prints of the day show what the new Ginza should have looked like: leafy, colorful, and cosmopolitan. In fact, early photographs show it to have been nothing of the sort. With the exception of the willows, the trees all withered and died. The houses, although attractive, were badly built. They were damp and dangerous. Or at any rate, they were believed to be damp and dangerous, and, one imagines, with good reason, considering the unsuitability of inexpertly built brick houses in a country of damp summers and periodic earthquakes. Several of the new residents fell ill with dropsy, lizards and centipedes proliferated, and an old woman inhabitant committed suicide. Worst of all for the authorities was the fact that the number of uninhabited houses was steadily increasing, and acrobats, jugglers, and other itinerant entertainers—including dancing dogs and wrestling bears—were moving in and staying put.

The authorities were forced to take drastic measures to attract back to the area the former residents from whom they had forcibly purchased land and houses, virtually paying them to return and give brick a chance. By about the year 1882, nearly all the houses, even in the back streets, had occupants. In particular, two kinds of establishment were attracted by the easy terms offered by the municipal authorities: the geisha houses of Komparuchō near the new Shimbashi Station, and newspaper offices. By 1877, there were already eleven newspaper offices in Ginza and the number went on rising, including the *Yomiuri Shimbun,* the *Hōchi Shimbun,* and several other of the country's most illustrious newspapers. Although many of these had moved away by the end of the Meiji era, Ginza remains the area where a large majority of the provincial newspapers have their Tokyo offices.

In 1881 rails were laid down the middle of the main street, and the horse-drawn trams made their first runs from Shimbashi to Asakusa. Until 1903, when electric power replaced horsepower, the coachman's horn and the weary plod of the two overworked horses in charge of the pulling department were an inseparable part of the Ginza scene. By 1887, the willows had won the day and taken over from the unfortunate pines, cherry trees, and maples. The willows, however, were dwarfed by the telegraph poles. Ginza had finally come of age. In 1894 Ginza's most famous monument, the Hattori clock tower, was erected on the site where it stands today, the northwest corner of the Ginza 4-chōme crossroads.

With the keenly refined mercantile instinct of the Japanese and the advanced state of the retail trade in Edo-period Japan, Ginza soon became the site of shops that befitted its role as symbol of Western culture in Tokyo. Pride of place goes to the bakery Kimuraya, which opened up a branch in Ginza in 1874 and found an appreciative customer for its bean-jam bread in the person of the emperor. A hundred and more years later, Kimuraya is still there, on the west side of the main street in Ginza 4-chōme, next door to Wakō (the postwar name for Hattori) and directly across the road from the site where it was first located. Many of the other shops in Ginza in the Meiji era sold Western goods: suits, hats, spectacles, beef, and such exotic items of furniture as the *iburu,* which looks for all the world like a *teburu* (table) but may have become semantically confused with an *isu* (chair).

This last item was advertised by Chibayao furniture shop in an 1885 brochure.

Several of the shops of modern Ginza have a history as old as this century's or older. Koyanagi, on the west side of Ginza's main thoroughfare, in 1-chōme, is a shop of Meiji vintage selling ceramic ware. Jūjiya in 3-chōme and Kyōbunkan in 4-chōme, both on the west side of the main street, sold musical instruments and books respectively in the last century, as they still do today. Hattori, on the northwest corner of the 4-chōme crossroads and now known as Wakō, has added jewelry to its original line of watches and clocks (K. Hattori and Co. are the owners of Seiko). Three buildings up from Wakō is a shop almost as old and even more famous, Mikimoto, which sells the cultured pearls whose perfectly rounded shape is the fruit of the experiments of the company's founder, Mikimoto Kōkichi. South of the great divide of the 4-chōme crossroads, on the west side of the main street (in 5-chōme) is Kyūkyodō, one of those shops selling the various delightful products made from Japanese paper. Upstairs, Kyūkyodō sells incense and writing brushes and all the other appurtenances of *kōdō,* "the way of incense," and *shodō,* calligraphy.

By now, we are indulging in that archetypal Ginza custom, *Gin-bura,* strolling aimlessly—*burabura*—through Ginza. *Gin-bura* was the rage through most of the first forty years of this century, when Ginza was in full bloom and the earlier indiscriminate cultural borrowing of the Meiji era had given way to a more careful selection and thorough absorption of those elements of Western culture that appealed to the Japanese. A leisurely stroll in the shade of the willows of Ginza in those sunny Taishō and early Shōwa years before the catastrophe of militarism and the war—what could have been more delightful than a *Gin-bura*? But beware! Even such an apparently innocent pastime has its snares and pitfalls. To start with, the very term *Gin-bura* itself. According to the painter Matsuyama Shōzō, who in 1911 opened Ginza's most celebrated café, the Plantan, when the term *Gin-bura* first came into use (at about the same time that the Plantan opened), it referred to idlers, ruffians, and other good-for-nothings who hung around Ginza street corners. The writer Tanizaki Jun'ichirō, for his part, claimed that to use the term *Gin-bura* was a sure sign one came from the provinces.

The victim of this semantic trap would most probably have been a *mobo,* short for "modern boy," in town for the day in search of a sweetheart, whose gloves and earrings would have stamped her a *moga,* "modern girl," and whose bonnet would have hidden her hair while her short knee-length skirt revealed her legs for all the world to see. As if being exposed to ridicule was not danger enough, the provincial on his or her special *Gin-bura* day trip had the added worry of becoming the victim of *Gin-bura* criminals: pickpockets. "According to investigations made by the Tsukiji police," says a newspaper report of 20 June 1926, "the smartest operators of them all are the elevator pickpockets. As the elevator shoots up like an arrow and the provincials *ooh* and *aah* in stupefaction, the elevator pickpocket gets down to work."[8]

But not everyone in Ginza was a provincial, nor were shops the only attraction. Beer halls were early and exotic additions to the Ginza scene. Ebisu Beer Hall claimed the honor of being the first to open, in 1899, down toward Shimbashi. Beer there was cheap, ten sen for half a liter (at a time when rice cost twelve sen for a *shō,* 1.8 liters), and before the hall's first week of business was over sales of a thousand liters and more per day were being recorded. Other beer halls soon followed, one of the oldest of them being the Lion Beer Hall that now stands on the southeast corner of the Ginza Street crossroads between 6- and 7-chōme. Beer was not all that was served. The viands were important, and so, too, was the atmosphere, exotically but not excessively European. The same could be said of the cafés. Indeed, Ebisu Beer Hall called itself Café Shimbashi. Here already is an important difference between European and Japanese cafés: the latter served all sorts of food. Another essential difference—but hardly a very surprising one—was that the Ginza cafés were staffed by waitresses and not, as in Europe, by waiters. This had an important bearing on the development of the Ginza café, as we shall see.

The cafés were the focal point of life in Ginza during the first four decades of the century when Ginza vied with Asakusa and eventually replaced it as the center of the city's social life. The first cafés to open remained the most famous: Matsuyama Shōzō's Café Plantan on Namiki Street, which became a meeting place for writers and artists; and the Café Paulista, which opened in the same year and had a younger clientele. The Paulista failed to survive the Great Kantō Earthquake of 1923, while the Plantan was a casualty of the 1945 air raids. There was no lack of other famous cafés. The Colombin, *pâtisserie française*, on the west side of Ginza Street, 6-chōme, advertised itself with an eight-meter-high model of the Eiffel Tower. The ceiling of the Colombin was painted by a young artist, Fujita Tsuguji, who was to become one of the most famous painters in Paris and was eventually to become a French citizen, adopting the name Léonard Foujita.

The connection with France and with painting, the medium through which France made its most direct impression on the Japanese, is an extremely important one. Of all the cultures of the West, it is to the French variety that the Japanese have felt most attracted. Why? Perhaps because the two countries share a strong feeling of cultural homogeneity, and both temper their keen sense of refinement with an appreciation of human susceptibilities. Ginza, with its eyes directed toward the West and its streets lined with willow trees, was the showpiece for the rest of the country of what appealed to the Japanese in French culture. It should not be thought, however, that Ginza served up France undiluted. The Fūgetsudō, one of Ginza's oldest and most distinguished cafés (a real café, this one, in the Western sense of the word and still there at the corner of Namiki Street and Miyuki Street), was one of many places in Ginza where you could buy (and still can) *shūkurimu,* a typical Japanese linguistic mélange describing something normally referred to as *chou à la crème*.

The range of *kissaten* (to use the Japanese generic word for cafés and teahouses) in Ginza was immense. The Sembikiya fruit parlor on the west side of Ginza Street in 8-chōme is as old as the century, while Shiseidō (where the poet Takamura Kōtarō first drank Coca-Cola, an experience he later described in verse), Fujiya, and Morinaga have all had establishments on Ginza Street for many years selling Western sweets and desserts and coffee and tea. From one of these cafés with their apron-clad waitresses, the young man-about-town could move on to a dance hall. The Ginza Dance Hall, for example, charged ¥1.50 for each three-minute dance. When the band stopped playing, the young man handed his ticket over to his dancing partner, and that was supposed to be that, she being a taxi dancer, an employee of the hall whose job it was to initiate young men into the mysteries of the tango or the two-step. After a vigorous tango, some refreshment was called for, and this Ginza possessed in its most nutritious form: "Milk drinking," wrote Katherine Sansom, wife of the historian, in 1936, "became the fashion in Japan some few years ago, and 'milk halls' the vogue; so that for a time it was quite the dashing enterprise to meet there for a drink."[9]

When all this sauntering down the byways of Western culture became too much, one could always repair to a Japanese-style *kissa shitsu* (tea room) serving Japanese sweets such as *yōkan, mitsumame,* and other delicacies made from azuki beans. One of the largest and most famous of these tea rooms was the Shiensō in that hardy survivor, the Kōjunsha Building, which still stands in 6–8 Ginza.

From the start, the *suito gāru* (sweet girl) and *gāru boi* (*boi* meant "waiter") were one of the attractions of the coffee shops of Ginza, so it was inevitable that some of them would degenerate into establishments of a more ambiguous nature. "Suddenly, from about the early twenties," wrote Nagai Kafū about the Ginza waitresses, "they came into vogue and held sway over the world, and along with movie actresses, took away the popularity of stage actresses. Today, however, a decade after the earthquake, the vogue of the café girls would seem to be passing. And their passing is the reason for my *During the Rains*."[10] Kafū's *During the Rains* portrays the tacky, raffish world of the Ginza cafés in much the same way as the earlier *Rivalry* had done the world of the Shimbashi geisha houses. The central character of his novel, Kafū tells us, "although, like courtesans and geisha of old, ...a woman whose charms were for sale, ...was quite different from them. She was more like the unlicensed prostitutes so abundant in Occidental cities."[11] However, we may be sure that not all the waitresses in the cafés of Ginza put their charms up for sale. Most of the sweet girls restricted themselves to a sweet smile.

The 1923 earthquake flattened Ginza and deprived it of the last of its original brick houses. The earthquake and the subsequent fire also put an abrupt end to a highly controversial move by the municipal authorities that had seen the replacement of Ginza's willow trees (not all of which found Ginza's soil ideal) by tougher ginkgo trees. The gods had not thought well of the plan, and so the willows were restored to their proper places, bordering the streets of Ginza. The mental association of Ginza with willow trees remains to strong that it seems hard to believe that today only one of Ginza's streets—the one running between 2- and 3-chōme—is still lined with them. As for the other streets, they contain plane trees, maples, pagoda trees, phoenix trees, zelkovas, and cherry trees. Ginza Street itself has no trees.

In 1930, Ginza expanded southward, and Owarichō, Izumochō, and the nearby areas became Ginza 5-, 6-, 7-, and 8-chōme. In 1932, the new Hattori (Wakō) appeared, an imposing seven-story building with curved front and clock tower, the same building that can be seen there today. Opposite it, Mitsukoshi's new building was also seven stories high. Just down the road, Matsuya and Itōya went high-rise too. In nearby Sukiyabashi, the Nihon Gekijō (Nichigeki Theater) and the new Tokyo office of the *Asahi Shimbun* thrust their ungainly bodies seven, eight stories up. But before long there were intuitions of war. Foreign goods became scarce and then nonexistent. Bars closed down. In 1940 dance halls were banned, and cafés found themselves resorting to substitutes for proper coffee. Then in 1945, out of the rubble of the blitz, the occupying Americans appeared. Ginza's sturdy big buildings had withstood the bombing better than most. Hattori and Matsuya were taken over by the U.S. Eighth Army as post exchange stores. Goods gradually began to filter back into the shops, and one of the best places to buy watches, cosmetics, liquor, suits, and cigarettes was at the night stalls, the *yomise,* of Ginza. Ginza's night market was one of the liveliest of the city, but it fell victim to progress about the time of the 1964 Olympics.

Since the war, Ginza has changed size and shape, color and sounds, age and smell. Indeed, almost all that remains of its old visage is the Wakō building—and a few other prewar structures tucked away in the back streets. The trams, which seemed almost as irreplaceable a part of Ginza as the willows, went long ago, and the willows have been replaced, at least on Ginza Street, by street lamps that resemble an inverted Horse Guard's helmet, with a painful-looking prong on the top. Ginza has grown even larger than it was before, having gobbled up Kobikichō and other districts to the east. It is completely circumscribed by expressways, whose courses coincide exactly with its boundaries. Chūō Street is certainly not one of the world's most beautiful thoroughfares. But when it glitters under the cold refracting rays of winter sunlight, there is an invigorating, obdurate spikiness to it, like the bones of a fish's spine, a spikiness enhanced by the street lamps and clocks and precise mathematical lines of *katakana* letters on the neon signs. It is a street of lines and angles, and so best appreciated obliquely, looking up from a sidestreet, out of a window, or into the sun.

# # #

Tsukiji

Many of Tokyo's place-names have fascinating and sometimes tortuous derivations. Theories involving water sprites contend with interpretations deriving from shogunal visits. And then there is normally some rather prosaic explanation, always coming last in the guidebooks, stating that Takabashi, "High Bridge," derives its name from its height and Nakagawa, "Central River," from the fact that there are rivers on either side of it. In the case of Tsukiji, there is but one theory, too prosaic to be anything but plausible: Tsukiji means "Built Land," and that is exactly what it is—land reclaimed from Tokyo Bay.

The coastline of the bay at the beginning of the seventeenth century bore precious little resemblance to anything a citizen of Edo living at the end of that century would have recognized (let alone an inhabitant of the modern city). By the middle of the century, the greater part of the city's reclamation work had already been carried out. Tsukiji, however, had yet to make its appearance; the shores of the bay stood at a point now marked (how else?) by Expressway No. 1. After the Long-Sleeves Fire of 1657, however, it was decided that the city was too cramped, too many people and houses were confined to too small an area. Among the measures undertaken to improve the situation was the reclamation of land in the east of the city. So it was that Tsukiji came into being.

The newly reclaimed land, instead of being given over to the *chōnin,* the townspeople, who lived in wretchedly overcrowded conditions, was reserved for the residences of the feudal lords and, a small part of it, for temples. The largest by far of the temples to be built in Tsukiji was the branch temple in Edo of the Nishi Honganji in Kyoto. Among the nobles who came to have their residences in Tsukiji were the Okudaira, from the domain of Nakatsu in the northeast of Kyushu. Here at the Okudaira residence between the years 1771 and 1774 there occurred an event that became the catalyst for a reorientation of Japanese culture, an event that can almost be compared in its importance to the presentation of Buddhist sutras to the court of Japan in the sixth century. The event concerned is the translation from Dutch of a book on anatomy, *Ontleedkundige Tafelen,* the first serious attempt to translate a book on science or medicine from a European language into Japanese. This was a pioneering work on the human anatomy written originally in German by Johann Adam Kulmus, *Doctor en Natuurkunde in de Schoolen te Dantzich,* and translated into Latin and French as well as Dutch. The book had been acquired in Nagasaki by Maeno Ryōtaku, a physician in the Okudaira fief.

Interest in the ways of the West had grown sporadically in the first half of the eighteenth century, spurred by the easing in 1720 of strict restrictions on the importation of foreign books (imposed as part of the attempts to quash Christianity). The first great promulgator of Dutch studies (*rangaku*) was Aoki Kon'yō, known as Kansho Sensei, "Doctor Potato," for his successful promotion of the sweet potato as a new staple food. Maeno Ryōtaku studied under Doctor Potato and first went to Nagasaki in 1770, a year after his teacher's death. It was while he was in Nagasaki that Ryōtaku acquired a copy of *Ontleedkundige Tafelen* and struggled to gain a passable knowledge of the Dutch language. The following year in Edo, Ryōtaku attended with his friend Sugita Gempaku an autopsy conducted on the body of a convicted criminal at the execution ground of Kozukappara in the north of the city. The two physicians were astonished to find similarities between what they observed with their own eyes and the diagrams they had seen in the Dutch book on anatomy. It was this experience that prompted them to undertake the task of translating the book into Japanese.

The importance of this endeavor is both actual and symbolic: actual in that it served as a stimulus to and an influence on the inquisitive minds of younger scholars, and symbolic because it represents a subconscious repudiation of Chinese learning and the beginning of Japan's intellectual examination and absorption of the civilization of Europe. The Meiji Restoration of 1868 marks the start of Japan's political and social transformation, but the intellectual groundwork had been laid in the century or so between the publication in 1774 of *Kaitai shinsho*, the title given to the translated version of *Ontleedkundige*

Tafelen, and the Meiji Restoration. Although the country's social structure remained fossilized for these ninety-four years, a revolution had occurred in the intellectual alignment of radical Japanese.

Maeno Ryōtaku himself epitomizes this spirit of inquiry into a vastly different cultural world. After the publication of *Kaitai shinsho,* he launched himself into a whole series of translating ventures, including works on astronomy, geography, and military science as well as medicine. He was known by the sobriquet Ranka, which might be translated as "the Hollandicized one," and his appreciative master, the lord of Nakatsu, under whose auspices he worked, dubbed him "our Dutch freak."

The translation of *Ontleedkundige Tafelen* must have been an extremely arduous task when one remembers that between them Ryōtaku and his colleagues could only muster a few hundred words of Dutch and they had no aids in the form of reference books and the like. Indeed, deciphering is probably a more accurate description of the process. Their exertions are chronicled by Sugita Gempaku in a book called *The Beginnings of Dutch Studies,* one of several works Gempaku wrote on Western learning and medicine.

The youngest of the physicians who gathered at Ryōtaku's home in the Okudaira residence in Tsukiji was Katsuragawa Hoshū, who was but twenty years of age when the project was begun. Hoshū had already been appointed two years earlier to the post of physician to the shogunate, the fourth member in his family to hold this hereditary post. The family residence was also in Tsukiji, another bond between Tsukiji and the introduction of Western learning. As well as his important medical work for the shogun, Hoshū found the time to write and translate works on Russia and geography (the connection perhaps resulting from the Russian thrust eastward, of which the Japanese were becoming increasingly aware), to import a microscope and conduct pioneering experiments with it, and to undertake diplomatic work for the shogunate.

Another young member of the remarkable coterie of talented, inquisitive, and energetic physicians and scholars of Dutch learning that gathered around Sugita Gempaku and Maeno Ryōtaku was Ōtsuki Gentaku, whose chosen personal name derives from those of his mentors. Gentaku lived for many years in nearby Kyōbashi, where he ran his own academy, the Shirandō, and where in 1794 he and his associates celebrated *Oranda shōgatsu*, the Dutch New Year, the first-ever celebration in Japan of New Year according to the Gregorian calendarand (so the story goes) the first time knives and forks were ever used in Japan. He wrote an introduction to Dutch learning, *Rangaku kaitei*, and in later years issued a revised and fuller version of the pioneering work of his teacher, *Kaitai shinsho*. Himself a prolific writer and translator, Gentaku was appointed to the shogun's translation bureau in 1811.

In 1815, Sugita Gempaku had presented Gentaku with the manuscript of *The Beginnings of Dutch Studies*. This very same manuscript turned up in a roadside bookstall in 1868 and was published the next year at his own expense by one of the luminaries of the movement to learn from the West, Fukuzawa Yukichi. Fukuzawa Yukichi was the son of a lowly retainer of the lord of Nakatsu, the same domain that Maeno Ryōtaku had served in the latter part of the preceding century. When at the age of twenty-three he was sent by the lord of Nakatsu to open a school of Western learning, the place where he conducted his teaching was none other than the Nakatsu residence in Tsukiji. Ten years later, in 1868, the school was moved to Shiba (and then a little further south to Mita) and renamed Keiō Gijuku.

Tsukiji's early contact with Westerners—as opposed to the culture they embodied—was not, however, a very happy one. In the north of Tsukiji, a special area was set aside for the houses of foreigners, a district that symbolized, because of the extraterritorial rights enjoyed by foreigners, all that was iniquitous in Japan's ties with the outside world. Here, in 1868, a hotel was built for the foreigners. The Tsukiji Hotel was an elegant two-story brick building with a view across the bay to the hills of the Bōsō Peninsula. It boasted verandas and blinds, 102 bedrooms, a billiard room, a dining room—in short, it was a type of building that the citizens of Tokyo had never before clapped eyes on. It was not, however, a success, and it was never rebuilt after being destroyed by fire in 1872. Most foreigners seem to have preferred to stay in Yokohama. The Tsukiji Foreign Settlement never counted more than one hundred eighty or so residents, despite the presence there of the American Legation, and the district reverted to normal status in 1899 with the repeal of extraterritorial rights for foreigners. Even the brothel quarter that had been set up with the blessing of officialdom in nearby Shintomichō never managed to prosper despite the reputedly amorous dispositions of many of the foreigners who lived there, some of whom in those early days seem to have been unusually high-spirited, not to say rowdy and boorish.

An interesting sidelight to the Foreign Settlement was provided by the need to satisfy another of the foreigners' appetites, that for milk and butter. It was to this end that a dairyman called Niihara Toshizō settled here in 1883. Nine years later, his wife, Fuku, gave birth to a son but shortly afterwards lapsed into a state of insanity; the son, Ryūnosuke, who was to become a famous writer, author of such works as *Kappa* and *Rashōmon*, was adopted into the family of his maternal uncle, Akutagawa Michiaki.

In the later years of the century, the Foreign Settlement became home for a large number of missionaries, teachers, and doctors, one of whom, a Scottish pastor named Henry Faulds, opened a hospital, worked to help the blind, and wrote a paper on fingerprints and their use in Japan, showing for the first time that no two persons' fingerprints are the same and thereby providing an invaluable contribution to criminology. There was an orphanage and a school run by nuns in the settlement, as well as the forerunners of several prominent colleges, including Rikkyō and Aoyama Gakuin universities. In 1900, the year after the disbandment of the settlement, Saint Luke's Hospital was built here in the newly named Akashichō. The present building, which was completed in 1933 and still dominates Akashichō and the surrounding area, houses one of Tokyo's most prestigious general hospitals, embodiment of the historical link between Tsukiji and Western medicine. But apart from the hospital and several commemorative plaques, there is no trace remaining of the Foreign Settlement, neither of its houses, hotels, nor schools.

Tsukiji is nowadays famous throughout Japan as the home of Tokyo's wholesale fish market. The grounds of the fish market, part of which in the nineteenth century had been the site of a beautiful garden built for his retirement by the politician Matsudaira Sadanobu, were known in the years either side of the advent of the Meiji regime in 1868 as Kaigungahara, "Navy Plain." In 1857 a shogunal school was started here for instruction in navigation, and then in 1869 the new Navy Ministry bought up land near the site of the school, built a port, and set up several colleges, including an academy for the training of naval officers. The academy was moved to Hiroshima in 1888, but it left behind it the memory of Tsukiji's role as the site of Japan's first attempts to launch a modern navy.

Dutch learning, foreign settlers, Western medicine, a fledgling navy—Tsukiji has one more historical connection, a fairly recent one, with drama, and principally with Kabuki. Kabuki is the traditional drama form of the children of the city. Its golden age in Edo and then in Tokyo coincided more or less with the time when the culture of the city was at its most vigorous and productive. For most of the middle of the nineteenth century, the three Kabuki troupes licensed to operate by the shogunate were sent to pasture in distant Asakusa. But not long after the advent of the new Meiji government in 1868, one of the three took the opportunity to move back. The troupe, run by one of Kabuki's greatest reformers, Morita Kan'ya XII, moved into the Shintomiza, built on the site of what should have become the licensed quarter for foreigners. The Shintomiza lived through chequered days, suffering from fire and from the myriad sorts of difficulties that inevitably accompany controversial innovations.

Kabuki had been a strictly plebeian form of theater, but in the Meiji era it rose above its station, and, thanks largely to the reforms of people like Morita Kan'ya XII, it attained a loftier rank. The Shintomiza was not alone in bringing about this ascent in the world of culture. In 1889 a theater opened to the east of Ginza that was to steal the reforming thunder from the Shintomiza and lead Kabuki forthrightly to the position it now holds among the performing arts of Japan. This theater was the Kabukiza. The outside of the theater was built—ironically, but not unusually for buildings of this period—in European style, a Renaissance neoclassical style with three grand arches at the entrance and pillasters on the second story. It was a brightly lit theater, quite unlike those of the Edo period. It incorporated many of the innovations of Morita Kan'ya XII and Ichikawa Danjūrō IX at the Shintomiza and of Ichikawa Sadanji II at the Meijiza in Hamachō. It still, however, adhered in part to the old system of teahouses, allowing them into the building as caterers if not as the monopolistic ticket agents they had once been. The years after the completion of the Kabukiza were great ones for Kabuki, led by the performances of the triumvirate of actors known as Dan-Kiku-Sa: Danjūrō IX, Onoe Kikugorō V, and Sadanji II.

In 1912, the management of the Kabukiza was taken over by the giant Shōchiku company, and in 1925 a new building replaced the old, a building that still houses the theater today. The new building, designed by Okada Shin'ichirō, is in the Momoyama style, a style whose richness and flamboyance derives from the great castles of the Momoyama period, the half century centered about the year 1600.

Tsukiji's historical connection with drama extended to the Western stage. Three hundred meters south down the road from where the Shintomiza had stood until it was destroyed in the Great Kantō Earthquake is the site of Tsukiji Shōgekijō, a much smaller theater with a strange romanesque facade built in 1925 by Hijikata Yoshi and Osanai Kaoru, who was himself a playwright of distinction. The two of them put on modern Western plays by dramatists such as Ibsen, as well as staging plays by the leading lights of the Shingeki ("New Drama") movement in Japan. After Osanai's death in 1928, the theater lost its central position in the Shingeki movement and was never resuscitated after its destruction in the 1945 air raids.

Like all land built out of water, Tsukiji's first affinity was with the element from which it had arisen. Today it is miles away from both Tokyo's port and the open sea, but in the days when the city breathed and sweated through its waterways, Tsukiji was one of its busiest and most exciting places. Some of the early Western residents of the city have left descriptions of the waterbound traffic of the days before land transport predominated. This is how Ernest Satow, who in later years became British minister to Japan, described his first impressions: "Curious duck-shaped boats of pure unpainted wood, carrying a large four-square sail formed of narrow strips of canvas loosely tacked together, crowded the surface of the sparkling waters. Now and then we passed near enough to note the sunburnt, copper-colored skins of the fishermen, naked, with the exception of a white cloth around the loins, and sometimes a blue rag tied across the nose, so that you could just see his eyes and chin"[12] A few decades later, Mary Fraser, wife of the British minister to Japan, described Tsukiji: "When I drive down there, it always delights me to watch the junks, with their huge sails, white or saffron, moving along the wide canal on the incoming tide, to watch the woodmen piling timber in the yards along the banks, to see the crowded ferry-boats carry the people from shore to shore."[13]

One of these ferryboats continued conveying people from Tsukiji to the stretch of reclaimed land known as Tsukishima for the following half century or so. For many years plans had existed to build a bridge linking Tsukiji with Tsukishima, but first the price of steel had been too high and then the metropolitan authorities had been too heavily in debt. Eventually, in 1940, the bridge was finished. It was called Kachidokibashi in honor of a famous Japanese sea victory over the Russians in 1905, and it was a double drawbridge, like Tower Bridge in London, which raised its two sections to let ships through to the nearby Sumitomo and Mitsubishi warehouses.

# # #

Tsukudajima

In the beginning there were two islands, two mudflats really, at the mouth of the Sumida River formed by deposits of silt. At different times in the first half of the seventeenth century, the mudflats were built up into proper islands, the northern one being called Ishikawajima, the other, Tsukudajima. In 1872, four years into the Meiji era, the two islands were joined together, and twenty-one years later reclamation work was finished on a large area of land to the south of Tsukudajima that came to be known as Tsukishima. Not long after that, a bridge was built connecting Tsukudajima with Fukagawa to the north. It was now possible to make one's way by road to the southern tip of Tsukishima. However, in order to make the more direct journey to the center of the city, a ferry ride was still called for. Indeed, it was not until the completion of Tsukuda Ōhashi in 1964 that the ferry service linking Tsukudajima to the mainland made its final crossing.

Despite these asphalt tentacles connecting Tsukudajima to the mainland, part of the former island remains conspicuously different from the rest of the city—part, but not all, because the northern portion, the former Ishikawajima, is now high-rise residential and miles away in spirit from the rest of Tsukudajima. It has fast become a second Shinjuku, complete with skyscrapers housing hotels and conference centers. Old Tsukudajima has been left untouched, but a sleepy old town has been turned into a museum piece, its social fabric and charm lying prone and ready for sacrifice on the altar of unchallenged modernity.

In referring to Tsukudajima, one must differentiate between the original island, which has become Tsukuda 1-chōme, and the reclaimed land to the north and east of it, which form 2- and 3-chōme. Here in 1-chōme among potted plants and shrubs and trees—such a profusion of vegetation that it seems to be growing out of walls, windows, and roads—old houses sit back to back in a cosy, affectionate fashion, the narrowest of alleys running in between them with a water pump at its head. It would all be too much like a film set if it were not for the saving grace of a pile of rubbish here, an obtrusive, modern building there, and that particular sort of scruffiness that accompanies that particular sort of neatness and epitomizes the Japanese landscape, be it urban or rural.

What is it about the place that has enabled it to retain such a distinctive atmosphere? In the first place, as an island it remained largely untouched (with a devastating exception in 1866) by the scourge of Tokyo: conflagrations. This explains the greater age of its houses—always a relative and recent matter in Tokyo—but not the distinctive atmosphere. For a clue here, we need look no further than the island's name: Tsukudajima, "Island of Cultivated Rice Fields"—strange name for a colony of fishermen where never a paddy was seen.

It was, so the story goes, the shogun's appreciation of a good dish of whitebait—those tiny fish whose English name explains their color and the use to which they are normally put—that led to the establishment of Tsukudajima. About 1615 Ieyasu or his son Hidetada ordered a community of skilled whitebait fishermen to pack up their nets and their other belongings and move from their native village of Tsukuda in Settsu province (now within the confines of Osaka) to the country's new military capital to fish in the bounteous waters at the mouth of the Sumida River. That was the official story. The real reason was rather less ingenuous: these fishermen were spies, seasoned navigators of the waters of the Inland Sea. Their brief was to keep the shogun's censors informed of any suspicious movement of boats in the bay. And while they were about it they were to net a good breakfast of whitebait for the shogun. A hundred years later, the eighth shogun, Yoshimune, followed this precedent, bringing with him from his domain, the province of Kii, a platoon of gardeners, the *niwaban*. The *niwaban* were supposed to be highly skilled at pulling up weeds and pruning plants, but everyone knew that their real talent lay in entering the gardens of the feudal lords unseen, carrying out their nefarious deeds, and then leaving the way they came.

The fishermen-spies were granted a recently reclaimed mudflat at the mouth of the Sumida, which they named Tsukudajima in memory of their old home. For the next two and a half centuries, the fishermen-spies put out in their flat-bottomed skiffs with billowing sails on winter nights to fish for whitebait. In the stern of their boats they placed beacons in the form of firewood inside a metal basket, and this became one of the sights of the bay, depicted in woodblock prints and chronicled in the old guides of the city. Of their spying activities we hear less.

The fishermen-spies of Tsukudajima were more than just skillful fishermen and artful spies. They were also the originators of a delicious method of preserving and serving the fish they caught, boiled in soy sauce and salt, known as *tsukudani*. Not only whitebait but goby and other small fish, shrimps, and seaweed caught in the bay were cooked in this way. Before long, an enterprising shopkeeper started serving *tsukudani* to the warehousemen and sailors who gathered at Nihombashi and called in on Tsukudajima to visit the shrine to Sumiyoshi Myōjin, protector of those at sea, a branch of the Grand Sumiyoshi Shrine in Osaka.

How different from Tsukudajima's history is that of its neighbor to the north, Ishikawajima. This island had been granted to a certain Ishikawa Hachizaemon, controller of the shogun's ships, and was also known as Hachizaemon's Isle. In 1790, Matsudaira Sadanobu decided that the island would make an ideal detention center, and to this end he expropriated and enlarged it. Here he sent troublesome masterless samurai and vagrants and political miscreants. Ishikawa must have been a success, for in 1870 it was turned into a proper prison, and so it remained until 1885, when it was transported—lock, stock, barrel, and inmates—to Sugamo in the northwest of the city, where it was to have a long and famous tenure. Not all of Ishikawajima was thus treated, however. In 1854, the Mito branch of the Tokugawa family was entrusted with the task of building a shipyard in the north of the island. This they did, and the shipyard they built became, in 1876, the first privately owned yard for the construction of Western-style ships and the forerunner of the modern shipbuilding and heavy-engineering firm, Ishikawajima-Harima Heavy Industries, IHI, which now has its dry docks across the waters in Kōtō Ward.

The prison and its inmates have left, but many of the descendants of the shogun's fishermen-spies still live in Tsukudajima and work at the Tsukiji wholesale fish market. With the market in danger of being moved, however, and the island under threat from the developers, who knows how much longer Tsukudajima will be able to hold onto its distinctive ways.

# # #

Ningyōchō and Hamachō

These two neighboring districts represent two different traditions in entertainment. Both had their heyday in the vigorous and inquisitive world of Meiji and Taishō Tokyo but have now lost out to more fashionable parts of the city. Their differences spring from the fact that Ningyōchō belonged to the plebeian traders' part of town, while Hamachō, between Ningyōchō and the Sumida River, was the site of several houses belonging to members of the military class.

In Edo's earliest days at the beginning of the seventeenth century, Ningyōchō was a swamp on the city's confines. Despite, or perhaps because of, the less than ideal nature of the terrain, it was chosen in 1617 as the site for the city's licensed quarter, which became known as Ashiwara, "Plain of Reeds." This name necessitated a smart change of characters. The Chinese character normally used to write "reed" is pronounced *ashi,* which can also, when differently written, mean "badness." *Ashi* was therefore changed to *yoshi,* whose meaning is unmistakably auspicious, and the Plain of Reeds became the Plain of Auspiciousness. Later the authorities decided that to have the licensed quarter so near the center of the fast-expanding city was not too auspicious after all, and they moved it, name and all, to the paddy fields north of Asakusa, where it remained. (One of the roads that nowadays bisects Ningyōchō is known as Ōmon Street after the quarter's gate and is thought to mark the location of the first Yoshiwara.)

The departure of the bordellos did not, however, deprive Ningyōchō of all its repertory of entertainment. Two of the city's great Kabuki theaters were situated in this part of town, the Nakamuraza in

Fukiyachō and the Ichimuraza in Sakaimachi. Clustered around these two leading theaters was a gaggle of lesser theaters, most of them offering puppet dramas. The puppeteers in turn attracted craftsmen skilled in the making and repairing of puppets. So it was that this area came to be called Ningyōchō, "Quarter of the Puppets," a name that finally won official recognition this century and has only recently eliminated all the various other names by which the respective parts of this district were known.

The puppets and puppet-masters vanished long ago, and the Kabuki theaters were banished to Asakusa in 1841 by the prurient Mizuno Tadakuni. Nevertheless, Ningyōchō provides the location for one of the most famous scenes in Kabuki. The scene is from the play popularly known as *The Scarred Yosa,* written in 1853 by Segawa Jokō. Yosa, whose scars tell of his misfortune, is unexpectedly reunited, after many years, with Otomi, the woman whose love led him into a life of crime. Now he unwittingly finds himself on the point of making her his next blackmail victim. A scene of furious recrimination ensues, in which Yosa berates Otomi for her callous treatment of him and laments the injustices he has suffered as a consequence. The scene occurs in a row of houses known as Gen'yadana, the "Gen'ya shops. " Okamoto Gen'ya was a doctor from Kyoto who successfully prescribed a bath of saké as a cure for the shogun's smallpox in 1629 when all other remedies had failed. Gen'ya's descendants followed in his shoes and continued to occupy the family house in Ningyōchō.

Hamachō, on the other hand, found a different sort of entertainment, more in keeping with its higher-class affiliations. *Machiai,* restaurants to which geisha were summoned, took over from the houses of the samurai, and Hamachō became, thanks to its proximity to the river, one of the most elegant geisha districts of Meiji Tokyo, a rival to Yanagibashi, a little way upstream. In the hot summer months the geisha and their customers would set off from Hamachō up the busy river as far as the cooler reaches of Mukōjima, the geisha plying their patrons with music and witty conversation as they went. In cooler weather they would sit indoors and admire the river view. These pastimes were the very height of the Eastern Capital's own stamp of *fūryū,* "elegance and refinement."

While the geisha served the fledgling Meiji businessmen with saké, children swam along the banks of the river. Every summer, huts were built out over the river and children were allowed to splash about near the bank until autumn came, when the children disappeared and the huts were knocked down. Each year, too, on 6 July, there was a display of water acrobatics, with swimming contests and displays of acrobatic skills on logs, rafts, and floating ladders.

Ningyōchō carried on its plebeian traditions, in keeping with its position at the entrance to one of the city's most important shrines, Suitengū. In the Meiji, Taishō, and early Shōwa eras, when a visit to the shrine became a regular custom among the people of Shitamachi, theaters, variety halls, and dance halls provided popular means of entertainment in Ningyōchō. Like the theaters but unlike the dance halls, the variety halls (*yose*) had been a highly popular part of the scenery in Edo days. They were cheap, and they were fun. They were where the Edokko, the child of the city, went for diversion when he did not want to go to the bathhouse. During the golden age of the Edo variety hall, there were as many as a hundred in the city, and in the Meiji era more people than ever before went to see the comedians, storytellers, and jugglers of the *yose*. Nowadays, people watch comedians on television, and the variety halls have all but disappeared. There are a couple of halls left in Asakusa, one in Shinjuku, and two in Ueno (the Hommokutei and the Suzumoto Engeijō). The last of Ningyōchō's variety halls, the Suehirotei, finally gave up the ghost in 1970.

One of the theaters, however, still flourishes, attracting large audiences to many of its shows. The Meijiza, in Hamachō, was founded in 1893, the year of the death of the foremost Kabuki playwright of the time, Kawatake Mokuami. In its early days, it was closely associated with the plays of Mokuami and with the career of one of Mokuami's favorite actors, Ichikawa Sadanji II. The Meijiza, which was the first theater in Japan to be equipped with electric lighting, became the home of Shimpa, the "new wave" of Kabuki. It can be argued that the Kabuki of the Meijiza was no longer a part of the plebeian tradition of the Kabuki of Ningyōchō and the troupes of Edo—that, in common with the world of Meiji drama in general, with its social and artistic airs and aspirations, it was an art more of the upper classes than of the townspeople, an art that belonged in upper-class Hamachō.

On 10 March 1945, the Meijiza was the scene of an unprecedented real-life tragedy. The theater was at the time the only ferroconcrete building in the district, and when the fires touched off by cluster bombs dropped from the B-29s started sweeping through the area, thousands of people sought refuge in the theater, only to be steamed alive in the heat generated by the burning building. Although both Ningyōchō and Hamachō had been razed to the ground in the conflagration that followed the Great Kantō Earthquake of 1923, much of Ningyōchō managed to avoid meeting the same fate in the air-raid fires of 1945, which swept on south from Hamachō but stopped at Ōmon Street, the wind having suddenly changed directions.

Ningyōchō, therefore, boasts several blocks of houses of prewar vintage. It is only a tiny morsel from the giant pie of Tokyo, quite small enough to be swept away with the crumbs in any other city in the world, but it is almost all there is. And it gives the visitor a chance to examine the architecture of the early Shōwa years. This was a time when, in order to strengthen the constitution of houses (and display one's wealth), it was the custom to cover the outside walls with copper plates. Great skill was called for in the application of these plates (known as *dōgawara*), for if they did not overlap to a sufficient depth, they would let in water. Although they are supposed to be good for a hundred years, the copper soon changes color, turning green with verdigris. Some of the houses with copper tiles have been painted, but most of them still sport their attractive patina, which blends well with the green of the ubiquitous plants. Many of Ningyōchō's houses are crowned by flat-topped roofs and geometric and mock-Egyptian structural motifs that one associates with the 1930s. Other houses are built in a more traditional style, the poorer ones with weatherboarding (*shitami ita*), others with plaster and lath. For some decades now, permission to build houses with weatherboarding or copper plates has no longer been granted in Tokyo, and the same applies to three-storied wooden houses, of which a very rare example can still be seen in Ningyōchō (on the right-hand side of the second street to the left walking toward the Hakozaki terminal from the main Ningyōchō crossroads). Ningyōchō is full of alleys, where the facing rows of houses look as if they would rub shoulders in an earthquake. Some of .hese rows of houses are late examples of *nagaya,* the tenement houses in which, until quite recently, the lower classes of the city lived.

It is ironic that in this little haven of old Tokyo was born, in 1886, the novelist Tanizaki Jun'ichirō, who turned his back on his native city and took refuge in what he regarded as the relatively unwesternized world of Osaka and Kyoto. Tanizaki had a youthful and brief flirtation with the ways of the West. It was about this time that the Great Kantō Earthquake occurred, and Tanizaki, who happened to be out of town at the time, recorded his expectations for the new city that was to rise out of the ruins of the old: "Orderly thoroughfares, shining, newly paved streets, a flood of cars, blocks of flats rising floor upon floor, level on level in geometric beauty, and threading through the city elevated lines, subways, street cars."[14] This flight of fancy was not to be realized, at least not for many decades, and Tanizaki's infatuation with modernity cannot have lasted long, for a year or so later he wrote *A Fool's Love,* with its satire of a Japanese girl besotted with the West. The attraction of Ningyōchō nowadays lies precisely in the fact that its thoroughfares are not orderly and its streets not newly paved.

# # #

Bakurochō-Yokoyama and Ryōgoku Bridge

After the Long-Sleeves Fire of 1657, in which thousands were trapped and burnt to death when officials refused to open the Asakusa Bridge Gate, a bridge was built across the Sumida. This, the first bridge across the river south of Senju, was known simply as Ōhashi, "Great Bridge." But when Shin Ōhashi, "New Great Bridge," was built a few decades later, the citizens of Edo decided to call it Ryōgokubashi, "Bridge of the Two Provinces." They called it this because it connected the west bank, which was in the province of Musashi, to the east bank, in Shimōsa. And yet, in point of fact, Shimōsa had by this time withdrawn its borders to the Edo River east of here, and the land between the Sumida and the Edo River had already become part of Musashi province.

Never mind the provinces. Ryōgoku was the great city bridge. It was the bridge from which the river was officially "opened" for the summer every year with a gorgeous display of fireworks. The *kawabiraki,* or "river-opening," was first held at the beginning of the eighteenth century to drive away the evil spirits that were spreading the scourge of *korori* (cholera) among the inhabitants of the city. The evils spirits eventually obliged, but the ceremony stayed. From then on, it was held every year on the twenty-eighth day of the Fifth Month. Between that day and the closing ceremony, on the twenty-eighth day of the Eighth Month, the river was full of boats aboard which the citizens of Edo entertained and were entertained by the geisha from Yanagibashi and Shimbashi, and generally immersed themselves in that exhausting pleasure of a Japanese summer, the job of keeping cool.

The fireworks were produced by two houses, Kagiya and Tamaya, who were locked in fierce competition to produce the most elaborate and dazzling displays. Kagiya won by default, as it were, when a fire started on the premises of Tamaya in 1834 and it was closed down. The scene on the river on the day of the opening was an enchanting one, a pageant of boats—big boats with roofs and horn-shaped prows (*yakatabune*) and small boats propelled by a scull at the stern, *choki bune*. The revellers needed refreshment, and this was provided in abundance by traders in their little *nitari* boats selling rice cakes, saké, dumplings, watermelons, and much else besides. Many fine *ukiyo-e* prints show the scene on the river as the fireworks shoot up and fan out into the night sky. The scene is described by Clara Whitney in her diary of life in Tokyo in the first years of Meiji rule: "The river was alive with lanterns of every color and shape, and musical with the notes of the samisen.... Now and then, a gay party would glide by singing and playing, or a theater boat would announce by large lanterns and a band of drums and fifes their attractions.... The fireworks...consisted of rockets, comets, Roman candles...a Fuji, a lady, umbrellas, dogs, men, characters, and other things, which I could not make out. There was great clapping all the time."[15]

After the Long-Sleeves Fire, when the Great Bridge was built, a firebreak had been made by widening the road and keeping it clear of houses. Instead of houses, however, stalls were set up, and Ryōgoku Hirokōji, as the open space was called, became the site of a giant amusement district, with Okuyama in Asakusa, the largest in the city. Amusement was to be found in wealth and variety on both sides of the bridge, but the west side here was regarded as being superior in the nature of its displays. Foremost among these were dramatic entertainments, which featured puppets and women and other sights not seen on the stages of the three officially licensed Kabuki troupes. These unlicensed performances were known as "hundred-day theater" or as *odedeko shibai*. The *odedeko* themselves were something slightly different, but they, too, were to be seen here. *Odedeko* were sophisticated Jack-in-the-boxes—sophisticated, because it was not Jack but a different puppet that sprang out each time the box was opened. There were storytellers, too, here in the Ryōgoku firebreak, and no lack of preachers and sermonizers. Other attractions were less mobile but no less fascinating: magnificently intricate models of Dutch galleons, parrots, plum trees, lanterns, giants, and goblins made out of glass or shells or even vines.

This all went on in the booths that lined the road to the east of Asakusa Bridge Gate, between it and Ryōgoku Bridge. On the west of the gate, the sights were less appealing. On the south bank of the Kanda River here, an earthen embankment had been formed and willow trees had been planted on it, whence its name of Yanagibara, "Willow-Tree Field." Yanagibara was one of the best-known haunts of the lowest class of prostitute, the "nighthawk," *yotaka*. It was also bedroom for *hinin*, "nonpeople," beggars and outcastes who had lost or been stripped of their place in society. A hovel was built for them here in 1675 by a benevolent city magistrate.

In the daytime, Willow-Tree Field was full of traders selling off old clothes on the cheap. And although the nighthawks have disappeared, trading in clothes is again today the staple of this part of the city, for this is now the giant Yokoyama-Bakurochō *sen'i ton'ya gai,* "textiles wholesale street," Tokyo's largest wholesale district. But clothes were not always the dominant theme. Bakurochō was originally, from even before the foundation of the shogun's capital at Edo, a marketplace for horses, and this is how it got its name, Bakurochō, "District of the Horse Dealers." The chief of the horse dealers was one Takagi Gempei, who became a *nanushi,* "district chief." The horses came from the north down the Ōshū Kaidō to Asakusa Bridge Gate. Also from the north, as well as from other directions, came the *gundai*. These were the bailiffs who administered the land under the direct control of the shogun, collecting taxes and settling court cases. They had their official residence here in Bakurochō inside Asakusa Bridge Gate. The shogun's bailiffs brought with them a lot of business, and as a result they entertained many visitors from the provinces. These visitors needed a place to stay, and they had no lack of choice. Bakurochō contained a large number of inns. Indeed, it was famous for them. If the guests of the inns lacked diversion, they had only to cross the road, for there was one of Edo's archery ranges, like others of its kind in Asakusa and Fukagawa, a front for prostitution. Or they could go to the firebreak at Ryōgoku and admire the puppets and models, the freaks and the wild animals.

As for clothes, these, in the Edo period, belonged within the sphere of Nihombashi, where the rich and powerful merchants from Ise had been given a quarter of their own in Ōdemmachō. There, between Nihombashi and the prison at Kodemmachō, they congregated and they flourished until before long the streets were lined with nothing but shops selling material. Bakurochō and Yokoyama, however, were that much further from Nihombashi. Instead of prestige shops selling the finest cloth, the streets here were lined with stores selling candles and paper and *tsukegi,* little wooden and sulphur charms against fire. There were all sorts of shops in Yokoyama and Bakurochō selling all sorts of products, but they were shops belonging to poor townspeople, not to the rich migrants from Ise and Ōmi who set up business in Nihombashi and Ōdemmachō. Bakurochō and Yokoyama belonged to Kanda, to the Edo of the impecunious townsman who had to struggle to make ends meet. Nihombashi was the domain of the prosperous and successful merchants like the Mitsui family from Ise.

Nowadays there are no more horses in Bakurochō; nor are there any more inns. There would be no room for the horses, and hotels prefer more fashionable locations. But still one senses that this is the heart of the city, land which has been occupied and exploited to the last square millimeter for centuries past.

4
Taitō Ward and the North

Kuramae and Yanagibashi

Between Edo Street and the river is the site of the shogunate's rice
storehouses (*okura*). Here in the early seventeenth century berths were
cut into the banks of the river, and the tributary rice from land under
the shogun's direct control was shipped here and stored in the
granaries. Much of the rice in the shogun's storehouses was destined
to be delivered to the shogun's retainers, the *hatamoto,* who formed
almost a quarter of the samurai population of the city and who were
paid most of their stipends in rice. They were paid three times a year,
but the problem arose of where to store their rice-wages. The solution
was provided by the men who ran the teahouses around the shogun's
granaries, who had already been providing the shogun's retainers with
a useful delivery service. They began to store the rice themselves, and
then to pay the shogun's retainers a sum (minus commission) in lieu
of rice-wages, which they stored and sold at their own convenience.
From here it was a short step to providing loans to the samurai in
advance of receipt of the rice.

The dichotomy created by an economic structure where wages were
paid in rice but goods and services were purchased with copper and
gold or silver necessitated the existence of the rice brokers, who were
known as *fudasashi.* Their role was acknowledged in the first half of
the eighteenth century, when they were given an official license by the
eighth shogun, Yoshimune. Because of the nature of their business
and the effect of weather on the price of rice, the *fudasashi* rice brokers

were able to amass great fortunes. If Kinokuniya Bunzaemon and his fellow timber merchants represented the first generation of outstanding Edo spendthrifts and profligates, they had worthy heirs in the rice brokers from the district "In Front of the Shogun's Storehouses," Okuramae. Yoshiwara was not far down the road, and the stories of debauchery attributed to such legendary *fudasashi* rice brokers as Ōguchiya Gyoyu, one of the Eighteen Great Connoisseurs of the licensed quarter, were to furnish material for playwrights and storytellers for generations to come.

If the trip north to Yoshiwara were too irksome for them, the brokers flush with rice needed only to turn south to the neighboring district of Yanagibashi, "Willow-Tree Bridge," which was to become one of the city's more elegant pleasure quarters in the nineteenth century. Divining origins is a hazardous business in Tokyo, but the origins of Yanagibashi's history as an entertainment district can be traced with some confidence to its links with Yoshiwara. It was from here, from the mouth of the Kanda River at Yanagibashi, that the boats known as *chokibune* pulled off with passengers aboard bound for the licensed quarter of Yoshiwara. With typical Edo adaptability, an unlicensed quarter soon sprang up so that there should be no need at all to embark on the journey.

The banks of the Kanda River, as well as providing moorings for chokibune bound for Yoshiwara, contained houses for the boats aboard which geisha regaled their patrons during the summer months, when the river was officially "open" for the pursuit of idle pleasures. Like Shimbashi, the pleasure quarter of Yanagibashi became gradually less water-oriented as the nineteenth century wore on. And it lost some of its elegance too, although it is debatable whether this is to be blamed on the influx of prostitutes from Fukagawa after the great cleanup of 1841 or on the advent of a new type of client in the form of the Meiji nouveaux riches. The Tokugawa official turned Meiji satirist Narushima Ryōhoku was already lamenting the decline in standards in the Yanagibashi houses in the early Meiji years. Half a century or so later, in 1916, laments were still to be heard, but by then the Meiji era was depicted as a golden age.

# # #

Ueno

For over a hundred years now, Ueno has been known far and wide as the name of a railway station (opened on 28 July 1883) from which trains run to and from the north of Japan. Ever since the beginning of the Meiji era the inhabitants of the impoverished northern prefectures of Japan have looked toward Tokyo for employment and the hope of a less arduous life for themselves and their children. The gravitational pull of Tokyo has been strong for many reasons, not least because there are few large cities in the north. The effect has been reciprocal: Tokyo's cultural and social tendrils stretch strongly to the north. The main port for this traffic has been and still is Ueno Station, from where trains leave for and arrive from Sendai, Morioka, Aomori, and Iwate, as well as Nagano, Niigata, and Kanazawa. It is, therefore, on the platforms of Ueno Station that many Japanese first set foot in the nation's capital.

With the dislocation of normal life in Japan at the end of the war, Ueno became a giant bedroom, an enormous lodging house for thousands of people without homes to return to. Among them were a large number of children who had lost their parents, or who had no recollection of where their home was. In the worst years of hardship, 1945 and 1946, Ueno was a grim sight, with well over a thousand people huddled together sleeping in the underground passage that leads up from the subway station toward the main station building. Eventually cheap lodging houses began to appear, and with the return to a makeshift sort of normality the number of homeless people sleeping out in Ueno began to decrease.

In those months of desperate shortage after the end of the war, anyone with something to sell gathered beneath the tracks near Ueno Station. To the ruins of Ueno, where hardly a building had been left standing by the air raids, they came, carrying little bundles of goods. They unwrapped their bundles and sold pots and pans, crockery and clothes. A few months later, the black marketeers moved in. They put up stalls, where they sold white rice and noodles and roots at ten times the price that the same goods would have fetched had they been available in the shops. Police raids were frequent, but murders and reprisals were carried out with impunity.

By 1948, the rice was back in the shops and so were other necessities. People now had a craving for the most elementary of luxuries, sweets. Ueno supplied them. At the peak of Ueno's confectionery boom, there were up to three hundred stalls selling various forms of sweets, most popular of which were *imo-ame,* sweet potatoes wrapped in candy. This is why the market came to be known as Ameya Yokochō, "Confectioners' Sidestreets," when it was legalized and its stalls given licenses. At about the same time, however, the Korean War broke out, and the Confectioners' Sidestreets were inundated with all sorts of goods that had mysteriously made their way out of the post exchanges of the American forces. Jeans, cameras, pens, watches—all the manufactured products of a nascent modern economy—joined the candy on the shelves of the Ueno booths.

Like many stations that serve poorer agricultural areas, Ueno and its environs have always been home for more people without a roof over their heads than elsewhere. They gather on their chosen benches on Ueno hill, some of them sullen and out-of-sorts, others demonstrative and garrulous, all of them observing their own rigid hierarchy. The tramps leave behind them, in Tokyo as in any other city, a trail of old newspapers. To judge by the profusion of out-of-date newsprint, one of their favorite haunts is an unprepossessing mound with the hyperbolical name of Suribachiyama, "Mortar Mountain." This hillock, like others that bear the same name, is a tumulus thought to mark the grave of a wealthy family of the fifth century A.D., owners perhaps of some of the rich farmland at the foot of the hill and along the shores of the bay.

Centuries later, a shrine was built on the mound, and there are occasional references in medieval documents to Gojō Tenjin shrine and the hill on which it was built. However, the great transformation of Ueno hill, which until then had been largely the abode of foxes, occurred with the establishment of the shogunate in Edo at the beginning of the seventeenth century. Tokugawa Ieyasu gave over a large chunk of land on the hill to a feudal lord called Tōdō Takatora. Takatora, who built his residence here, was one of the greatest castle builders in the country, a man of many parts who had fought in Korea, taken the tonsure on Mount Kōya, been lured back to secular life by Toyotomi Hideyoshi, and fought on the victorious Tokugawa side at the Battle of Sekigahara in 1600. Takatora it was who master-minded the construction of Edo Castle, the largest castle in all of Japan.

The other figure whose name is linked with that of Ueno is the abbot Tenkai, who was born in 1536 and lived to the venerable age of 107. Tenkai played an instrumental part in the deification of Ieyasu and was a close political adviser both to Ieyasu and to his two successors. He was asked in 1624 by the second Tokugawa shogun, Hidetada, to supervise the construction of a temple on Ueno hill. The temple was to be built here on this hill because Ueno stood at the northeast corner of the shogun's new capital, at the devil's gate—the northeast being regarded, according to the old Chinese ideas of geomancy, as an unlucky direction. Thus both Nara and Kyoto had large temples built to guard their northeastern approaches, Tōdaiji at Nara and the great monastic complex of Enryakuji on Mount Hiei, the mountain to the northeast of Kyoto.

Tenkai's grandiose plan was to build here on Shinobugaoka (the name by which the hill was known at the time) a temple to rival Kyoto's Hieizan. The new temple was called Tōeizan Kan'eiji, and in the next couple of decades the hill was transformed: a gate was built, as well as halls of all shapes and sizes, and a pagoda and a shrine to Ieyasu, both of which still stand in their original places. Funds and labor for this burst of temple building were provided by the feudal lords eager to curry favor with the Tokugawa. To complete the transformation of the hill, Tenkai had a hall built in imitation of Kiyomizudera in Kyoto. Next door to the hall, Hayashi Razan, "court Confucianist" to the early Tokugawa shoguns, built an academy which was later moved to nearby Yushima.

Although the Tokugawa adhered to the Amidist Pure Land sect of Buddhism and Kan'eiji belonged to the Tendai sect, they chose it as their family temple, along with the Pure Land temple Zōjōji in the south of the city. In 1647 Kan'eiji's status received imperial acknowledgment when the retired emperor Gomizunoo's third son was sent there to become the temple's first imperial abbot in residence. By the end of the seventeenth century, Kan'eiji had reached its apogee. It now had a magnificent main hall befitting its status and 36 subsidiary buildings as well as 36 subsidiary temples within the 119 hectares of its precincts.

A temple as large and important as this attracted a stream of visitors—priests, officials, pilgrims, and, not infrequently, the shogun himself. Kan'eiji lay beyond the gates and the moats of the city, but houses and shops lined the way to the foot of its hill, and for most of the two hundred fifty years of the Edo period it fell within the confines of the urban sprawl. The road that led out to Ueno passed by Kanda market, where the shogun's cooks bought fruit and vegetables for the castle, and through Sujikai Gate. The road continued straight as an arrow almost as far as Ueno hill. It ran slightly west of the modern Chūo Street, but where Chūo Street bears to the right (just south of Matsuzakaya department store), it veered right in a right angle and then again left to end up covering the same ground as the present-day street.

Travelers of old, like the residents of the modern city, now found themselves in the orbit of Ueno. They passed several landmarks that would be to some extent familiar to the inhabitants of modern Tokyo. A couple of hundred meters in to the right (east) were the quarters of the shogun's infantry escort, his *kachigumi,* men who headed his procession and accompanied him on hunting expeditions and other forays from the castle. Now, in modern Tokyo there are two stations with names unusually euphonic to mark the site of the residence of the shogun's runners, Okachimachi Station and Naka Okachimachi Station. Immediately on the right our travelers passed a dry goods shop that has since expanded somewhat, Matsuzakaya, the name giving away the origins of its founder—Matsuzaka was in the province of Ise. On the left, down the road that runs along the south bank of Shinobazu Pond, among the teahouses that served rice steamed in leaves from the lotus plants of the pond, stood a shop selling combs and ear-cleaners laboriously fashioned out of boxwood. And here the shop still stands It was founded in 1736 by an archery instructor from the north who called his new shop Jūsanya, "Thirteen," which is what nine and four add up to, and nine and four are pronounced *ku-shi,* the Japanese word for a comb. But *ku* can also mean "suffering" and *shi* "death," and no one would want a shop by that name.

Back on the main road, we find another station name that links past to present, Ueno Hirokōji. The road here is still quite broad, but it was once a good deal broader, which is why it was given the name Hirokōji, "Broad Little Road." The Broad Little Road at Ueno was one of three big firebreaks and many smaller ones created after the catastrophic Long-Sleeves Fire of 1657. Most famous of these firebreaks was the one at Ryōgoku, but Ueno's Broad Little Road lost nothing in broadness, nor in the intriguing way it was put to use.

Broad open spaces were too valuable in such an overcrowded city to be left unexploited. Ueno's soon filled up with stalls and booths and roadside preachers, dancers, actors, acrobats, tightrope walkers, puppeteers, sword-swallowers, and peculiar characters known as *hōka* priests. These eccentric itinerants dressed up as priests and tied branches of bamboo in various suggestive shapes on their backs. They strapped drumlike affairs to their chests which they beat with their arms in time to the songs they sang. All this was by way of accompaniment to their main act—juggling. In the narrow streets behind the booths and shops and teahouses of Ueno Hirokōji dwelt Ueno's own type of prostitute, the *kekoro*. The *kekoro* lived two or three to a brothel, and there were up to fifty *kekoro* brothels. The hallmark of the *kekoro* was her apron, and she was often referred to as the "apron from under Ueno hill," *yamashita no maedare*.

The Edo-period visitors to Ueno now found themselves at the foot of three small bridges that no longer exist. Mihashi ("Triple Bridge") led over the waterway that flowed into Shinobazu Pond. The wider, central bridge, it is said, was reserved for the shogun on his visits to Kan'eiji. Beyond the Triple Bridge was the same sort of three-way crossroads that still exists today at the entrance to the subterranean Ueno Keisei Station, where trains leave for Narita airport. The road that branched off to the left was taken by visitors to the shrine to Benten in Shinobazu Pond and to the restaurants and the *deaijaya,* the Edo-period trysting houses whose verandas looked out over a sea of lotus leaves.

Straight ahead was Kuromon, the "Black Gate," entrance to Ueno hill and Kan'eiji. This is the gate that priests and pilgrims would take, as well as the parties of sightseers and pleasure-seekers come to enjoy the cherry blossoms or the view of Shinobazu Pond and the famous pine tree with hooped branch. The shogun had his own gate beside the Black Gate, which was not worthy of his exalted status. The avenue of cherry trees leading up the hill from the Black Gate to the main hall of Kan'eiji passed below, as it still does today, the Kiyomizu Hall dedicated to Kannon. A little way further up was the main temple gate, Niōmon. Beyond that on the left stood a bronze statue of a Buddha, Edo's answer to the *daibutsu* ("Great Buddhas") of Nara and Kamakura, part of which still exists somewhere in one of the thickets behind Ōkuma Ujihiro's equestrian bronze statue of Prince Akihito, founder of the Japanese branch of the Red Cross. The Great Buddha itself seems to have survived the battle at Ueno in 1868, but body and head melted away in the air raids of 1945. The face alone remains, in its own little stupa-shaped hall, and the face is quite enough to reassure us that the destruction of the rest of the statue was no great loss to mankind. Beyond the Great Buddha towered the "Supernatural Lantern," Obake Tōrō, which now stands by the entrance to modern Ueno's most substantial link to the past, the shrine to Tokugawa Ieyasu, Tōshōgū. Finally, pilgrims in the Edo period arrived at the temple's main hall, Kompon Chūō, named after the main hall of the mother temple on Mount Hiei. Kan'eiji's Kompon Chūō was not built until 1698, at least fifty years after most of the other halls of the temple, and it failed to survive the 1868 battle on Ueno hill.

Supposing our travelers had been making not for the Shinobazu Pond on the left, nor the temple straight ahead, but for the post station of Senju or—who knows?—perhaps even the shrines at Nikkō, they would then have followed the road round to the right, much as they would now on their way to the main entrance of Ueno Station. Here was another broadening out of the road, a firebreak created in 1737, and known as Ueno Yamashita ("Under Ueno Hill"). This, too, was crowded and bustling with entertainers and customers of the shops and restaurants. The shops here, selling paper, brocade, medicine, oil, bonito shavings, tea, confectionery, and candles, were known as *hotokedana,* "Buddha stores," because, perhaps, of their proximity to Kan'eiji. Some of the Buddha stores sold those services in which the *kekoro* specialized.

Ueno's great citadel of Buddhism disappeared in flames on the fifteenth day of the Fifth Month of the fourth year of the Keiō reign period, 1868. The surrender of Edo Castle had been successfully negotiated by the imperial forces advancing from Kyoto, and there had been no bloodshed. But the takeover of the city which owed its existence to the Tokugawa family and their system of government was not to be effected totally without the firing of guns and the drawing of swords. The diehard Tokugawa loyalists, numbering about two thousand, rallied on Ueno hill and engaged the imperial forces by Kuromon, the "Black Gate." Surrounded on three sides, vastly outnumbered, and out-gunned by modern artillery, the Tokugawa loyalists, known as the Shōgitai, were thoroughly routed. But as they died or turned to flee, they decided to take with them into oblivion the magnificent buildings of Kan'eiji. The imperial troops all but finished off the work the Shōgitai had begun, putting to the torch those halls left standing, symbols of the prestige of the Tokugawa family. Ironically, one of the few buildings that escaped the flames was the Tōshōgū, the shrine honoring the memory of Ieyasu, the first Tokugawa shogun.

Now victor and vanquished share space on the crowded slopes of Ueno hill. Saigō Takamori, the general from the south of Kyushu who himself died a rebel against the government he had fought to install, is immortalized in bronze, bull-necked and full of swagger but with a humorous glint in his eyes. Because of the ignoble circumstances of his death, Takamura Kōun statue, cast in 1893, has him in the casual clothes of a countryman accompanied by his dog, rather than in the uniform of a general.

Not more than fifty meters behind the victorious general is a memorial to the Shōgitai—Ueno nowadays is a pragmatic place not concerned with taking sides. When the imperial forces eventually gained control of the hill, they left the corpses of the defeated Shōgitai to rot where they had fallen. However, priests took pity, collected the dead bodies, and cremated them. Most of the ashes were taken away to a temple in Minowa, north of Ueno, but some were buried here at the site of the pyre. Six years later the authorities relented and allowed the burial spot to be marked by a gravestone. It was the result of the efforts of one of the Shōgitai who survived, a certain Ogawa Okisato, that the gravestone was erected, and his descendants still tend the grave and look after the documents and mementos kept on display in a small gallery beside the grave.

The original intention after the installation of the Meiji regime had been to build a hospital on Ueno hill, but a Dutch doctor in the employ of the government managed to persuade the authorities that a park would be a better idea. So it was that Ueno—along with Asakusa, Shiba, Fukagawa, and Asukayama—became the site of one of the nation's first public parks. It was never, however, a park for the enjoyment of nature but more a place for the cultural instruction and advancement of the citizenry. In 1877, the first national exhibition for the promotion of industry and commerce was held here in imitation of similar exhibitions in the West. The exhibition was a grand affair,

with more than eighty-four thousand items on show. During its thir-
teen-week run, it attracted over four hundred fifty thousand visitors. It
was followed five years later by a second national exhibition, a second
great showpiece for the fruits of civilized progress. The art gallery
used on this occasion became in the following year the main hall of
the precursor of the present-day Tokyo National Museum. The zoo
was opened at the same time as the museum, and three years later, in
1885, Tokyo Library, forerunner of the National Diet Library, was
founded on Ueno hill. On the left of the north gate of the present
Tokyo University of Arts, one of the original red-brick library buildings still stands. Another early Meiji feature of the Ueno landscape
was the Seiyōken, one of Japan's first Western-style restaurants
(together with that of the Grand Hotel in Yokohama). The Seiyōken
still stands on Ueno hill, but it bears a functional look that belies its
distinguished history.

# # #

Negishi

The day trip, you might think, was an invention of the age of the
automobile. But in the last hundred years of the Edo period and still
in the Meiji era, when feet and later rickshaws were the only means of
locomotion available to the common people, the idea of the day trip to
a famous site in the suburbs was refined into an act of some ceremony.
And judging by the intrinsic merits of the places chosen, it must all
have been great fun. Lest we doubt this, we have only to look at some
of Hiroshige's prints of picnickers under the cherry blossoms of
Asukayama in Ōji or of people sipping tea under the mini Mount Fuji
in Meguro. But as Hiroshige unerringly shows, one of the favorite of
destinations was the bluff of land under which the Yamanote Line now
runs, behind Ueno hill.

To get there meant walking up the Nikkō Kaidō from the direction
of Kanda, round Kan'eiji and its dozens of subsidiary temples and the
mortuary halls of the Tokugawa shoguns, and skirting the hill more or
less as the Yamanote Line does now. Like the railway, the people of
Edo on an excursion would arrive at Uguisudani, "Valley of Bush

Warblers," where they might pause to contemplate the beauty of this name and try to figure out its derivation. This was something the compilers of the Edo-period gazetteers never managed to agree about. Some say the birds were a gift from Nikkō and others that they were sent from Mount Hiei in Kyoto. But they do agree to the extent that a flock of bush warblers was released in the area and took up domicile in the trees here. The birds have left us one of the world's most enchantingly named train stations.

The travelers would now have arrived in Negishi Village. At last away from the noise of the city, they could relax in semirural surroundings. A journey to Negishi might have several destinations. An estimable one was (and still is) Sasa no Yuki, "Bamboo-Grass Snow." When the imperial abbot arrived from Kyoto and took up residence at his new temple of Kan'eiji, he soon found that he lacked an essential of civilized life, the silken soft sort of bean curd known as *kinugoshi* tofu. He had an expert tofu chef brought over from Kyoto, and so pleased was he with this man's tofu that he said it was "as beautiful as snow lying on *sasa* bamboo." The restaurant founded by the chef from Kyoto came to be known as Sasa no Yuki, and to this day Sasa no Yuki serves nothing but its silken snow.

Another of the travelers' destinations might have been Tennōji, to try their luck in the temple lottery, or they might have been going on a little further to Nippori, another mellifluous name with one of those derivations so charmingly convoluted as to be possible only in Japanese. Nippori is the Chinese-style reading of three characters otherwise read *hi o kurasu no sato,* or *higurashi no sato,* phrases which, in typical fashion, are roundedly suggestive rather than pointedly precise in meaning. "Village living from one day to the next" is one of several possible renderings. Not that any of this has much bearing on the derivation of the name itself. Until the 1780s, two completely different characters, meaning "new ditches," had been used to write the name. According to one theory, the new ditches were built in 1557 by a vassal of the Hōjō family, the dominant power in the east. It seems certain, however, that the residents of the land by the new ditches decided to adopt characters for the name with more salubrious connotations. From Nippori, and in particular Suwa Shrine, there was a view over the fields and the Sumida River as far as Mount Tsukuba. There were teahouses on the bluff here, where people gathered to view the snow in winter, the cherry blossoms in spring, and the moon in autumn. Hiroshige drew the scene, as he did a hill two hundred meters to the north where insect-listening parties would often be held late in summer. This hill, just northwest of Nishi Nippori Station, was—and still is—called Dōkanyama, after a fortification built here by Ōta Dōkan, "father" of Edo.

All these enticingly rustic names were an irresistible attraction for the literati of Edo. They built their country retreats (or perhaps we should call them suburban villas) in Negishi and Nippori and in the fields of Shitaya to the east. Shitaya and Negishi, indeed, became the site of quite a colony of artists and writers seeking the fresh breezes of the field and the gentle murmurings of water in the paddies. The artist and connoisseur Sakai Hōitsu, inheritor of the tradition of Ogata Kōrin, had a retreat in Negishi and lived here many years at the beginning of the nineteenth century. Kitao Shigemasa, a contemporary of Hōitsu and founder of the Kitao line of *ukiyo-e* artists, and Kameda Hōsai, the Confucian philosopher and another Edo-born contemporary, both lived here as well.

Among the neighbors of these luminaries of Edo culture were some of the most celebrated courtesans of the licensed quarter. Yoshiwara lay a short walk away across the paddies, and the wealthier Yoshiwara houses built villas in Shitaya, Negishi, and Nippori, where their treasures could convalesce after illness and pregnancy. The change of regime in 1868 had no immediate effect on the fortunes of the area. On the contrary, so popular did Negishi become as a home for men and women of letters that a group of writers and a school of tanka poets were named after it.

The most famous of Meiji poets to live in Negishi was Masaoka Shiki, modernizer of the haiku and tanka forms. In Negishi, just north of Uguisudani Station, Shiki lived out his last years, bedridden with consumption. In an entry in his diary written shortly before his death in 1902, he listed "the things I would most like to see for the first time: moving pictures; bicycle races and stunts; lions and ostriches in the zoo;...automatic telephones and red letter boxes; a beer hall; women fencers; and Western-style theater. But I haven't time to list them all."[1]

# # #

Ōji

Ōji once stood beside a hill clad with cherry trees and a meandering stream and a waterfall, under which people took cleansing showers. Now the stream's course has been changed so that it no longer meanders, and its bed and banks are encased in concrete. The cherry trees were planted by the eighth Tokugawa shogun, Yoshimune, an enthusiastic admirer and planter of cherry trees, on land he granted to the nearby Ōji Shrine. In 1873 this land was made into one of Tokyo's first five public parks, Asukayama Park, and for many years it was among the favored destinations for excursions, to view the cherry blossoms in the windy days of early April and the azaleas in the warm sunshine of early May.

Across the main road, across the city's last metropolitan tramline, across the stream from Asukayama Park stands the Ōji Shrine, on a hill overlooking the park. A few blocks behind Ōji Shrine is another shrine, this one called Ōji Inari Shrine. This is the main shrine in the east of Japan to Inari, the deity who protects the farmers' rice fields but who was later coopted by the merchants to keep a protective and promotional eye on their money-making activities. Inari's messenger and embodiment is the fox, a creature the Japanese held in awe for its ability to change into human shape and bewitch. It was probably this power the fox had that gave rise to the tradition of the hackberry tree across the fields from the Ōji Inari Shrine. Every year deep in the night of New Year's Eve, the foxes of the eight provinces of east Japan would gather under this tree to change into their best clothing before paying their respects at the shrine. The scene was depicted by several artists of the Edo period, but by none so hauntingly as Hiroshige. He shows a group of them clustered under the tree, and tens of others making their way across the fields to the shrine. From each of their mouths issues a flame, the *kitsune-bi,* or "fox fire." According to the *Illustrated Gazetteer of Famous Places in Edo,* all the flames together were "like a parade of numerous pine-branch torches, or like large quantities of fireflies all set free and flying away."[2] It was said that the local farmers could tell what the next year's harvest would be like from the size and the brightness of the flames. The farmers, it seems, knew where to look to see the fox fires. Other people, however, according to the *Gold-Dust Tales of Edo,* "come from afar to see this, and many of them return home disappointed. But if you stay all night long it is said that you are bound to see them."[3] Indeed, Kikuike Kiichirō, in his Edo almanac *Illustrated Accounts of Edo Customs,* remembers going to Ōji and seeing hundreds of them.

Stories about foxes were legion, but one in particular has come down to us, kept alive by the traditional *rakugo* storytellers. It concerns a young man of Edo who, on his way to worship at the Ōji Inari Shrine, spied a fox in the act of transforming itself into a voluptuous woman, something that foxes, like serpents, were liable to do. He decided that the fox-woman was too beautiful to ignore and took her to a nearby restaurant, the Ōgiya, where he regaled her with food and drink. He fled, and she fell into a drunken stupor. When she awoke, she found herself back in fox form and being chased out of the restaurant by a waiter armed with a broom. The next day, the young man, feeling thoroughly contrite, bought a peony-shaped rice cake wrapped in leather and called on the fox at her burrow. One of her little cubs came to the mouth of the hole, listened to the man's apologies, accepted his offering, and brought it down to his mother, whose head was still throbbing painfully from all the alcohol she had so recently consumed. On seeing the rice cake wrapped in leather, the voluptuous woman of the day before, now a harassed vixen with a large litter to look after, furrowed her eyebrows and said to her little one in a tone full of motherly circumspection: "Careful now. It's probably horse dung."

Fox stories did not always end so well for the victims of the fox's powers.

In the Meiji era, foxes began their retreat from Ōji. Factories moved in, print works and armament factories to the fore, transforming the area into an important industrial district. Its location was ideal: close to that great conveyor of traffic, the Sumida, and far enough north of the city for land to be plentiful. Leading the way was Japan's first Western-style paper mill, which was opened in 1875 by the Ōji Paper Manufacturing Company. Thousands of curious visitors came to gaze at this strange red-brick building. Although the mill was moved out of Tokyo some time ago, Ōji retains its links with paper in the form of the Paper Museum, a fascinating little shrine to paper and all things made of it. That other shrine, which foxes used once to visit in the depths of the night on New Year's Eve, welcomes large crowds of human visitors every year on the first Day of the Horse in February, when its grounds at the top of a steep flight of steps are full of stalls selling kites of all kinds but in particular kites representing the valiant firefighters of Edo. The kites have survived where the foxes and their fires succumbed.

# # #

Asakusa

Asakusa's day was Tokyo's day. For a hundred years and more, this northern suburb and its temple, Sensōji, better known as the Asakusa Kannon, was the city's cultural lodestar, a hundred years when the whole city was in a mood of confidence and vitality that enabled it to relish the new and at the same time to bask in the old. For most of the hundred years, between about 1840 and 1940, Asakusa ruled.

Asakusa had something for everyone. And never more so than in the year 1920, when the novelist Tanizaki Jun'ichirō wrote of its "innumerable classes of visitor and types of entertainment, and its constant and peerless richness preserved even as it furiously changes in nature and in its ingredients, swelling and clashing in confusion and then fusing into harmony." Asakusa possessed a cornucopia of pleasure: it had "old theater, song theater, new theater, moving pictures, things Western, things Japanese, Douglas Fairbanks, Onoe Matsunosuke [Japan's first idol of the screen]; ball-riding, equestrian acrobatics, Naniwa chanting, girlie theater music, merry-go-rounds, Hana Yashiki [a sort of garden-cum-zoo-cum-outdoor entertainment parlor]; the Twelve Stories tower; air-gun shooting; prostitution; Japanese food, Chinese food, Western food, Rairaiken [a Chinese restaurant], wonton, noodles, oysters, rice, horse meat, snapping turtles, and eels."[4]

Like the phoenix, Asakusa rose out of the rubble of the Great Kantō Earthquake of 1923 (minus its Twelve Stories tower) and resumed its business of providing pleasure with all the abandon of earlier days. The 1945 air raids, however, dealt it a more serious blow. It was not so much the physical devastation that did the damage as the city's cultural transformation. It is fashionable nowadays to write off

Asakusa. But if Asakusa has lost out in the rat race of fashion, so much the better. Let the hordes go to Roppongi and Shibuya. There will always be a welcome for the discriminating in Asakusa.

Asakusa's roots are planted in the extravagant, escapist, but dangerous soil of grudgingly licensed but barely tolerated entertainment of the Edo period. The licensed quarter, Yoshiwara, had been banished to the paddies north of Asakusa in 1657 and the Kabuki theaters were sent packing to Asakusa in 1841. *"Yoshiwara to shibai wa sai no ura omote "* ("The licensed quarter and the stage are but two sides of the same coin"), it was said in the Edo period, and both of them were deemed to be wicked places. As was the case with the brothels, the authorities had always tried to pen the theaters in for nefarious purposes of surveillance. Of the three officially recognized Kabuki troupes, the Nakamuraza had spent most of the Edo period in Sakaimachi, the Ichimuraza in Fukiyachō (both in Ningyōchō), and the Moritaza in Kobikichō (Tsukiji).

The sentence of exile to Asakusa was passed down on the theaters by Mizuno Tadakuni, the shogun's all-powerful adviser, as part of the sumptuary edicts known as the Tempo reforms. He imagined, perhaps, that by banishing the theaters to this distant part of town, he could put bounds on the adoration shown by the public for its thespian heroes and ensure that less time was squandered by the townspeople in these frivolous pursuits. For a while, it seemed that he might succeed. The coincidence of sudden geographical isolation and a dearth of new dramatists led to a few lean years for the troupes. But, as had happened almost two hundred years earlier when the licensed quarter was moved north, the customers soon followed, and before long the new theater district in Asakusa became one of Edo's main attractions.

Asakusa itself, although well to the north of the center of the city, had long been a place of some importance. Archaeological evidence shows that a temple existed here from the seventh century, making the Sensōji just about the oldest temple in the east of Japan. This was also one of the oldest crossing points over the lower Sumida River.

As well as being strategically placed by the banks of the Sumida River, Asakusa straddled the road that led to the north of the country. When Tokugawa Ieyasu and his successors ringed the city with moats and gates at the beginning of the seventeenth century, Asakusa fell an hour's walk north of the nearest gate at Asakusa Bridge. For most of the next few centuries it remained an outlying suburb rather than an integral part of Edo, connected to the city by the built-up corridor of the Ōshū Kaidō, the road that led to the north. The process by which village became suburb was initiated with the construction in 1620 of the shogunal rice depots along the west bank of the Sumida River between Asakusa Bridge Gate and Asakusa itself. The same process was hastened by the replanning of Edo that was undertaken after the Long-Sleeves Fire of 1657, when most of the city's temples were moved and relocated in areas like Asakusa outside the walls.

As for Yoshiwara, the licensed quarter, it was moved to land beyond the shogun's rice godowns, beyond the little temples that had been replanted outside the city walls, and beyond even Asakusa's temple to Kannon, to a site in the paddy fields north of Asakusa. Asakusa now lay directly between the houses of the pleasure-loving citizens of Edo and the one place where they were officially allowed to indulge in one sort of pleasure. This was to Asakusa's immense benefit, as those of the patrons of the licensed quarter who preferred to make their journey by land rather than up the river by boat were more than likely to stop at Asakusa to make an offering at the temple and have some tea and cakes at the temple gate.

By the time the theaters were banished to Asakusa in 1841, the temple and its environs were a lively and well-established suburb of the city, and it is not surprising that the troupes only suffered a temporary setback. The area to which they were consigned was renamed Saruwakachō after a style of comic entertainment originated by the founder of the Nakamuraza when he first came to Edo in 1624. Saruwakachō covered the southeastern part of the present-day Asakusa 6-chōme. Each of the three main troupes occupied its own block, which it shared with manifold other more impromptu setups, in particular, puppet theaters. They stayed here, however, for a surprisingly short time: Moritaza, the first to go, moved to Shintomichō in 1872. The others followed suit soon after. Nevertheless extravagant, escapist Kabuki had taken root in Asakusa, and after the fall of the shogunate in 1868, restrictions on the number of theatrical troupes were eased somewhat and other Kabuki theaters opened in Asakusa. One in particular, the Miyatoza, survived almost until the Second World War and became a stronghold of the untainted Kabuki of Edo, a theater for Kabuki connoisseurs.

Kabuki's arrival in Asakusa was both appropriate and timely. Asakusa, like Yoshiwara, was the scene of several of the most popular plays. Many of the exciting incidents in *The Last Days of Chōbei of Banzuiin* take place in Asakusa, where Chōbei of Banzuiin himself lived. Chōbei is the archetypal Edo hero, valiant and kind, strong and generous, a romantic and swashbuckling character who devotes himself to the righting of innumerable wrongs as leader of a band of worthies and who eventually falls victim to the callous and contemptible Mizuno Jūrōzaemon. So, at least, the play would have us believe. In fact, Chōbei of Banzuiin was a rogue, leader of the *machiyakko*, gangs of townsmen who imitated and brawled with the *hatamotoyakko*, similar gangs composed of samurai. Chōbei was killed in 1650, and Jūrōzaemon, the son of a well-known military family, was eventually captured and executed in 1664. Their gangs, products of a warrior society becalmed in peace and of a city that had grown too fast for its own good, were a growing menace both to peaceful citizens and to the authorities until they were finally stamped out in the third quarter of the seventeenth century. On account of their flamboyant clothes and long whiskers, these ruffians were known as *kabukimono* (perverse, or wayward, ones). Later, they were glorified and celebrated on the stage, and referred to as *otokodate* men of style and valor.

Their extravagant habits and exaggerated actions provided the perfect vehicle for the kind of Kabuki that developed in Edo in the eighteenth century. The principal distinctive feature of the Kabuki of Edo was *aragoto*, a style of acting developed by Ichikawa Danjūrō I, involving bravado and exaggeration in expression and action. It was just the sort of entertainment (*aragoto* means "wild things") to suit the tastes of the robust, vigorous citizens of Edo, so much less refined than the townspeople of Kyoto and Osaka. The Kabuki of Edo reached its maturity in the nineteenth century, in the first three decades of the century, when Tsuruya Namboku IV was producing such masterpieces as *Tokubei of India* and *The Ghost Story of Yotsuya,* and again during the 1850s and 1860s, when the playwright Kawatake Mokuami was writing his blood-curdling depictions of the underworld of gamblers, thieves, and extortionists. This last period coincided with the sojourn of the Kabuki troupes in Saruwakachō, Asakusa.

In a manner similar to the Yoshiwara of these years, the Kabuki of

Saruwakachō was steeped in excess and extravagance and elaboration of well-worn themes. It hinged on the adulation shown by the audiences for the leading actors. The personality cult was as much a part of Edo Kabuki as of the various modern, Western forms of entertainment that took Kabuki's place in the public esteem in later years. "It is related that in the year 1833," wrote A. B. Mitford in his *Tales of Old Japan,* "when two actors called Bandō Shūka and Segawa Rokō, both famous players of women's parts, died at the same, time the people of Yedo mourned to heaven and to earth; and if a million riyos could have brought back their lives, the money would have been forthcoming." Mitford visited Saruwakachō during its heyday and was struck by the great throng of people who came to watch the plays: "As soon as the sun begins to rise in the heaven, sign-boards all glistening with paintings and gold are displayed, and the play-goers flock in crowds to the theatre.... The place soon becomes so crowded that the heads of the spectators are like the scales on a dragon's back."[5] Performances used to begin early in the morning and to last until dusk. The theaters were very dark, and they needed all the natural light they could get. The actors had their faces lighted by candles held by attendants who dogged their footsteps. As for the spectators, apart from the wealthier ones who had boxes, they sat on mats in small compartments divided by narrow gangplanks along which the waiters of the theater's teahouses skillfully made their way delivering tea and refreshment to their customers. With performances lasting as long as they did, a lot of chat and banter went on, and wooden clappers were used to draw the spectators' attention at moments of high drama. The clappers have survived down to the modern day, but the rest of Kabuki has undergone a radical transformation.

Saruwakachō was not the only place where entertainment was offered in Asakusa, nor was Kabuki the only form of entertainment available. Behind and on either side of the main hall of Asakusa's great temple to Kannon was Okuyama. Here were stalls where tea, saké, and other refreshments were served. "Here, too," wrote Mitford, "are all sorts of sights to be seen, such as wild beasts, performing monkeys, automata, conjurers, wooden and paper figures, which take the place of the waxworks of the West, acrobats, and jesters for the amusement of women and children."[6] Okuyama was not the only area of its kind, not Edo's only version of a Western fairground (although was ever a fairground as full of marvels as the Okuyama of Edo?). There were others in the streets that had been broadened to act as firebreaks after the Long-Sleeves Fire of 1657, as well as in the approaches to temples, such as at Shiba around Zōjōji and at Fukagawa, but Okuyama was the only one of them to survive well into the Meiji era.

Okuyama was already established by the 1770s. There was an archery range which turned out to be a brothel, as well as over seventy teahouses, some of whose waitresses served more than just tea. There were *komabutsu* stalls, which sold cosmetics, ornaments, hairpins, combs, and all the various devices women used in the Edo period to enhance the attractions of their appearance. There were *yōji* stalls, selling apparatus of all sorts for beautifying and blackening the teeth. Other stalls sold plants, medicines, toys, and sweets, often advertising their wares with exhibitions of swordsmanship such as the *iai nuki,* a sort of Japanese sword version of the "quick draw" of the cowboys of the Wild West. Some of the acrobatics and juggling make modern practitioners look tame if not timid: a child hanging perilously from the branches of a plum tree supported by the upheld arms and feet of a recumbent human "root"; or a "bridge" from the ends of which acrobats hung suspended from their feet, the bridge being perched on the top of two long bamboo legs balanced on an acrobat's upturned feet. Often these acrobatics were accompanied by the spinning of tops, a form of entertainment that had originated in Hakata in the north of Kyushu and had made its way to Edo via Kyoto at the end of the seventeenth century. In Edo it was popularized by one of the most famous prestidigitators, Matsui Gensui. Top-spinning was performed against the background of a curtain depicting, for example, a dragon or an enchantress. The heavy iron tops would be spun on the projecting whiskers of the dragon or locks of the enchantress. Or they would be spun on the rim of the performer's fan or on the tip of his sword.

Perhaps the most splendid of all the acts and objects on display at Okuyama were the papier-mâché dolls, some of them life-size, depicting scenes from Kabuki and folk stories. The old hag of Adachi Moor, who lived centuries ago and lured travelers to her lonely hut where she robbed and murdered them, was shown about to slay her own daughter by mistake. Red-haired barbarians made perfect subjects for puppets. When Clara Whitney visited Okuyama in the summer of 1875, she was amused by the familiarity of some of the puppet scenes: "We then...saw a show of life-sized puppets dressed like foreigners—all having red hair and blue eyes. A lady and a gentleman with flame-red hair and azure eyes were standing arm in arm, ...a red-haired beauty rode a velocipede, one walked with a crutch, and another swept while a gardener very lifelike sat by a flower bed smoking an English pipe, and a little boy had a string of balloons. It was all very well done. Wonderfully lifelike—even the redheaded individuals, who were ugly to be sure, looked like some I have seen before."[7]

Among the novelties that foreigners brought with them was the camera, and, since no one likes novelties and gadgets more than the Japanese, it was not long (in 1875, to be precise) before camera studios started appearing in Asakusa's Okuyama. In this way, the home of some of the country's most bizarre and wonderful forms of entertainment became one of the first places to turn its eyes to the exotic West and help ensure that Asakusa as a whole remained the entertainment center of the city. Indeed, in the Meiji and Taishō eras, Asakusa was to show a vitality and exercise an appeal that drew the crowds in their tens of thousands in a way that the city never witnessed before or since, with the temple, too, a great crowd-puller and the best of pretexts for a visit, if pretexts were needed.

Several important changes occurred in Asakusa between the years 1873 and 1890. The first of these was the designation of the precincts and environs of the Asakusa Kannon as one of the city's first five public parks. A few years later two ponds, Ōike ("Large Pond") and the larger Hyōtan'ike ("Gourd Pond"), were created on the west side of the main temple hall, and these were to survive until 1951. Two years later, in 1884, the park was divided into seven sections, the fourth and fifth sections covering the two ponds, Okuyama, and Hana Yashiki—a garden of plants and animals in cages and entertainers in their booths that has now become an amusement park. The sixth section, Rokku, was the section of theaters and opera houses, cinemas and music halls, the section where the cultural life of Meiji and Taishō Tokyo unfolded its brightest blossoms. The following year, 1885, saw the construction of two rows of red-brick buildings to house the famous old Naka Mise, "Inside Shops," that lined the approaches to the

Asakusa Kannon. Finally, in 1890, Asakusa's—indeed, the city's—most distinctive landmark was completed, a tower so tall that it dwarfed all the other buildings in Tokyo, including the temple's recently repaired pagoda. This tower rose to a height of about sixty meters, and it had seven more stories than the pagoda. It was named Ryōunkaku, the "Cloud-Surpassing Pavilion," but was known to all as Jūnikai, "Twelve Stories." In a country that, until twenty-five years earlier, had no building over two stories high apart from castles and pagodas and that even in 1890 boasted only a handful of three-story edifices, the potency of the impression made by the Twelve Stories can be easily imagined.

The Twelve Stories was octagonal, built of red bricks with a wooden frame, and designed by a Briton, W. K. Barton. It contained a viewing platform and shops selling goods from all over the world, and it was owned and operated by a private company. Its most unusual feature was an elevator, the first in Japan to be open to the public, although not for long. It was considered hazardous and was closed down a few months later. In 1894 the inevitable earthquake occurred and had the Twelve Stories rocking dangerously. As a result, it was reinforced with a steel frame and steel girders which did their work so well that eight stories of the twelve remained standing through the Great Earthquake of 1923. That was not, however, enough to save it from the dynamite of professional demolishers.

This great tower of fabulous height became overnight the supreme symbol of Asakusa, presiding benignly over its great jamboree. It presided, first of all, over a warren of alleys at its foot where prostitutes plied their trade under the flimsy guise of operating bars known as "famous-brand liquor houses." These tiny brothels, the successors of the Edo-period unlicensed quarters of Fukagawa and elsewhere, aroused the resentment of the houses of Yoshiwara, and repeated protestations to the police finally led to the area being cleared after the 1923 earthquake. The prostitutes, however, regrouped in Tamanoi and Kameido, where they carried on their trade until the war. The Twelve Stories also presided over the Panoramakan. Built at about the same time as the Twelve Stories itself on the site of one of the city's many mini Mount Fujis, the Panoramakan was a white wooden building with a long, dark corridor and a staircase that led into a battlefield. Painted scenes of battle decorated the walls; in the foreground life-size models represented soldiers and generals first from the American Civil War and, after 1895, from the recent Japanese war with China.

The Panoramakan was not alone. The Twelve Stories presided over a whole district of novelty and distraction. Until the arrival of moving pictures in 1903, the staple entertainment in Rokku consisted of juggling and acrobatics, and narrative chanting known as *deroren* and *musume gidayū*. This last was by far and away the most popular, with audiences made up of young people driven to the point of frenzy by the chanting—to musical accompaniment in the *gidayū* style—of girls in the flower of youth. As the young singer, reclining languidly on an armrest and removing provocatively the various ornaments from her hair, approached the climax of her recitation, her admirers in the audience would shout out in feverish adulation, "*Dō suru?*" "*Dō suru?*" ("What to do? Oh, what to do?"). These devoted fans came to be known as the *Dō suru-ren,* the "What-to-Do Band." In the year 1900, the education minister decided that the What-to-Do Band was not a healthy phenomenon, and so he instructed the theaters to ban students from their doors during performances of *musume gidayū*.

The advent three years later of moving pictures—first shown at the Denkikan, a hall that until then had exhibited electronic gadgetry of various types—brought with it new problems of an unexpected sort. These problems were caused by the fact that the performances took place in almost total darkness. The nature of the problem can be left to the reader's imagination. The solution was that lights should be left on, that seats for men should be divided from those for women, and that the usherettes should at all costs wear underpants. From the year 1903, films were all the rage, and to cater for the public's insatiable demand many more cinemas were opened in Rokku, which soon became the film-goer's Mecca. In 1912 a French detective film proved to be such a success that young admirers of the film's great bandit hero started brandishing toy guns and staging mock holdups in the street. The police decided to halt all screenings of the film and others like it, causing considerable financial loss to the cinemas. Later, when the talkies arrived, the cinemas faced a different sort of problem. The narrators and musical accompanists made redundant as a result of the new talkies called a strike of cinema workers in 1932, thus bringing about the temporary closure of the Rokku cinemas. These narrators and accompanists were skilled performers, and many of them moved into the variety halls. A stone to their memory stands in the western part of the grounds of the Asakusa Kannon.

The moving pictures did not have the field all to themselves. An unlikely challenger to their hold on the public fancy arose in the form of opera. It was called Asakusa opera, and it did indeed resemble the real thing, which had first been performed in Japan without much success a few years before it caught on in Asakusa. The first performance of what was called opera but would better fit under the name Tanizaki gave it, song theater, was staged at the Tokiwaza in 1917. This was the beginning of the Asakusa opera boom. For the next few years song theater dominated. It ranged from serious opera (*Salome* and *Carmen*) to operetta to musical skits. The fervor of the fans of Asakusa opera knew no bounds, and, in a manner reminiscent of the What-to-Do Band of twenty years earlier, they would shout out the names of their favorite singers, regale them with balloons, and crowd around their dressing-room door. They came to be known as *peragoro,* short for *opera gorotsuki,* or "opera ruffians."

After the earthquake of 1923 and its subsequent fires, which claimed all of Asakusa apart from the temple to Kannon, opera gave way to cabaret and revues. The hero of Asakusa revues was a singer and comic called Enomoto Ken'ichi, known to most of Japan elliptically as Enoken. In 1929, he returned to Asakusa after several years spent touring the country and joined the Casino Fōri (Bergères was beyond the capabilities of the Japanese tongue). In the same year a young novelist whose story *The Izu Dancer* had just been published moved to Sakuragi on Ueno hill and started writing articles for the *Asahi* newspaper on Asakusa. The writer of these articles was Kawabata Yasunari, and so popular did they become among the middle classes and others who had until then looked askance at Asakusa that a Casino-Viewing Club was formed, and gentlemen from plush Yamanote suburbs made their way to Asakusa to watch little Enoken, with his husky voice and ad-lib gags. Their journey to Asakusa had been made easier, for in 1927 Tokyo's first subway line was opened, between Asakusa and Ueno. This was later extended to Shimbashi and Shibuya. Now known as the Ginza Line, it was Tokyo's only subway line until the completion in 1959 and 1960 of the Marunouchi Line and part of the Toei Asakusa Line.

Like the rest of Asakusa, including this time the temple, Rokku was razed to the ground following the air raids of 1945. But whereas people have returned in their droves to the temple and brought prosperity back to the shops and restaurants at its gates, Rokku has been neglected. In part, this is a result of the slow demise of the Japanese cinema, which itself is largely attributable to the rise of television. Rokku had long been famous for its colossal billboards advertising films, but nowadays the lurid depictions of bloody battle at sea or of bounteous breasts and faces contorted in grimaces of pleasure attract little more than a handful of spectators. The citizens of Tokyo no longer go to Asakusa to see films. If anything can be said to have replaced cinema in Rokku, it is the strip show, but even the strippers now find the air of Asakusa too chilly for their liking. There are still, however, a few variety halls left in Rokku, two on Rokku's main street and another two under the same roof, between Rokku and the temple.

Another survivor of Asakusa's days of glory is to be found on the street corner near Azuma Bridge. This is Kamiya Bar, Tokyo's first bar to be called a bar. Here, with the ghosts of Nagai Kafū, Tanizaki Jun'ichirō, and Kubota Mantarō, doyen of Asakusa writers, one can drink that galvanizing concoction Denki Bran, "electric brandy," consisting of vermouth, curaçao, gin, and wine added to a brandy base. It is said that Kamiya Bar used to be on the second floor, but so many customers had trouble negotiating the stairs on their way back down that eventually the bar moved itself downstairs.

# # #

Yoshiwara

Apart from during the war years, there have always been more men than women in the city, but never was the imbalance more pronounced than in the Edo period. Not only among the military classes, but among the townspeople, too, men predominated. Men outnumbered women to the tune of two men to one woman in the middle of the eighteenth century, although the imbalance slowly decreased until, by the middle of the following century, it had almost reached the modern level of near parity. Men have always outnumbered women in large cities, but for the townspeople of Edo, this situation was exacerbated by the nature of their function in the city: to trade, to sell, and to manufacture goods for the military class.

Not all was provided by men. While male prostitution became quite common, especially around the big temples, Edo had from its birth a predictably large number of women of the streets. This was not to the liking of the rulers of the country's military capital. In 1617, in answer to a proposal put forward by a certain Shōji Jin'e-mon, a special quarter was built on the outskirts of town east of Nihombashi. It was called Yoshiwara, and it was one of the country's three licensed quarters (excluding the post stations, whose status was less clear-cut), the other two being the Shimabara quarter in Kyoto and Shimmachi in Osaka. Prostitution and the management of brothels in other parts of Edo were banned. The pleasures of the flesh, and their concomitant perils, were thus safely immured, and Yoshiwara became not just a citadel of sex but the generator of an alternative culture and social system where merchants could brush sleeves with samurai and the stolid Confucianism of officialdom could be safely lampooned.

As Edo continued to grow, it soon engulfed the Five Streets of Yoshiwara, a situation not to the liking of the prudish authorities. Two new sites were suggested, one across the river in Honjo, the other to the north of the city near Asakusa. No bridge had yet been built across the Sumida River to Honjo, and so the paddy fields of Asakusa were chosen by the reluctant proprietors of Yoshiwara's houses. It was in the same year, 1657, shortly after the order to move that the Long-Sleeves Fire occurred, destroying more than half the city and giving rise to the first of Yoshiwara's many periods of dispersal to surrounding districts, which thrived on this occasional "patronage" and became prosperous as unlicensed and illegal brothel quarters. Yoshiwara was one of the most fire-prone parts of the city, and the casualty toll was often made worse by the habit of closing the gates to prevent the girls' escape. These periodic decampments—evacuations—became a feature of Yoshiwara, and they were greatly welcomed by the girls of the quarter because, despite the cramped and makeshift conditions, the atmosphere was carefree and they were allowed to come and go as they pleased.

By the middle of summer in 1657, Shin Yoshiwara, the new Yoshiwara, was ready. In those days, Asakusa was outside the city confines, and Yoshiwara, deposited there in the middle of the fields beyond Asakusa, was at first a lonely, rather eerie place. Despite a considerable increase in size, business was bad. Nevertheless, the city was growing ever larger and its inhabitants more prosperous, and before too long the new Yoshiwara was quite as lively as its predecessor. The problem of distance was overcome by the provision of a boat service. Boats left from moorings in Yanagibashi and several other spots along the Sumida River and deposited their passengers in San'yabori, a waterway that has only recently been completely covered up, and left them to make their way the short distance up Nihonzutsumi, an embankment built to protect Yoshiwara and the surrounding flatlands.

The entrance to the Five Streets of Yoshiwara (which by now had become seven) was marked by stores and drinking houses and a row of ten shops on each side of the road that rented, and later came to sell, *amigasa,* hats of plaited straw, to customers who wished to conceal their identity. A drawbridge let the visitor over Ohaguro-dobu, the "Ditch of Black Teeth" (married women and courtesans were so adorned), and through Ōmon, the "Great Gate," into the ceaseless festivity of Yoshiwara. Only two or three times a year, on the days of the Niwaka and Tori no Ichi festivals in summer and autumn, were the other gates thrown open and women of all sorts allowed into the quarter. The girls themselves, of course, were not allowed out except on the days of the Tori no Ichi festival in the Eleventh Month. Although the former Yoshiwara near Nihombashi had been open for business only in the daytime, the new Yoshiwara kept more liberal hours. The gate was closed late at night and opened again at dawn, when customers who had tarried too long were a common sight slipping out of the quarter and bracing themselves for the long journey home.

The main street, which ran the length of the quarter from the main gate, was called Naka no Machi. Along it several shops had been built (there was need for them out here in the fields north of the city). A little more than halfway down Naka no Machi on the right was Ageyamachi, where the customer with means would head. The *ageya,* which were grouped together in Ageyamachi, were rendezvous teahouses (nothing as base as a brothel) where a *tayū,* a high-ranking courtesan among the prostitutes of the quarter, would betake herself to meet a client. The *tayū* expected to be treated with some ceremony and at considerable expense. There were never very many of them, and their numbers soon fell into a rapid decline. Already by the last decade of the seventeenth century, there were fewer than ten *tayū*. Their customers increasingly were men from the merchant class like Kinokuniya Bunzaemon, and seldom did they find themselves trysting with the great military lords like Date Tsunamune, whose liaison with the celebrated courtesan Manji Takao led (it is said) to her assassination and his early retirement and formed the background of the play *Meiboku sendai hagi* ("The Disputed Succession").

A fall in standards was the constant plaint of the licensed quarter. As the number of *tayū* and *kōshijorō*, one notch down on the scale, decreased, so the continual influx of girls without training and skills raised the proportion of lower-class prostitutes, most of whom, far from being escorted by servants to meet a client they were at liberty to reject, sat behind the latticework window of a brothel in one of the back streets using their physical charms to attract customers in the time-honored way of the red-light district. By 1751, things had come to such a pass—the *tayū* had ceased to exist and the *ageya* were no more than a memory—that a distinction was made between the girls who catered to men's sexual needs, the *yūjo,* and those who restricted themselves to social and cultural forms of entertainment, the *geisha.*

Like many a good resolution, this reform was less than successful, and by 1779 the geisha were extending the range of their work into what should have been the exclusive preserve of the *yūjo*. This situation so angered Daikokuya Shōroku, the proprietor of one of the oldest establishments in the Five Streets, that he decided to set up an office in order to control the activities of the girls in Yoshiwara. His idea won immediate acceptance, no doubt because others were losing money—as he himself had been—as a result of the "extracurricular" activities of the geisha. Daikokuya himself was appointed "comptroller" of Yoshiwara (the district came in theory under the direct supervision of the Edo city magistrates). His first action was to set about regulating the activities of the geisha, checking up on their conduct, their clothes, and their standards of decorum. The rule that a customer was never to be entertained by one geisha alone but always by a group of three was strictly enforced, and any *hikitejaya* (the rather less decorous successor to the *ageya*) found encouraging a geisha to sell her body was to be closed down forthwith, along with both its neighboring houses. The new office met with considerable success in the enforcement of the rules, and it extended its activities to all areas of administration in the quarter, financing itself by taking increasingly larger and onerous contributions from the houses.

The last hundred or so years of the Edo period were marked by two disastrous famines, in the 1780s and 1830s, both of which were followed by attempts at reforms that involved on the one hand inept measures to stamp out institutional corruption and on the other sumptuary edicts, among whose chief targets were the unlicensed quarters that had sprung up all over the city. The result of these measures was an influx of prostitutes to the licensed quarter. These new arrivals were invariably untrained and without skills, and so they found themselves consigned to the lowest class of brothel, where they lived in miserable conditions. By the middle of the nineteenth century, there were over ten thousand girls in the licensed quarter. This must have meant wretched overcrowding, as Yoshiwara had not been allowed to expand by even one block since it was moved to the Asakusa paddy fields.

In this final century or so of Tokugawa rule, and particularly in the last twenty years of the nineteenth century, the fame of the Five Streets reached a pinnacle. Yoshiwara exerted a peculiar but irresistible appeal, and it became the center of attraction for the cultural luminaries of the city. It gave birth to fashion in dress, to faddish jargon, to style in deportment, and to an exhaustive etiquette of entertainment. Its music, costumes, festivals, and patois represented the essence of all that was modish and most desirable, and a thorough and up-to-the-minute knowledge of them was the hallmark of a *tsū*, a denizen of the quarter, a man-about-town whose sophistication and urbanity, whose profound knowledge of the houses and sensitivity for their inhabitants singled him out as worthy of that highest token of respect, emulation. But great danger lurked here, for a breach of etiquette or sign, however slight, of unfamiliarity with the newest fad would give the lie to a patron's best and most strenuous efforts to prove his qualities as a *tsū*.

In all this lay the seeds of social satire and comedy. The most famous writer to exploit these possibilities was Santō Kyōden, whose wit and verve and versatility found fruition in his descriptions, both literary and artistic, of the licensed quarter and of its *tsū* and not-so-*tsū* patrons. In his stories and narrative cartoons he delved into and described every type of custom and all the most arcane details of life in Yoshiwara. He pilloried the impostors and lionized the true *tsū*. As an *ukiyo-e* artist, under the name of Kitao Masanobu, he depicted the beauties of the licensed quarter in the style of Katsukawa Shunshō and Kitao Shigemasa, whose joint picture album of famous courtesans, *A Mirror of Lovely Images: Matching Beauties of Yoshiwara,* was to become a classic of its kind. The prints in this album were also to have a crucial influence on the work of the greatest portrayer of the licensed quarter, Kitagawa Utamaro. Utamaro, in series like *Contemporary Edo Dancers Arrayed for the Yoshiwara Niwaka Festival* and *A Collection of Reigning Beauties,* gave such poignant color and form and style to his portrayals of the inhabitants of the quarter that the impression he made on the canons of artistic taste was to be lasting and worldwide.

In this way, Yoshiwara came to be a refuge for men of means and a modicum of culture, a place where they could escape from the stifling class distinctions of Edo-period society and the stern and unimaginative morals of the official school of Confucianism. It was an effete, decadent, self-absorbed atmosphere, an elaborate party game for adepts. It represented both an abnegation of serious political and literary responsibilities (with all the dangers of persecution that they entailed) and at the same time an embracing of the spirit of the "floating world," that approach to life, Buddhist in origin, which arose out of a realization of the evanescence of human existence, the impermanence of human achievement, and the futility of human effort.

The dilettante writers in their "green towers" (*seirō,* one of the euphemisms for a brothel) strike us as having been surprisingly unimpressed by the nature of the establishments in which they spent so much of their time. Neither were they (allowing for the few inevitable exceptions) sexual profligates, nor were they particularly concerned about the dissipation of others. (In this sense, the *shunga*—erotic drawings—of Utamaro and others are reminders of the true nature of the place.) The plight of the prostitutes and the squalid circumstances in which most of them lived never enter the picture. Indeed, one finds oneself resisting the relentless gaiety and decorum depicted in these Edo-period portrayals of Yoshiwara. For accounts of the licensed quarter that evoke a more realistic picture we must turn to the eyewitness descriptions of foreigners and the literature of the Meiji era.

"The time to see Yoshiwara to the best advantage," wrote A. B. Mitford, "is just after nightfall, when the lamps are lighted. Then it is that the women—who for the last two hours have been engaged in gilding their lips and painting their eyebrows black, and their throats and bosoms a snowy white, carefully leaving three brown Vandyke-collar points where the back of the head joins the neck, in accordance with one of the strictest rules of Japanese cosmetic science—leave the back rooms, and take their places, side by side, in a kind of long narrow cage, the wooden bars of which open to the public thoroughfare. Here they sit for hours, gorgeous in dresses of silk and gold and silver embroidery, speechless and motionless as wax figures, until they shall have attracted the attention of some of the passers-by, who begin to throng the place."[8] Not all of the prostitutes were quite so docile, if one is to judge by the fact that one of the quarter's back streets was named after the harlots' habit of desperately lunging out for passers-by and refusing to let go of anyone who fell into their clutches.

In the last decade of the nineteenth century, Yoshiwara was portrayed in a series of evocative vignettes by a young woman writer, Higuchi Ichiyō. In a story called *Growing Up,* she describes the children who live in the shadow of the Five Streets, the festivals of the quarter—the annual summer carnival and the Tori no Ichi—and the gang fights of the children. Ichiyō left her home in Hongō and spent a year with her aunt, who lived in the streets behind Yoshiwara. It was shortly after her return home in May 1894 that she wrote *Growing Up.* Ichiyō is a writer for whom many Japanese feel great affection, in part because of her early death, at the age of twenty-four in 1896.

Another writer who described the quarter was Nagai Kafū. His descriptions, written some decades after the time of Higuchi Ichiyō, are steeped in wistfulness, in nostalgia for the samisen, the dances, and the festivals of Yoshiwara in days gone by. "In the autumn of 1908, when I came back from several years abroad, I felt like an old devotee for whom the rules had been turned upside-down. There were beer halls on the old central street of Yoshiwara, and the harmony of 'the two rows of lanterns, that first sign of autumn,' had already been destroyed. The rows of ladies waiting in the houses had disappeared. The Five Streets were dark, the rickshaws along the embankment were conspicuously fewer in number."[9]

The Meiji government had brought with it an order of life in which there was no natural place for a licensed quarter. It is a measure of Yoshiwara's appeal, therefore, that it survived as long as it did into the modern era. In 1900, when a law was passed enabling the girls of the licensed quarter to leave whenever they pleased, at least four hundred of them took immediate advantage, and by the end of the year Yoshiwara found itself eleven hundred women poorer. Many houses had to close their doors for good. At the same time, geisha houses in Hamachō and Shimbashi, which catered to the new prosperous class of businessmen, industrialists, and politicians, attracted more and more of the *oiran,* the high-class heirs to the tradition of the *tayū.* Nearby Asakusa, however, was flourishing as never before and had become the center of entertainment in Tokyo. It was only a short rickshaw ride from Asakusa to Yoshiwara, and so even if the Five Streets had lost something in style they retained much of their racy vigor. Nevertheless, the Yoshiwara that survived in such jaunty fashion the fires and disasters of the Edo period succumbed in the end to a way of life that was basically inimical to its continued existence. It was formally dissolved, disbanded, on 31 March 1958. That is not such a long time ago, and there are plenty of people who remember the quarter well and who, with a knowing, proud twinkle in the eye, are more than willing to recall the place.

The present Senzoku 4-chōme covers almost exactly the extent of the former licensed quarter, and within Senzoku 4-chōme are the successors to the Miuraya, Ōgiya, Tamaya, and the other great Edo-period houses. But these modern establishments are unworthy heirs. Their names give them away: Monroe, Acapulco, and Quartier Latin. They are supreme examples of modern international bordello kitsch, and slightly passé at that. It is easy, of course, to romanticize the past, and it would be hard to deny the assertion that Yoshiwara was in many ways a more squalid place than Senzoku 4-chōme, but Senzoku 4-chōme could be anywhere in Japan—anywhere in the world—and it has nothing to do with Yoshiwara.

The districts between Yoshiwara and the Sumida River—Nihonzutsumi, Higashi Asakusa, Kiyokawachō, Imado, and Hashiba—are among the most depressed in Tokyo. Their shabbiness makes them one of the few parts of the city that stand comparison with the poorer regions of cities in the West. In the years not long after the end of the war, the part of this area known as San'ya became the site of a large number of cheap lodging houses, dilapidated wooden structures where a bed for a night cost the same as a bowl of ramen noodles. In 1961, there were three hundred or so hostels, home for an estimated twenty thousand people, most of them day laborers called *nikoyon,* because they earned ¥240 a day (and ¥100 was popularly referred to as *ikko*). The area became known as the San'ya Doyagai, *doya* being a not so cryptic anagram for the word *yado,* "lodging."

In several enclaves in San'ya lived those people who fell outside recognized society, the pariahs of the feudal world. Their descendants, the *burakumin,* who are *de jure* treated as equals with the rest of society, live mainly in the west of Japan. It was from the west, from the province of Settsu (Osaka), that the family of Danzaemon, hereditary leader of the outcasts, was said to have originated. For many years Danzaemon had his quarters near Nihombashi, in Muromachi, but he and his fellow outcasts were moved early in the Edo period to land that is now part of Imado 1- and 2-chōme. Here they were further from the Kodemmachō prison, where their duties included the administering of torture, but nearer the execution ground at Kozukappara and the licensed quarter of Yoshiwara, although the licensed ladies of the Five Streets, unlike their unlicensed colleagues, were not members of the pariah class.

There were in the Edo period two types of outcasts. There were the "nonpeople," *hinin,* whose number included beggars and prostitutes, people who had fallen upon hard times but who, with a little money and luck, might be able to "wash their feet" and return to the recognized strata of society. The leader of the nonpeople was called Kuruma Zenshichi, but his role was eventually taken over by Danzaemon. Danzaemon was leader of a slightly higher but permanent class of outcasts, the *eta.* Twenty-eight professions are said to have come under Danzaemon's sway, including fortune-tellers, monkey-trainers, mendicant entertainers, lion-dancers, and puppeteers. Some of these, however, would have been non-people rather than *eta.*

The *eta* were involved in ritually unclean work. One such task was the slaughter of animals. Near San'ya in the Meiji era, an abattoir was built. Another of the jobs traditionally associated with the *eta* was tanning and other work that involves handling leather and hide. Among the host of small commercial and light-industrial enterprises in this part of Tokyo are many that deal in hides and leather goods. Indeed, the area in the triangle formed by Yoshiwara, the Asakusa Kannon, and the river remains to this day one of the most important centers for the country's wholesale network of footwear.

# # #

Senju

"When we disembarked at Senju, my heart grew heavy at the thought of the thousands of miles that lay ahead, and tears welled from my eyes on leaving my friends in this world of illusion." This is how Bashō, the great haiku poet, described his departure on a journey to the north of Japan recorded in his masterpiece *Narrow Road to a Far Province*. Bashō had made the short trip from his house in Fukagawa by boat up the Sumida River in the company of his friends. From here the poet set out along the road to the north, stopping on his first night at a place called Sōka.

Sōka, which is now safely within the suburban confines of Saitama Prefecture, was the second staging post on the Ōshū Kaidō, one of the four roads out of Edo (off which a fifth, the Nikkō Kaidō, branched at Utsunomiya). The first staging post was at Senju, and indeed, if Bashō had wanted to spend the night there, he would have had no trouble. Only a few decades after the poet's death (in 1694), there were seventy-two inns at Senju. Although regulations had been drawn up restricting the number of serving girls each inn was allowed, at least one part of Senju became a flourishing brothel quarter.

Senju, originally written with characters meaning "Thousand Hands" (named, legend has it, after an image of Thousand-Armed Kannon that was picked out of the river here in 1328), is the site of the first bridge to have been built over the Sumida River. Ōhashi ("Great Bridge") was built in 1594 at the order of Tokugawa Ieyasu to link his new castle town of Edo with the north, and for over half a century it remained the only bridge over the lower reaches of the river. The original structure was so strong that, although it was damaged several times, it stood firm until 1886, when it was swept away by a flood.

The bridge that once carried all the traffic and travelers bound for

Nikkō and the north is now modern and inconspicuous beside an array of similar bridges and carries traffic bound for the most part, no doubt, for places only a few kilometers away. Senju still straddles the river, as it did in the days when it was a post town, with most of it in Adachi Ward north of the Sumida but with Minami Senju, an area including several unlikely monuments, south of the river in Arakawa Ward.

Between the northernmost suburbs of the city of Edo and the post station of Senju lay one of the city's two execution grounds, at a place called Kozukappara. The other execution ground was at Suzugamori to the south near Ōmori on the Tōkaidō. Kozukappara, here in the north, stood on the Ōshū Kaidō. The position of the two execution grounds, on the main roads leading out of the city, was intended to serve as a salutary reminder to travelers, among whom there was always a certain number of fugitives from shogunal justice. Burning at the stake was the punishment for arson; decapitation or crucifixion, for various other crimes including murder and robbery. The criminals had become outcasts and were therefore not allowed to have their bones buried beside those of their family in the family temple. But they were not completely disregarded. In 1662 a temple was set up beside the Kozukappara execution ground where their memory could be preserved.

This temple was a subsidiary of the Ekōin built in Honjo to honor the tens of thousands of people who perished in the Long-Sleeves Fire of 1657. It was known as the Kozukappara Ekōin, and it still stands on its original site, although its grounds have been sliced by railway lines. Near it is a large statue of Jizō, serene in countenance but with the lugubrious name Kubikiri, or "Head-Chop," Jizō. The temple has an interesting connection with the spread of European learning in the Edo period. It was here that Sugita Gempaku, Maeno Ryōtaku, and a few friends conducted autopsies on the bodies of executed criminals. They found that their observations concorded with the treatise on anatomy which they had been translating from the Dutch.

Ironically, among the unfortunates to be buried at the Kozukappara burial ground near Ekōin was Hiraga Gennai, the most versatile, learned, and accomplished of the Edo-period scholars of European learning. As wayward as he was talented, Gennai was a close friend of Gempaku, and when he died in prison after killing one of his followers and was buried with the outcasts at the Kozukappara execution ground, it was Gempaku who tried to have him given a decent grave. Gempaku's efforts bore fruit, for Gennai does now have a grave, enclosed by an elegant wall situated not far from Ekōin in Hashiba, Taitō Ward. Gennai was indeed a versatile man: he was a tireless collector of medicinal herbs and plant life, and he helped to arrange the first exhibition ever to be held in Edo, in 1757, and then arranged his own exhibition, finally cataloguing the products—animals, plants, and minerals—in an encyclopedia. He encouraged mining for iron and gold, fashioned a heat-resistant asbestos cloth, and re-created a friction electric motor. His curiosity was insatiable, and his other activities included sheep farming and the introduction of Western techniques of pottery. Gennai was also an accomplished writer and painter who is said to have been the first person to use the term *gesaku* ("worthless works") to describe the supposedly frivolous, light-hearted pieces written by men of letters. He himself was a prominent writer of Bunraku puppet plays and comic and satirical works, in which he denounced contemporary society for its lack of enterprise. As a painter, he was important in the spread of Western oil-painting techniques, and he taught Shiba Kōkan, who became the most prominent Edo-period oil painter. For all this, Gennai was unsuccessful, and bitter at his lack of success and recognition. "An extraordinary man who was fascinated by extraordinary things, conducted himself in extraordinary ways, and died a most extraordinary death": this was the epitaph that his friend Sugita Gempaku wrote for him.

Senju and the area to the south between it and Asakusa seem to have had a natural sympathy for victims, outcasts, and losers. In 1868, the imperial forces stormed Edo, and the losers in a brief but fierce encounter on Ueno hill were members of a band of Tokugawa loyalists known as the Shōgitai. Several of those of the Shōgitai who died in the fighting were later given proper graves by sympathetic priests of Entsūji, a temple in Minami Senju not far from Kozukappara. In 1907, a gate whose name is inextricably linked to the memory of the Shōgitai was moved to the grounds of Entsūji. The gate is Kuromon, the "Black Gate," which once stood at the foot of the approach to Kan'eiji on Ueno hill. It was around this gate that the Shōgitai rallied during their last stand against the imperial forces. The gate can still be seen in the temple grounds, but it has been so heavily repaired that it no longer bears the look of historical veracity.

5

Kōtō Ward and
the East

Fukagawa

Ask most inhabitants of the modern city of Tokyo where Fukagawa is and they will shake their head, suck in air, and hazard the view that it is probably somewhere the other side of Asakusa. Ask them what Fukagawa represents, however, and the hesitation will evaporate: Kiba (the timber merchants' district), they will say, and a raffish line in geisha, and, in general, the raucous happy-go-lucky atmosphere of plebeian Edo. In this way, historical and cultural remoteness—a feeling that the things of Fukagawa no longer belong in the modern city, if they still exist at all—has given rise to the myth of geographical inaccessibility, as if Fukagawa were somewhere beyond the pale, when it is in fact not an hour's walk from Nihombashi. It is, however, the other side of the river, and for this the inhabitants of Fukagawa had to suffer the scorn of the townspeople from the more prosperous districts of the city.

If it is true to say that the waters of its rivers and the sea conditioned the city's existence right up toward the end of the nineteenth century, this is especially true of Fukagawa, which was born from water, received its livelihood from water, and—many would say—died when its waterways lost their commercial importance. It prospered because of its waterways, and it suffered for them too. Flooding was endemic in Fukagawa, just as were fires in the rest of the city. Already in the first half of the seventeenth century, before even Fukagawa had been fully reclaimed from the sea, steps were taken to divert the flow of rivers to facilitate navigation and especially to curb the floodwaters. Until then, the Tone River, mightiest of the many rivers of the flatlands of the east, had flowed into Tokyo Bay through several mouths with courses and names that changed bewilderingly through the centuries. The aim of these river-diverting projects was to make the main course of the Tone River flow into the Pacific Ocean at Chōshi. The Edo River, which now flows into the bay between Tokyo and Chiba, became a subsidiary mouth, while the Arakawa, which is known in its lower reaches as the Sumida, had its course diverted so that it should no longer be a mouth of the Tone River but part, instead, of the flow of the Iruma River. In its details the whole business is highly complicated; in its aim of making the Tone flow east instead of south it is quite simple; and in its results it must be judged to bedevil the lives of the inhabitants of Fukagawa and surrounding areas throughout the Edo period.

River-flooding in preindustrial times was, on the whole, a menace that people could learn to live with. The level of the waters rose slowly, as a rule. People were prepared for the worst, and they had time and boats in which to evacuate. Ironically, the worst two floods occurred at the beginning of the twentieth century, when most of the people of the area no longer depended on the rivers for their livelihood. Although these floods were unusually severe, some of the damage may have resulted from the fact that there was much more to damage—more houses and new factories in the area—than there had been half a century earlier in the Edo period. The year after the second and more severe of these two floods, that of 1910, work was begun on the greatest river-diverting project yet undertaken. Over the next nineteen years a new course was built for the Arakawa running close by the old course, starting up in Saitama Prefecture and finally reaching the bay between the modern Kōtō and Edogawa wards. This new mouth is known at the Arakawa; the former course retains its former name, Sumida.

The new outlet for the Arakawa was successful in putting an end to flooding from the river, but Fukagawa had always been prey to a more sudden and ruthless foe, the combination of typhoon and high tide. The floods of 1742 and 1791 were particularly bad; the second of the two wiped out the whole of the entertainment district of Susaki, an appendage of Fukagawa. In 1854 a tidal wave of terrifying dimensions swept through Fukagawa, shattering most of its rickety houses, and no sooner had they been rebuilt than another flood washed through the area. This second flood, like the earlier one, followed an earthquake, the Ansei earthquake of 1855, which caused untold damage and the loss of over ten thousand lives. No wonder the citizens of Edo thought that the end of the world was nigh and that the recently arrived red-haired barbarians in their Black Ships were harbingers. Typhoons and tidal waves have continued to visit suffering on Fukagawa, even since the war, but in recent years a tidal boom has been built and the banks of Fukagawa's waterways have been reinforced, so the chances of floods have been considerably reduced.

The Fukagawa that has undergone untold ordeals by water suffered its greatest catastrophes from fire. In 1923, on 1 September, it was one of the first districts to be razed by fire after the Great Earthquake had shattered the city that day. Twenty-two years later, Fukagawa was the prime target of the heaviest air raids that any Japanese city had to endure in the Second World War. The raids of March 1945 were not the first. Bombs had been falling on the city all through the winter, one of the coldest on record, with the mercury under zero for forty-five consecutive days. The raids of the night of 9 and 10 March were the climax, although bombs were to continue to rain down on the city until well into the summer. All through the day of the ninth, a strong wind had been blowing, and people knew full well what would happen if the Americans chose that night to launch another raid. The Americans knew well, too. They went about their job with thoroughness; there was no need to hurry. They dropped incendiary cylinders that the Japanese called "Molotov flower baskets" to mark the target area and then let the first bombs fall on the periphery of this area. Inside it were the most heavily populated parts of the city, those parts that had made up the townspeople's quarters of Edo: Fukagawa, Nihombashi, Kanda, and Asakusa, as well as districts that in more recent years had become important industrial centers like Senju and Mukōjima. The industrial areas were the most densely populated, and few save children had been evacuated.

The statistics of the raid are as follows: over three hundred B-29s took part, each carrying seven or eight tons of a newly developed incendiary bomb. Between midnight and three o'clock in the morning alone, seven hundred thousand bombs were dropped, ten times greater in weight than the bombs dropped on London by the Luftwaffe in the raids of September 1941.¹ The ferociously hot winds that the fire bombs engendered, the inflammability of what was supposed to be protective gear, and the fallen utility poles and debris that made escape impossible—all this meant a most horrible end for anyone caught within the target area. It was never possible to make more than a rough estimate of the dead, but out of a total of over seventy-two thousand victims, about a third were in Fukagawa. Some 40 percent of Tokyo was laid to waste in this one raid, and Fukagawa was obliterated. Eight days later, when relatives and the few survivors were still sifting through the rubble, they were joined by a slight, bespectacled man in army fatigues. The emperor had come to examine the damage for himself, the only time he ever left protocol behind him and saw with his own eyes the terrible trials that the war had inflicted on the ordinary people of his country.

Fukagawa has every right to claim the title of most disaster-prone district in this disaster-prone city. Disasters, however, brought prosperity as well as suffering. "When the wind blows, the cooper wins," the saying went. In Fukagawa was the district where the timber merchants had their wharfs and warehouses, the district known as Kiba, "Place of Wood." Edo had had several "places of wood," with the main timber district situated in Nihombashi. In the aftermath of the Long-Sleeves Fire of 1657 they were gathered together and sent across the river, and after several decades of peregrination on the east bank, they settled down in Fukagawa. Before the Long-Sleeves Fire, Fukagawa had been little more than a collection of fishing villages, and indeed not many decades earlier it had not existed at all. The earliest works east of the river had been initiated by Tokugawa Ieyasu not long after he first arrived in Edo in 1590. His new city, he realized, would need salt, and so he had a canal built from the tidal flats at Gyōtoku (in modern Urayasu, Chiba Prefecture) across to the Sumida so that salt could be conveyed in quantity to meet the anticipated demand. This canal, called the Onagigawa, still exists, in the north of present-day Kōtō Ward. But at the beginning of the sixteenth century, the east bank of the Sumida stretched little further south than this. Gradually, over the next fifty years, the borders of terra firma were pushed south, the swamps and tidal flats being solidified with earth excavated for the construction of canals and with the city's garbage. Fukagawa sits, in fact, on a giant bed of detritus. A shadowy figure called Fukagawa Hachirōemon seems to have been in charge of much of the reclamation work.

By about 1655, work had been carried out as far as it was going to be for the next few hundred years, to a line just south of Eitai Street and including the modern districts of Eitai, Monzen Nakachō, and Tomioka. At this time, or to be precise a little earlier, eight men arrived on the scene from the west of Japan, from the province of Settsu, where the modern city of Osaka now stands. It seems likely that these eight men and their families were moved from the west in the same way and for the same reasons as the fishermen of Tsukudajima: to teach the primitive fishermen of the east a thing or two about fishing techniques and to keep a weather eye on the movement of vessels in the port. Unlike the fishermen of Tsukudajima, the island at the mouth of the Sumida just downriver from Fukagawa, the eight men of Fukagawa eventually found more profitable vocations for themselves. They became warehousemen. Each of the eight had been given his own little district, and each district was named after that one of the eight who lived there. Collectively the eight districts were known as Ryōshimachi, "Fishermen's Town." In 1695, the names of the districts were changed, and of the names that were new in 1695 one still exists, Saga. But by then the fishermen had become warehousemen, and Saga and the other districts around it contained many of the city's wharves and warehouses. There was an inevitable preponderance of warehouses for rice, but many of these stored unhulled rice for use in an emergency. Fukagawa was the central district for oil wholesalers (both vegetable and animal oil); in 1851 there were twenty-five wholesalers with warehouses here. As well as oil, other commodities such as beans, saké, and salt were unloaded and stored in Fukagawa warehouses. So, too, was the fertilizer made from sardines known as *hoshika,* much of which was transported by boat from Chōshi on the Pacific coast and stored at special wharves belonging to that town.

But of all the wharves and warehouses of Fukagawa, the most famous were those of the timber merchants, who eventually settled in the district still known as Kiba, just to the east of the center of Fukagawa. Timber was a commodity of immense importance to everyone in the city, and many of the large shops in Nihombashi and the wealthier parts of town kept a sort of prefab spare frame in Kiba so that when the inevitable happened and their shop burned down it could be rebuilt in the shortest time possible. Kiba has lost its sturdy, white-plastered storehouses, and it is in the process of losing its sweet-scented timber yards, most of which have already moved to their new quarters, Shin Kiba, some three or four kilometers further south. Logs are being moved away from the canals of Kiba, and the "raftmasters" in their *happi* jackets are becoming an ever rarer sight. The raftmasters had the tricky job of steering the logs down from the mountains and then through the busy waterways of the capital. They would hop nimbly from log to log, guiding them with a long pole and punting them under bridges and down busy waterways.

Along with the timber yards came the timber merchants themselves. Two timber merchants, in particular, were preeminent for their immense wealth and their unscrupulous business practices, Kinokuniya Bunzaemon and Naraya Mozaemon. Both of them had their main townhouses in the more prosperous districts near Nihombashi, but they had suburban villas in Fukagawa. Kinokuniya, indeed, came to know both sides of life in Fukagawa, for when his business collapsed in 1709 after an unwise venture into minting coins, he found himself living the life of a pauper near the entrance to the Fukagawa Hachiman Shrine. Another local tycoon was more enlightened: Sugiyama Sampu was a poet who offered a corner of his villa in Fukugawa to the haiku master Matsuo Bashō. Bashō made this his home and base in Edo, and from here he struck out on his travels to the north and to other parts of the country. In the garden of the poet's cottage in Fukagawa, a *bashō* plant grew. The *bashō* is a type of banana plant or plantain. It is scruffy, with no particular charm and with leaves that tear easily in the wind. It was for this very reason that the poet fell for it, named his cottage after it, and used it as his *nom de plume*. He made the plant the subject of one of his early haiku masterpieces:

> Plantain tree in autumn storm
> As I listen all night to
> Rain in a basin.

By the time Bashō arrived in Fukagawa in 1680, the settlement of the eight fishermen had already grown into a substantial suburb. Like so many others of the regions just beyond the boundaries of the city, its development was spurred by the Long-Sleeves Fire of 1657, after which many of the temples of the center of the city were moved to Fukagawa. When the first bridge across the lower reaches of the Sumida was built, at about this time, Fukagawa became easier of access. And then in 1693, another bridge, the Shin Ōhashi, was built a little way downstream. When it was completed, it made life much easier for Bashō, who expressed his appreciation thus:

> How grateful I feel
> As I step crisply over
> The frost on the bridge.

Five years later, a third bridge was built, Eitaibashi, from where convicts were loaded onto boats and shipped to penal colonies on the Seven Isles of Izu, as often as not never to return. Eitaibashi replaced an overworked ferry, but in 1808 it suffered catastrophically from overwork itself, collapsing under the weight of crowds of worshipers who were taking part in the festival of the Fukagawa Hachiman Shrine. A thousand people are said to have drowned or been injured in the accident.

Eitaibashi linked Fukagawa directly to the city's commercial center, Nihombashi. From that time on Fukagawa was an intrinsic part of the city, a fact that was recognized about twenty years later when it was placed under the jurisdiction of the Edo magistrates. In 1828, there were almost twelve thousand dwellings in the townspeople's parts of Fukagawa (which meant most of the district), and, calculating on the basis of four inhabitants per dwelling, its population at the time was almost fifty thousand.

Fukagawa had ceased to be a fishing village, but the fish served in its restaurants were among the best. And the very best of its restaurants was Hirasei, near the entrance to the Fukagawa Hachimangū. The fish served at Hirasei were of the freshest from the bay "in front of the city" (Edomae). No reputable restaurant in Edo would have served anything but the freshest fish from Edomae, and Edo-style sushi, known as *Edomae-zushi,* became the pride of the city's cuisine. At Hirasei the speciality was sea bream, and in common with other high-class restaurants the great culinary event was the first bonito of the year (*hatsugatsuo*), a predeliction of the Edokko. Restaurants like Hirasei, however, were beyond the means of the ordinary townsman, and they were, in any case, few in number.

Sushi caught on in Edo, according to one theory, at the end of the sixteenth century, and Fukagawa possessed one of the two most famous of the city's few sushi restaurants, Kashiwaya. Kashiwaya served *maze-zushi*, mixed sushi, with chopped seafood and vegetables added to the rice; it also served *hayazuke,* prepared a day earlier, and *kirizuke*, something like the pressed sushi of Osaka. Loaches were great favorites among the people of Edo; a stone's throw from the site of Kashiwaya stands Iseki, one of the city's last two loach restaurants. More common than loaches and sushi and all the rest was *soba*, served at countless roadside stalls as *ni-hachi soba,* or "two-eight noodles," so named because the noodles consisted of two parts wheat flour and eight parts buckwheat flour.

Of all the dishes served in the teahouses of Fukagawa, none was as popular as *kabayaki,* grilled eel. The people of Edo have always liked their food well impregnated with soy sauce, and this was how the Fukagawa teahouses served their eels, broiled and oily and salty. "The eels of Fukagawa are seldom large," it is written in the *Gold-Dust Tales of Edo* of 1732.[2] "They are, most of them, medium-sized or small, and they taste delicious." In the *Illustrated Gazetteer of Famous Places in Edo* of 1836 we find the following passage: "The three or four blocks along the west side of the road inside the first of the [Fukagawa Hachiman] shrine's arches are lined with teahouses and restaurants where the sound of singing to the accompaniment of the samisen never ceases. Most popular of them all with the pleasure-seekers are the restaurants nearest the shrine known as 'the two teahouses.' Oysters, mussels, clams, eels, and other fish are the specialities of the district."[3] "The two teahouses" were Iseya and Matsumoto, whose fame spread throughout the city in the first half of the eighteenth century. They were famous, as we have seen, for their eels and oysters and clams, and also for their elegant gardens and for their excellent saké. But the special ingredient was social and musical, not culinary. It was the charm and musical skill of the teahouse girls.

Edo was a city in which men outnumbered women, and it was also a city in which the authorities tried to regulate every aspect of the life of its inhabitants, including the sale of sex. Licensed prostitution was confined to the licensed quarter, Yoshiwara, but unlicensed quarters had sprung up all over the city. In Fukagawa there were more unlicensed quarters than anywhere else, seven in all. They were called *oka basho*, "hill places," as opposed, so some people say, to the "bitter sea" of the licensed quarter. They seem originally to have found Fukagawa fertile ground because it was outside the jurisdiction of the city magistrates. The "seven hills" of Fukagawa benefited too each time fire struck at Yoshiwara, which it did with some regularity, for the houses of the licensed quarter would then have to seek refuge under the roofs of their unlicensed competitors. But the seven hills of Fukagawa were quite different from the licensed quarter. They were the result not of an administrative plan to confine pleasure within walls but of spontaneous growth in response to demand. The higher-class prostitutes of Fukagawa called themselves geisha, "entertainers," but there was not the distinction that the smart houses of the licensed quarter tried hard to preserve between the geisha, skilled in the samisen or in dancing or in some other feminine accomplishment, and the *yūjo*, the "pleasure girls." The geisha of Fukagawa were prostitutes, a fact drummed into them by a sort of double contract that some of them were made to sign with the proprietor of their establishment. One part covered the sale of *gei*, entertainment, the other, of *iro*, sex.

The top-class prostitute of Fukagawa was summoned to a teahouse by a prospective customer, but she was given the chance to examine the man through the door and reject him if she thought he looked like a *hyōtare* (Fukagawa argot for a bad customer) or a *yūdeku* ("country bumpkin"), or again if he had a mug like a *chira*, a "deceitful man." How often they exercised their right of rejection one can only guess, but it is unlikely to have been very often, given the nature of their trade. So the woman, who was herself often known as a *kodomo*, or "child," would return with her customer to the *kodomoya*, the "house of children," the ironic name that custom gave to the brothels of Fukagawa.

The "children" of the seven hills were famous for a number of eccentricities, one of the most uncomfortable of which was that they never wore *tabi*, socks, not even in the coldest days of winter. *Tabi* would have hidden their toenails, which they painted red. As if to compensate for a chill in the feet, however, they kept their breasts wrapped up warmly in *haori*, a jacket originally worn only by men.

They did so for reasons connected with the stage. In the seventeenth century women had been banned from appearing on the Kabuki stage, and so men took on female roles as well. The handsome young *onnagata* actors, whose popularity grew to great proportions, would wear—when behind stage maybe, or after a performance—a *haori* on top of their women's stage clothing. It was in an attempt to cash in on their popularity and associate themselves with these paragons of feminine charm that the Fukagawa geisha took to wearing *haori* and even adopting men's names such as Yonehachi and Eikichi. They were therefore known as *haori* geisha. They were also known as *tatsumi* geisha, *tatsumi* meaning "southeast" according to the points of the old zodiacal compass (Fukagawa was in the southeast of the city).

On many occasions, notably in the so-called Kansei reforms of 1787, the shogunate tried to stamp out illegal prostitution. In Fukagawa it met with little success until Mizuno Tadakuni introduced his sumptuary edicts, those same that saw the Kabuki troupes banished to Asakusa in 1841. During one of the campaigns against the seven hills of Fukagawa, the city authorities banned the use of *haori*. The geisha simply stopped wearing them and took instead to plucking their eyebrows so that they could pass off as married women. The *tatsumi* geisha, hardy though they once were, are scarce indeed today. There are said to be still over twenty of them, but their number dwindles by the year.

In the days when Fukagawa was by the sea, a fishing expedition was an excellent pretext for a visit to the seven hills. Fishing has long been one of the most popular recreations in Japan, as well as an important means of livelihood, and a fishing trip off Fukagawa often ended up on dry land in one of the Fukagawa teahouses. It was not always necessary, however, to disembark and make for a teahouse, there to summon one of the Fukagawa "children." There was one type of prostitute, known as a *funa manjū*, "boat dumpling," who invited customers onto her boat, where she dispensed her services at a slightly lower price than her colleagues on land. These latter, the low-class prostitutes, were known as *kekoro* ("kicks"), *maruta* ("logs"), and lowest in this hierarchy, the *yotaka* ("nighthawks"). As for Fukagawa, it had its own type of low-class prostitutes, known as "ducks," *ahiru,* a name they shared with their "hill." The land on which the Ahiru quarter stood belonged to the fishermen-spies of Tsukudajima, who had petitioned the shogunate for more land on which to spread out their nets. The link with Tsukudajima is preserved to this day by a small shrine in 3–12 Botan, a subsidiary shrine of Tsukudajima's Sumiyoshi Jinja.

A footnote to the unlicensed quarter of Fukagawa is provided by a district called Susaki (since renamed Tōyōchō), two kilometers or so southeast of the center of Fukagawa. The land that became known as Susaki was reclaimed from the bay toward the end of the seventeenth century, and it came to be a favorite spot in spring and autumn for one of the most popular of Edo recreations, that of shell gathering. Many prints show the scene on the flats of Susaki as women and children sift busily through sand and mud searching for clams and other garnishments for a good hot soup. Teahouses were opened in Susaki, and before long the waitresses of the teahouses took to other activities, brothels were opened, and Susaki became a flourishing appendage to the seven hills of Fukagawa. In 1791, however, a tidal wave lashed through the district, sweeping all away with it and restoring the mudflats to their former state. The city magistrates availed themselves of the opportunity and refused to allow permission for rebuilding in Susaki. It was not for another 108 years that houses were built on the mudflats, and these were once again brothels, this time, ironically, moved to Susaki with official sanction from Nezu. From 1899 until the Pacific War, Susaki prospered again, most of its customers coming from the new industrial zone that had grown around it.

The teahouses of Fukagawa and most of its seven hills stood along the approach to the main shrine east of the river, the Fukagawa Hachiman Shrine, and the temple that stood in its grounds, Eitaiji. Fukagawa was far from being the only place in Edo where teahouses had sprung up at the gates of a temple or shrine and then become houses of assignation. But, as with the other, lesser unlicensed quarters of the city, a visit to the teahouses and brothels of Fukagawa was nonetheless quite different from a trip to Yoshiwara. People visited Fukagawa for all sorts of reasons. Many came for archery practice. On the far side of the Hachiman Shrine stood a hall of thirty-three bays built in imitation of the celebrated Sanjūsangendō in Kyoto. Fukagawa's Sanjūsangendō was similar to Kyoto's in most respects, but its bays were shorter (in Japanese architecture, the standard bay is equivalent to 1.8 meters) and it contained only one image of Thousand-Armed Kannon, a thousand fewer than the hall in Kyoto. Unlike the hall in Kyoto, where the custom of shooting arrows from one end of the hall's veranda to the other had developed incidentally, archery was the raison d'être of the Fukagawa hall. Behind the Sanjūsangendō in Fukagawa there was a lawn, and it was here that retainers of the feudal lords practiced *kyūdō*, the "way of the bow." The long hall with its thirty-three bays existed through most of the Edo period, but in 1872 it was moved elsewhere and then done away with altogether, a superfluity in the new age of guns. It was only in 1931, however, that the district in which the hall stood lost its old name of Kazuyachō, "Cheap Arrow Quarter." The primary school behind the Hachiman Shrine still bears the name Kazuya.

The Thirty-Three Bay Hall was not the only unusual building east of the river. Further out to the east, there was a temple called Ten'-onzan Gohyaku Rakanji, the "Five-Hundred Arhat Temple," which is now in Meguro. The story of this temple and its five hundred statues starts in the seventeenth century in Kyoto with a monk named Sōun, who was a carver of Buddhist images. The story is told in the *Gold-Dust Tales of Edo*. "Sōun, who made the Buddhist images in this temple, was originally called Kubei. He was a carver of Buddhist images by profession, a carver of considerable skill. He lived a care-free, idle life in Kyoto but eventually became a monk. Later, he moved to Edo and rented lodgings in the Hanakawado district of Asakusa. He would come every day to the bamboo gate in the lane behind the Asakusa temple, and there he embarked on his grand project: to create five hundred arhats".[4] By the bamboo gate he sat, begging for alms, one of his carvings beside him. After a time, people began to take note and offer food. Eventually his labors reached the ears of the pious Lady Keishōin, mother of the fifth shogun, Tsunayoshi. She prevailed on her son to give Sōun land to build a temple in which he could house his statues. A year later, in 1695, the Ten'onzan Gohyaku Rakanji was founded on a plot here to the east of the city. Sōun did not, however, finish the 536th and last of his arhats for at least another five years. Finally, he carved a much larger image of Shakyamuni, the historical Buddha, to whose sermon the arhats are all listening. In 1725, some years after Sōun's death, a large and impressive hall was completed for the statues. People traveled from all over the city to admire them.

The arhats came to play an unusual role for the citizens of Edo: when a member of the family died, his relatives would come to this temple, search out the statue most closely resembling the dead man, pray before it, and give offerings.

The people of Edo came to the temple for another reason, too. In its grounds stood a three-story building, and if this was not unusual enough in itself, it contained one hundred statues of Kannon, the goddess of mercy. The arrangement of these statues was unique: on the first floor were thirty-four images, each representing one of the thirty-four holy places of Chichibu; on the second floor were thirty-three images, one for each of the thirty-three holy places of Kantō; and on the top floor there were a further thirty-three images, one for each of the thirty-three places holy to Kannon in the Saigoku pilgrimage route of the Kyoto and Osaka area. In other words, by visiting this hall the good citizens of Edo were able to cheat (decently). Few of them could ever hope to do the rounds of the temples of these three pilgrimage routes in honor of Kannon, but they could at least come to this building, and so take part in a sort of vicarious pilgrimage. And when they got out onto the terrace on the top floor, they had a rare and marvelous view west toward the city and beyond, as far as Mount Fuji. Hokusai includes it among his thirty-six views of the mountain, and Hiroshige portrayed the Kannon hall, too. It was known as the Sazaedō, the "Turban Shell Hall," because of the wooden slope up which one wound one's way, anticlockwise, from Chichibu through Bantō to Saigoku. The Turban Shell Hall was to the citizens of Edo what Asakusa's Twelve Stories was to the citizens of Meiji and Taishō Tokyo and what (God help us!) Tokyo Tower should be to us inhabitants of the modern city. But in the middle of the nineteenth century, floods and an earthquake proved too much for the Turban Shell Hall. It succumbed to the disasters and was never rebuilt.

It was not everyone, however, who walked all the way out to the Turban Shell Hall to get a view of the city and the surrounding countryside. Some made do with the miniature Mount Fuji that stood in the grounds of the Fukagawa Hachiman Shrine. The view from the top of this miniature peak is described in one of the city's gazetteers, *Notes on Famous Places in Edo*: "Far to the east can be seen the mountains of Awa and Kazusa [in the Bōsō Peninsula]; to the south...are Shinagawa and Ikegami. Fuji's summit stands to the southeast and the castle to the northwest, while the view to the north is enlivened by the faint outline of Mount Tsukuba. Spread out along the northeast is Shimōsa [northern Chiba], and finally on the rocks by the shore, smoke from the salt furnaces wafts away in the wind."[5] While this is what one would have seen from the mini Mount Fuji in 1850, by 1900 the view would have been radically different. In the foreground the smoke would no longer be wafting up from the salt furnaces; instead, it would be belching from the chimneys of numerous factories.

Fukagawa was chosen as one of Tokyo's first industrial zones. It had the country's first Western shipyard, before even the fall of the shogunate, and this still exists in the south of Fukagawa, run by Ishikawajima-Harima Heavy Industries. It had the country's first cement works, and it had the country's first chemical fertilizer plant. In 1895 Japan's first sugar refineries were constructed east of Fukagawa. The area east of Fukagawa also had many foundries, although these had been there in the Edo period, and a large number of textile factories, whose women workers eventually rose up in revolt against the conditions of their employ. Fumes were disgorged over Fukagawa not only from these factories but also from a private temple crematorium. These latter were so acrid and unpleasant that the place was soon closed down.

The shipyards, factories, and cement works occupied land on the periphery of Fukagawa. In the center of the district was another first, one of the first five parks in the city, and, for that matter, in the country. Fukagawa's was the smallest of the five, and it did not bear much resemblance to what we would think of as a park. It did, however, contain some greenery, in the form of the garden of Narita Temple, a garden that existed until after the Second World War. The center of Fukagawa, the area in front of the Fukagawa Hachiman Shrine and the Narita Temple, known as Monzen Nakachō (the "Central Quarter in Front of the Gate"), retained much of its old Edo jauntiness and imperturbability. It was a part of the city that exercised its fascination over Nagai Kafū in his young days. "My longing to take refuge in Fukagawa was irresistible," he wrote in his *Song of Fukagawa,* published in 1909.[6] Fukagawa was the birthplace of two great Edo writers, both of whom Kafū ardently admired, Takizawa Bakin, author of immensely long moralistic romances, and Santō Kyōden, master commentator on the customs of the licensed quarter. Here too had lived Tsuruya Namboku IV, perhaps the greatest of Edo playwrights, and here, too, was born, not many years before Kafū wrote his *Song of Fukagawa,* the film director Ozu Yasujirō. Fukagawa, then, had a literary as well as a physical allure for Kafū in the years before the floods of 1910 and 1917 washed away so much of its history. Westerners, perhaps, were less adept at picking up the old Edo associations. Fukagawa is described in Murray's 1913 *Handbook of Japan* as "a maze of narrow streets, chiefly inhabited by the lower trading and artisan classes."[7]

Despite all that has happened around it, this little "maze of narrow streets" still exists, precariously, between the thunderous traffic of Eitai Street and the inevitable ribbon of a motorway. In the narrow streets are shops selling *sembei,* salty rice crackers wrapped in dried seaweed, which have replaced eels as the speciality of the area. They also sell *manjū*, another local speciality, and the *tsukudani* of nearby Tsukudajima. One thing that has changed, however, is the orientation of the shops of Monzen Nakachō. They no longer lead up to the Fukagawa Hachiman Shrine, now known as the Tomioka Hachiman. They look instead toward a temple that did not even exist here in the Edo period, the Fudō Hall of the great Narita Temple in Chiba Prefecture, which replaced Eitaiji in the Meiji era as Fukagawa's main temple.

# # #

Honjo

Since the beginning of the Meiji era, Honjo has shared its history with Fukagawa, a history compounded principally of industrialization and disasters. Industry arrived in the form of textile and leather factories, matchstick manufacturers and watchmakers, synthetic rubber plants and the city's first railway-carriage constructors. The disasters are those of water and fire. Six major floods have hit Honjo since 1868, the most recent of them in 1947 and the most devastating in 1910 and 1917, the first caused by swollen rivers and the second by the combination of a typhoon and high tides. On both occasions the streets of

Honjo were turned into rivers, and photographs show people punting their way down the streets on improvised rafts and boats beached on mud-encased streets from which the floodwaters have receded. Floods caused tremendous damage to property but relatively little loss of life. The fires were less discriminating, as population statistics reveal. In 1920, 256,269 people lived in the Honjo area. Five years later, after the Great Kantō Earthquake, the number stood at 207,074. By 1940 the population was back to 273,407. Five years after that, the bombings and large-scale evacuation had decimated the local population. In both cases the number of casualties in the area was so great that a comparison means little. However, of these two terrible disasters, the first, the earthquake, caused greater loss of life in Honjo.

A surprising number of those who perished in the 1923 earthquake died, not crushed under falling beams nor in the fires that engulfed the city for the next three days, but drowned in rivers ablaze with the flames of burning oil. Water, the element that should have been most resistant to fire, was a death trap. In Honjo, however, most people died in one fire, the single greatest disaster in the concatenation of disasters that the earthquake set off. This occurred in a six-hectare site north of Ryōgoku Station that had been used as a depot for military uniforms and had been sold the year before to the Tokyo municipal administration. Work was underway to transform the ground into a park, when at 11:58 in the morning of 1 September 1923 a powerful earthquake struck. It occurred at a time of day when gas burners were on in thousands of homes cooking people's midday meals. This is said to have caused many of the fires that broke out here and there in the city immediately after the first shocks.

Many of the inhabitants of the crowded and ramshackle wooden buildings of Honjo headed for the park, which was one of the few open tracts of land for kilometers around. Various figures have been given, but it is likely that almost forty thousand people sought refuge here. Fires were raging in the area, and inevitably the flames made their way into the site of the park, carried perhaps by the baggage of the panic-stricken crowds. Strong gusts of wind buffeted against the wall of flames creating a series of little whirlwinds that sucked people into the air and then dropped them down again as balls of fire. The whole park turned into a blaze of infernal proportions, hot enough to buckle steel and melt metal. Nearly everyone who had fled there was burnt to death, and afterwards the devastation was so complete that it was impossible to tell how many people had died.

Those who sought refuge in the grounds of the Asakusa Kannon, on Ueno hill, and in the outer gardens of the Imperial Palace escaped the blaze. The outer gardens of the palace and neighboring Hibiya Park became a vast encampment of homeless humanity. Lines of hungry people formed for food in the temple of Kannon the merciful. People slung up shacks made out of any material they could lay their hands on. In Ueno school classes were held in the open in front of the station, and the famous statue of Saigō Takamori became an impromptu noticeboard. For two days and two nights, as fires raged throughout the city, a pall of smoke hung over Tokyo that the rays of the sun could barely pierce, and people walked about with cushions and umbrellas over their heads to protect themselves from the dust and ashes that the winds were picking up and depositing elsewhere. The same winds blew the nauseating smell of corpses over the city.

The fury of the earthquake and fires led to an outburst of murderous insanity among certain sections of the stricken populace. Rumors were started that wells had been poisoned by Koreans. Gangs of right-wing thugs patrolled the streets and with the help of the police butchered thousands of Koreans. They carried off anyone who would not or could not sing the Japanese national anthem. Many of the inhabitants of the city whose houses had survived were too frightened to venture out of doors lest they be mistaken for the hapless Koreans. Eventually, the government stepped in, and on the 5 September it ordered that the carnage be stopped, but the killings seem to have continued for at least another five days. In recent years the remains of people thought to have been murdered at this time have been discovered buried in the embankment of the Arakawa waterway near Yotsugi Bridge in the north of Sumida Ward. As if mob violence and mass murders were not enough, black markets flourished, and many people returned to the site of their former home only to find someone else had laid claim to it. On the whole, however, people showed their customary patience and discipline in the face of disaster, and life in Tokyo was able to begin again far sooner than would have been possible in most other cities.

Since the two disasters of 1923 and 1945, Honjo has followed a course similar to Mukōjima to the north and Fukagawa to the south.

All three have become districts of small-scale businesses, and although they have few overt aesthetic attractions these days, their charm lies partly in the nature of much of the local enterprise, which is resolutely independent and impervious to the notion of economies of scale. The tradition of the townsman's Edo and of Shitamachi lies in the family business, and it is good to see it still thriving here. Nevertheless, Honjo, which was a ward in its own right (from 1878 until it was merged with Mukōjima to form the modern Sumida Ward in 1947), has a history different from that of plebeian Fukagawa to the south and rural Mukōjima to the north.

The banks of many of Honjo's canals, built in the seventeenth century, were lined with vegetable markets and vegetable wholesalers. Markets were held near the east foot of Azuma Bridge, from six to ten o'clock in the morning, and near Yotsumebashi, the "Fourth Bridge" (over Takekawa), where by the year 1825 twenty-five wholesalers bought vegetables such as lotus roots and radishes from the farmers of Kasai and sold them to the shopkeepers of Edo. The other predominant activity of the townspeople in Honjo was the baking of tiles. In the north of Honjo, on the banks of the Kitajikken waterway, several of the townspeople's quarters were given over to the production of tiles. In Nakanogō Kawaramachi alone there were 208 kilns in the year 1828.

The townspeople's quarters of Honjo were, most of them, strung along the banks of the canals. In the middle were the residences of lowly members of the military class, interspersed here and there with the storehouses and suburban villas of some of the important feudal lords, and several of the shogunate's warehouses. Among the lords who had villas here in the wilds of the east bank was Kira Yoshinaga, known as Kōzunosuke. He had the task of offering instruction in court ritual to Asano Naganori Takuminokami, lord of the salt-rich domain of Akō in Harima province, who had been chosen to receive and feast at Edo Castle emissaries from the emperor. Kira was an older man from a famous family of high status. He expected handsome gifts for his expert instruction in etiquette, but from Asano he received nothing. He took to insulting Asano, and eventually so goaded him and provoked his anger that Asano drew his sword in the castle precincts and took a lunge at Kira. This occurred on the fourteenth day of the Third Month, 1701. Asano was arrested, and a few days later was ordered to commit suicide. He was buried in the Asano family temple,

Sengakuji, in Takanawa. The Asano family was disinherited and its estates split up. The family retainers became *rōnin* ("wave men"), samurai without a master whose lives were at the mercy of wind and waves. Asano's leading retainer, Ōishi Yoshio, moved to Kyoto, where he arranged with forty-six other retainers to avenge the death of his lord.

Kira, for his part, had not escaped unsullied from the affair. He suddenly found himself out of favor and forced to live in his suburban estate in this unfashionable district east of the river. It was here on the fourteenth day of the Twelfth Month, with snow lying thick on the ground, that Asano's forty-seven loyal retainers fought their way into the Kira residence and caught and killed their man, while he was in the bath, it is said. They severed his head and carried it across the city past crowds of curious admirers to Sengakuji. There the triumphant retainers presented it before their lord's grave. They were duly sentenced to death, but being samurai were allowed to take their own lives and be buried beside their lord.

This is the story of the Loyal Retainers of Akō, as they soon became known, a story that attracted immense interest and sympathy even before its closing chapter had been written. Nowadays, a festival is held to commemorate this famous act of revenge on the site of Kira's house.

The houses of the military class started appearing east of the river in Honjo after the fire of 1657, when the layout of the city was reorganized and expanded. The fire, in which thousands of people were trapped along the west bank of the river and burned to death there or swept away in the river's current, prompted a reluctant shogunate to discard considerations of security and approve the construction of a bridge, Ryōgoku Bridge, the first over the Sumida River south of Senju. Firebreaks, too, were created, and one of the biggest of them was at the west foot of this new bridge. It came to be known as Ryōgoku Hirokōji, and it was the scene of all sorts of impromptu dramatic performances.

On the east foot of the bridge, known as Mukō ("Other-Side") Ryōgoku, entertainers of a lower class set up shop, building their little booths out of reeds and branches and charging a small entrance fee. Here on the east bank there were jugglers, acrobats, exotic animals, human freaks, peep shows, side shows, and every sort of diversion that human ingenuity could conjure up. How much more fun it must have been—and cheaper—than the noisy electronic gadgetry that fulfills a similar need for diversion nowadays! Camels, elephants, and tigers supplied by the Dutch were the pick of the wild beasts on show, with elephants being trained—if we are to believe contemporary drawings—to play the flute and the samisen and balance acrobats on their trunks. The east bank was famous for its mountebanks and charlatans who practiced all sorts of quackery and foolery, parading children with elongated heads who claimed to be Fukurokuju, god of wisdom, or presiding over roulette tables formed by a picture over which a pair of compasslike needles were spun, to the carefully calculated advantage of the spinner. The east foot of Ryōgoku Bridge was the place, too, for pornographic shows, vulgar and primitive in the extreme.

In the modern city, the area just south of Ryōgoku Station is where many of the sumo "stables" are situated. The Dewanoumi stable is here, so are the Isegahama, Tokitsukaze, and Nishogaseki stables, as well as about fourteen others. A walk down the back streets is likely to reveal the sight of a sumo wrestler heaving his enormous body out of a distressed taxi or the smell of *chanko nabe,* the wrestlers' stew, bubbling wickedly on a stove in the kitchen of one of the stables. Now, after a thirty-five-year sojourn at Kuramae on the west bank of the Sumida, the great sumo stadium known as the Kokugikan has moved back to the east bank, to a site directly north of Ryōgoku Station, the most fitting location for this sport whose roots are here east of the river.

It was in the grounds of a nearby temple, Ekōin, that sumo found its first permanent home in 1833. Before then sumo tournaments had been held at various venues, chief among them the Fukagawa Hachiman Shrine. Between 1833 and 1909, one hundred fifty tournaments were held at Ekōin, one in spring and one in autumn. Each tournament lasted ten days, providing rain held off. If it rained, the bouts for that day were canceled, and the tournament was extended by a day. Then in 1909, sumo was given a roof, known affectionately as the "great steel umbrella." This was the first Kokugikan, built next door to the temple. It was a great round structure with turrets and a flattish domed roof. It survived both the Great Kantō Earthquake and the air raids, but after the war it was requisitioned by the Occupation forces, and later it became a university lecture hall. It was knocked down not many years ago, but it is good to know that the spectacle it once housed has returned to Honjo, where it belongs.

# # #

Mukōjima

Mukōjima—"Yonder Isle," or "Island on the Other Side of the Sumida"—was once vegetable gardens and paddy fields and villages. Terajima ("Island of Temples") and Ushijima ("Ox Island") and Koume ("Little Plum Tree") were the names of the principal villages. The soil was fertile and the capacious markets of the city were nearby, but life was less than idyllic for the farmers of Mukōjima. It was their misfortune that their fertile fields lay in the path of one of the shogun's hunting courses, and the farmers paid a high price for the privilege of having the shogun and his retinue ride through.

The Tokugawa shoguns were quite as crazy about hunting with falcons as the average modern Japanese businessman is about golf. And like the company manager and his golf club membership, they used their falconing as a means of dispensing patronage: a parcel of hunting land here for a feudal lord in favor; a couple of falcons there for a leading shogunal official who had completed an onerous duty; special permission to Lord Hosokawa to go falconing to break his long journey back to Kyushu. Most of the fifteen Tokugawa shoguns went falconing. One of them, Tsunayoshi, the fifth shogun, banned it as part of his edict against the taking of life. Three shoguns—Ieyasu himself, his grandson Iemitsu, and the eighth shogun, Yoshimune—were little short of fanatical about it.

In 1628, Iemitsu assigned certain villages within a radius of twenty kilometers of Edo as hunting reserves for the shogun. He established nine reserves, each one of which was on village land near the city. Later Yoshimune reorganized these into six courses: Kasai to the northeast; Iwabuchi and Toda to the northwest; Nakano to the west; and Meguro and Shinagawa to the southwest. Each course had a game warden to administer it, and additional supervision came from an officer of the shogunate with the lugubrious-sounding title of "bird-watcher." The shogun's bird-watcher did much more than watch birds.

He superintended the whole of the shogun's falconing "industry": the two stables of falcons, one in Zōshigaya and the other in Sendagi, and their keepers; the catchers of bait for the falcons in their Koishikawa quarters of Tobizaka; the dispensers of bait for the pheasants, quail, and herons that formed the shogun's game; and of course the game wardens who administered the six courses. As for the poor peasants, they suffered in all sorts of ways, not least of which was having to live under the scrutiny of the game wardens as well as the bailiff of their village. They had to fell trees, delay their work in the fields, and even fill in their paddies if so ordered by the game wardens and bird-watchers. In addition, they had to supply manpower for the hunting expeditions. Kasai, which included villages in the modern wards of Sumida and Katsushika, seems to have been one of the shoguns' favorite reserves. Hidetada, the second shogun, built a villa on the banks of the Sumida River, and a century later Yoshimune used the two Mukōjima temples Mokuboji and Kofukuji as places at which to rest and refresh on his hunts.

For all the tribulations that Yoshimune, the "falcon shogun," inflicted on the farmers, he brought great pleasure to the citizens of Edo by planting cherry trees in the city and its environs. One of the sites he chose was the embankment of the Sumida. Mukōjima soon became a favorite pleasure resort, and crowds flocked here in spring to see the blossoms, as well as in early autumn to enjoy the sight of the harvest moon and again in winter to view the snow. The east bank of the Sumida has the extra advantage of being only a ferry ride away from Asakusa and its Kannon temple and from the licensed quarter of Yoshiwara, which itself was famous for its cherry trees, although there is no record of these having been planted at the instigation of the shogun.

There were at least two ferries to convey people across the river (not too many, as the authorities disapproved of anything that made travel easy). One of them pulled in near Mimeguri Shrine, from where a busy road lined with shops and teahouses ran for a kilometer or two to Akiba ("Autumn Leaf") Gongen Shrine. Hiroshige shows the grounds of the shrine: a large pond in a spacious garden surrounded by trees—their leaves an autumn shade of red. Another of Hiroshige's prints shows boats being hauled along a waterway that used to run nearby, connecting the vegetable fields of Kasai with the markets of Edo. In the background stands Mount Tsukuba, the mountain that once dominated the northeast of Edo as Mount Fuji did the rest of the city.

Around the beginning of the nineteenth century, the temples and teahouses of Mukōjima became a center of social and cultural life for the refined and witty and clubbish writers and artists of the day. They were given a new and unusual source of enjoyment in 1804, when a man called Sawara Kikū sold his curiosity shop in the center of Edo and bought a plot of land near the river here in Mukōjima. Then, together with his friends, he collected three hundred sixty plum trees and flowers and plants of all descriptions from every part of the country. Among these friends were Ōta Nampo, who wrote comic verses under the pen name of Shokusanjin; Kameda Hōsai, Confucian philospher; and the artists Tani Bunchō and Sakai Hōitsu—all of them true-born sons of Edo and among the foremost figures in the cultural life of the city. The flowers and plants they chose were all plucked from the pages of the classics of Chinese and Japanese literature, so that the park became a true garden for scholars. But being sons of Edo, they were not pedants. Their scholarship and their cultural refinement embodied the vigor and humor and whimsy of the city. It was Sawara Kikū and his friends who decided to create a pilgrimage circuit to the Seven Deities of Good Luck in Mukōjima, and it was they who allotted a temple or shrine to each of the seven.

It was as if the wit and refinement of Edo in the first half of the nineteenth century and the vigor and curiosity of Tokyo in the second half chose Mukōjima as its favored place for relaxation. When Edo gave way to Tokyo, the literati of the old culture made way in Mukōjima for the politicians and businessmen of the new, who built their villas along the river here. Two men with villas in Mukōjima whose active life straddled the great divide of the Meiji Restoration were Enomoto Takeaki, who held out for the Tokugawa in Hokkaido but later served in several Meiji cabinets, and Katsu Kaishū. Clara Whitney, the American girl who became a protégée and daughter-in-law of Katsu Kaishū, was among those invited to the Katsu villa. In her account of her visit to Mukōjima she describes the great crowd she encountered along the river: "a gaily dressed holiday crowd jostling along in holiday merriment, some stopping at the teahouses or refreshment booths which lined the way, others buying masks or toys, charms, hairpins, or ornaments.... In time," she continues, "we reached

Mr. Katsu's summerhouse, a lovely spot just out of reach of the noise and tumble of the carnival, yet surrounded by beautiful cherry trees. In the center of the large garden lies a lake on either side of which rise picturesque green and sloping hills."[8]

Not many decades earlier the chief concern of the inhabitants of Mukōjima had been the shogun and his falconing expeditions; now factories and their attendant problems began to occupy their attention. There were few parts of Tokyo where the transformation from agriculture to industry was so rapid. In the north of Mukōjima is an area known as Kanegafuchi, the "Bell Depths," so called, we are told, because a bell was once dropped in the Sumida River near here and was never recovered. This is the site of the first factory of a company called Kanegafuchi Bōseki, or simply Kanebō, and this is why that company's symbol is a bell. Although it later diversified into cosmetics and other fields, Kanebō's original line was textiles, and it was only one of several textile companies to set up factories in Mukōjima in the last decades or so of the nineteenth century. Factories now began to dominate the scenery in this part of the city, but at night one could still imagine they did not exist. "At night," Nagai Kafū wrote in 1913, "you cannot see the factories, ...and there is only the moon gently lighting the surface of the water, and, white in the mist beyond, the houses of Imado and Hashiba on the right bank, and the trees of Kanegafuchi and Komatsushima on the left."[9]

After factories, floods were the chief agents of Mukōjima's transformation. The first two decades of the twentieth century witnessed several devastating floods, including a particularly severe one in 1910. "In the Meiji period there were not a few people who loved Mukōjima and had their houses and gardens there," wrote Kafū, who himself loved the district, although he had his house elsewhere. "After the flood of early August 1910, however, almost everyone departed.... In the changing times since, as the outskirts of the city have moved on, the cherry trees along the river embankment have died one by one."[10] Kafū wrote in his customarily elegiac vein about this part of Tokyo and made it the scene of one of the most lyrical and successful of his stories, *A Strange Tale from East of the River.* The events of the tale are woven around the setting of a red-light district that had sprung up in a part of Mukōjima known as Tamanoi. The prostitutes came to Tamanoi after their "famous-brand liquor houses" at the base of the

Twelve Stories tower in Asakusa were destroyed in the earthquake of 1923. They moved to Tamanoi and to Kameido, a few kilometers to the south. The district prospered for a time, and Kafū was among its denizens. It went up in flames during the air raids of 1945 but reappeared under the more fashionable name of Hato no Machi, or "Pigeon Street." Pigeon Street was situated in Higashi Mukōjima 1-chōme, a few hundred meters south of Tamanoi. The red-light district disappeared with the ban on prostitution, enacted in 1958.

So what is there left now for the visitor to Mukōjima, apart from the stories? Not the red-light district. Not the waterway along which boats were once towed; although its course is marked and its name preserved by Hikifunegawa Street and by two nearby stations called Hikifune. Nor is there much left of Akiba Shrine; the shrine is still there, if you can find it, but the grounds are gone. The cherry trees are there, along at least a part of the embankment in Mukōjima, but, what with the expressway overhead, the muddy industrial waters of the Sumida River alongside, and a thick blanket of dust, they seem more like a travesty than the real thing. So what is there then? There is the atmosphere, still, of Shitamachi, a nebulous but pervasive feeling of a community which is happy to get on with things in its own way, a feeling transmitted by the houses and their occupants and their plants. Especially the plants, which express so much of the wisdom of the traditional Japanese attitude to nature and life.

And there are still those six curious gentlemen and one curious lady who add up to make the Shichifukujin, the Seven Deities of Good Luck, each with his or her own shrine or temple in Mukōjima. Daikoku, Ebisu, Hotei, Benten, Fukurokuju, Jurōjin, and Bishamon: they are an odd bunch, a product of a relaxed and contented outlook, symbols, in their different ways, of Edo optimism and wit. They once appeared in people's first dream of the year (maybe they still do). Hawkers would roam the streets on the first day of the new year crying "*O-takara, o-takara*" ("Treasure, treasure"). The pictures they sold of the Seven Deities, with bales of rice and bounty galore aboard their *takarabune,* "Treasure Boat," were placed under the pillow on the first night of the new year, and the dreams of that night would bring promises of a year of prosperity and well-being. Fukagawa, Asakusa, Nihombashi, and Yanaka all have "rounds" to the Seven Deities like Mukōjima's. The first week or so of the new year is the time to make a pilgrimage to the shrines of the seven, an invigorating winter morning's walk, with these plebeian deities the best of guides to plebeian Mukōjima.

# # #

Kameido

In Edo days and even in the Meiji and Taishō eras, the easiest way to reach the village of Kameido and its shrine to Tenjin was by boat from Yanagibashi or Asakusa. The boat made its way down the Kitajikken Canal as far as a place called Yanagishima, "Willow Tree Island," on what is now the boundary between Sumida and Kōtō wards. Here there was a well-known teahouse, Hashimotoya, and a temple to the Bodhisattva Myōgen, deity of the north star, which was a particularly popular place of worship among members of the acting fraternity. One of the woodblock prints of Hiroshige depicts the scene, a scene quite untranslatable into modern terms. The teahouse disappeared long ago, as did the temple's famous pine trees. The temple hall now finds itself on the first floor of a modern apartment block cheek by jowl with the residents' car park.

A few hundred meters further down the canal was a garden of plum trees known as Kiyogaoen. The eighth shogun, Yoshimune, stopped here while on a hunting expedition in the year 1720 or thereabouts. He was full of praise for the beauty of the plum trees, and from that time on their fame was assured. Some of the trees had branches so long and sinuous that they were thought to resemble reclining dragons, and were known as reclining-dragon plum trees, *garyūbai*. It seems, however, that the dragons reclined a little too far. Many of them failed to survive the floods of 1910, and those that did withered and died not long after as a result of the air of the locality, which had become steadily less congenial to the healthy, horizontal growth of reclining-dragon plum trees.

Back those few hundred meters to Willow Tree Island. There, the boat bound for Kameido and its shrine to Tenjin turned south under a picturesque crescent-shaped bridge into Yokojikken Canal, built like Kitajikken, in the seventeenth century and called a *kawa*, "river," like

the other canals of the city. A short way down the Yokojikken Canal
on its left the boat passed Ryūgenji, better known as Hagidera, "Bush-
Clover Temple." In the grounds of this temple there were once 126
varieties of bush clover; and in autumn, when the bush clover comes
into flower, the temple attracted a throng of visitors, including, on one
occasion, the poet Bashō. There are several stories explaining why the
bush clover was first cultivated at this temple. According to the most
attractive of them, thieves in this area were adept at stealing people's
clothes, indeed in literally tearing them off the backs of hapless
passers-by. The temple came, therefore, to be known by the inherently
unsuitable name of Strip Temple. Not surprisingly, the priests took a
dim view of this nickname and decided to plant some bush clovers so
that their temple could go by the less irreverent sobriquet of Bush-
Clover Temple—*hagi*, "bush clover," being a homophone of *hagi*, to
strip. The remarkable thing is that the bush clovers are still growing
in the temple's grounds. There are fewer of the plants than was once
the case, and it seems hard to believe that there are still 126 different
varieties. Nevertheless, the garden has a sort of leafy charm, with cats
dozing in the shade of miniature stupas and the untrimmed foliage of
the bush clovers tickling the visitor's hands and arms.

The west bank of the canal, in counterpoint to the quiet temple, is
carved up by giant apartment blocks. This is the site of a factory
belonging to Tōyō Muslin, one of the leading prewar textile companies, and it is here that many of the young teenage girls, angry at
being summarily dismissed, staged a protest in which local residents
joined and which was only put down by the combined forces of the
police and mobsters. This famous incident, which occurred in 1930,
was the culmination of several similar protests. The miserable conditions endured by these girls, most of whom came from poor farming
families, were described in a book called *The Pitiful Story of Factory
Women* written by Hosei Wakizō, a writer who himself was orphaned
at an early age and sent to work in a textile plant. (He died in 1925,
the year *The Pitiful Story of Factory Women* was published, aged
twenty-eight.)

In 1923 Kameido was the scene of one of the worst outrages that
occurred in the days of confusion after the Great Kantō Earthquake.
The police rounded up nine socialists, including a leading trade-union
official and polemicist, Hirasawa Keishichi, took them to Kameido

police station, and put them to death. These nine were not the only socialists to be killed in the aftermath of the earthquake. The most prominent victims were Ōsugi Sakae and his wife, Itō Noe, who were put to death, together with Ōsugi's young nephew, by a captain in the military police, Amakasu Masahiko, a nationalist fanatic, who was let off lightly and became one of the instigators of the Manchurian Incident of 1931, the first step in Japan's military encroachment into China. In both these cases not the slightest attempt was made to act in accordance with judicial procedure. It was all done with total impunity. Kameido was involved in these events, in the killings and unrest, because it was a working-class area, one of Tokyo's first large-scale industrial zones.

Back on board the boat from Asakusa, it was only a short ride on to the pier at Kameido. Here the passengers disembarked, some for the village, some for the shrine with its beautiful wisteria garden, and some no doubt for the famous teahouse, Funabashiya, which sold a confection made of *kuzu* starch, *kuzumochi*. It had been serving this since 1805, and still does today, on the main road, Kuramaebashi Street, between the entrance to the shrine and the canal.

6

Bunkyō Ward and
the Northwest

Yushima

Yushima stands on the very rim of the Yamanote hills with their long, sinuous ridges and steep but shallow escarpments, nowadays all too often obscured by overbearing apartment blocks. It is an area of old and venerable slopes with names that tell fascinating stories not only of Yushima's history but of the history of the whole city. For Tokyo is a city that lays great store by the names of its sloping roads, its *sakamichi*. There are over five hundred named slopes or hills in Tokyo, the subject of all sorts of learned disquisitions on their origins, their exact location, and still more arcane information.

The slopes of the city were first celebrated in the Edo period, when virtually no building stood over two stories high to obscure the view from even the most modest of salients. In those days, any sloping road or path, however insignificant it might seem nowadays, afforded a new view and a change of scenery and a breath of fresh air at the top. "Our road takes us through park and garden-bordered streets and lanes," wrote Sir Rutherford Alcock of the city of Edo in the middle of the nineteenth century, "alternating over undulating hills, high enough occasionally to give glimpses of the open country beyond."[1] This in itself must have been sufficient reason to treat the slopes with special regard. But in addition, there is that special Japanese love of place, be it a tree or a stone or a slope, manifested in haiku poems and landscape paintings, an attraction felt for places because they are exactly what they are and nothing more.

The names of *sakamichi* are full of surprises. There is never anything official about them. Far from it, most of them are informed by a humorous irreverence, a rough-and-ready quality that matches the houses lining the slopes and occasionally borders on the downright coarse. In the west of Yushima is Kasadanizaka, "Umbrella Valley Slope," whose name has two possible derivations. The first links the name to the shops of several umbrella makers in the locality and the second to the shape of the slope, which is in fact not one but two slopes, together shaped like an upturned umbrella. Be that as it may, the slope soon became known by a different name pronounced in the same way but meaning syphilis. Nearby Yokomizaka, "View-Across Slope," then took on the name of Yokonezaka, "Chancre Slope."

Not all is back street ribaldry. On a more elevated level, Tokyo's slopes tell stirring stories, too. Two slopes in Yushima, both named after Tsumagoi Shrine, refer to one of those myths involving gods whose names are of heroic proportions and whose deeds match their names. According to this myth, when Yamato Takeru no Mikoto journeyed to the east to subdue the barbarians, he went by boat across Sagami Bay. A storm brew, and in order to quell the wrath of the sea god, his wife, Ototachibana Hime, threw herself into the waves. When Yamato Takeru no Mikoto reached Yushima, he looked back, and in the distance saw the waters of Sagami Bay. Overcome by sadness at the thought of his wife's fate, he cried out, "*Azuma ha ya*!", "My wife, alas!" And this is why the shrine and these two slopes, Tsumagoizaka and Shin Tsumagoizaka, celebrate Yamato Takeru no Mikoto's love (*koi*) for his wife (*tsuma*).

With ridges and bluffs dropping suddenly down toward the shores of the bay and many springs of bubbling water, the hills of Yushima and surrounding areas held many attractions for the hunters and fishermen of prehistoric Japan, of a time before even that of the gods. There are many Stone Age remains in the area, normally in the form of conical mounds. Evidence of the hot springs is to be found in the names. Yushima means "Island of Hot Water," and nearby Ochanomizu (where a prehistoric mound has been discovered) means "Tea Water," from an occasion when tea that was brewed from the water of a spring at that place was offered to Hidetada, the second Tokugawa shogun.

One of Yushima's slopes, Mikumizaka, bears a historical connection with Hidetada's father, Ieyasu. *Mikumi* means "three groups" and refers to Ieyasu's retainers, who accompanied him on his last trip to retirement in his old stronghold of Suruga. When he died in 1616, his retainers—including his servants, his palanquin bearers, and his attendant dwarfs—returned to Edo, where special quarters were prepared for them on what is now Mikumizaka, the slope of the shogun's servants, bearers, and dwarfs. Near Mikumizaka is another slope with an interesting derivation, Gaizaka, otherwise known as Gomizaka (*gai* and *gomi* being different readings for the same character). Here the locals threw their *gomi,* their garbage, which was then carried away, loaded onto boats, and dumped in the bay to become reclaimed land.

Yushima's most famous slope belongs to a more recent day. Muenzaka named, it is thought, after a temple called Muenji that once stood at its foot is the scene of the novel *Wild Geese,* written by Mori Ōgai in 1912, which depicts Yushima and the overlapping district of Hongō as they were in 1880. The book describes the old Edo world of a woman forced by poverty into concubinage and the new world of a student of the nearby Tokyo Imperial University. The concubine loves the student from afar but can never meet him, except once under strange circumstances. It is a moving story sparsely told, like a haiku poem in novel form. Throughout the book, we are kept aware of its stage, of Yushima, and in particular of the part of Yushima where the concubine lives: "Even in those days, on the south side of Muenzaka stood the Iwasaki mansion, but the proud earthen wall that surrounds it now had yet to be built. Then there was nothing but a grimy stone wall, with ferns and horsetail sprouting out from the cracks between one moss-covered boulder and the next."[2]

Everything else about Muenzaka has changed. No longer is it used as a short-cut to Ueno by the students of Tokyo University, and no longer is it lined with lodging houses for them. But the stone wall is still there, still hiding from prying eyes the Iwasaki mansion. Built for the founder of Mitsubishi, this Meiji era monument to architectural syncretism is basically Jacobean but bears traces of every Western style in the book. Like many of the other large buildings of the time, it is the work of the British architect Josiah Conder.

Above all else, Yushima still has its shrine, Yushima Tenjin, one of the most attractive in the city. Two flights of steps, one on a mildly inclined Female Slope and the other on a steep Male Slope, cut through a grove of plum trees and up to the shrine, which has remained over the centuries one of the favored gathering points of the city's inhabitants. In the Edo period its grounds contained teahouses as well as plum trees and stone lanterns. Now on festival days it is crowded with stalls selling sweets and fried noodles and toys and masks for children. All year round, but particularly in spring, it is popular with students, who go to pray for success in exams to the ninth-century statesman and poet Sugawara no Michizane, deified as Tenjin, patron of the arts and of learning.

At the foot of the steps leading up to the shrine is a little collection of old buildings that include that greatest of rarities, a three-story wooden house, as well as a *dagashiyasan*, a cheap-sweets shop, where once children of Shitamachi bought toys and candy. This is the Tokyo that people reminisce about. It was part of the people's city. But from the top of the slope began the city of the military class and later of the prosperous middle classes. Yushima encompassed both.

# # #

Hongō

Like Yushima next door to it, the part of Tokyo now known as Hongō was one of the favorite dwelling places of the prehistoric inhabitants of this part of Japan. So strong is the connection that a whole era of prehistory, the Yayoi period, is named after a district on the northern border of Hongō. But the name Yayoi itself dates back only as far as 1828. In the Third Month of that year (Yayoi refers to the third month of the lunar year), Tokugawa Nariaki, lord of Mito, ordered that a stone monument be erected with a poem chiseled on it in praise of a view from a spot in Mukōgaoka. As a result, the district, which is now occupied largely by Tokyo University, came to be known as Mukōgaoka-Yayoi. And when, in 1884, a road was built down the slope toward Nezu, it was called Yayoizaka. In the same year an archaeologist named Tsuboi Shōgorō dug up from a prehistoric mound here some earthen pots which were sufficiently different from previously excavated prehistoric implements for them to be regarded as the products of a separate period. The period to which they were ascribed was named the Yayoi period to differentiate it from the earlier Jōmon period.

While much of Hongō nowadays is occupied by Tokyo University, in the Edo period it was known for a smaller establishment. There was a saying that "Up to Kaneyasu, Hongō lies within Edo," and no doubt in the early days of Tokugawa rule this was true. But Edo carried on expanding, and the saying stuck, a souvenir of the past. Kaneyasu was a shop founded in the seventeenth century by a dentist turned tradesman who reckoned he had found a winner in his "frankincense powder," red-colored toothpowder made with sand from the Bōsō Peninsula. He was right. His shop became one of the most popular in the city, and all the more so after 1702, because the shop's sign had been written by one of the forty-seven Loyal Retainers of Akō, Horibe Yasubei. Nowadays, Kaneyasu is still there, almost in the middle of the city, but Western cosmetics, baby clothes, and teddy bears have replaced its frankincense powder on the shelves.

Hongō these days is made of more serious stuff than red toothpaste. Hongō 7-chōme is the site of Tokyo University, the nation's premier institute of learning. The generous expanse of land on which the university now stands belonged in the Edo period to the wealthiest of all the feudal lords, the Maeda of Kaga province (Ishikawa Prefecture). It was the site of their main Edo residence. One red gate, the famous Akamon, which has become a sobriquet for the university itself, is all that is left of the Maeda mansion. It was built in 1827 to celebrate the entry into the Maeda house of Tomoko, twenty-first of the shogun Ienari's fifty-five children. With her in her bridal suite came no fewer than seventy maids. A hundred or so townspeople had to be moved to Ichigaya (where there is still to this day a Kagamachi) to make room for new buildings needed to house this vast retinue. The gate was built to the prescribed size and style for the people involved and the occasion, with two lateral guardhouses detached from the main portal.

Tokyo University, in one of its several former incarnations, moved to Hongō from Kanda in the 1880s. The steep, wooded banks of the university's small garden, on the site of the garden of the Maeda residence, surround a pond which has come to be known as Sanshirō

Ike after the title of a Natsume Sōseki novel whose hero from the provinces arrives to study here and finds himself star-struck by the city and by the university. The brigade of writers who have lived in Hongō is led by no less a figure than Higuchi Ichiyō, who wrote moving portrayals of the changing world of the Meiji era. During her short life, she looked wistfully back. It would be interesting to know what she would have thought, if she had lived a few decades longer, of her contemporaries who were looking boldly forward to a day of emancipation. It was in Hongō that Hiratsuka Raichō established the offices of her Society of Blue-Stockings in 1911, fifteen years after Higuchi Ichiyō's death at the age of twenty-four.

Despite police harassment, Raichō and her associates managed to publish fifty-two issues of their newsletter. "In the beginning, woman was the very Sun. Woman was genuine." This was their battle cry, and it went on, "Now woman is the Moon, living as an appendage of others, basking only in the light of others, a Moon with the pallid face of an invalid. We women must restore now our concealed, hidden-away Sun."[3] The Society of Blue-Stockings was sometimes referred to as the Hongō Group. Nearby, in Hakusan, the True New Woman's Society was formed in 1913. Free love and closer allegiance to radical Western thinking were the platforms on which this, the Hakusan Group, campaigned. The Hongō Group and the Hakusan Group formed the vanguard of the women's movement in Japan, and several of their members, notably Raichō and Ichikawa Fusae, were prominent members of the postwar feminist and peace movements.

Parts of Hongō are remnants of the days of Higuchi Ichiyō and of the Hongō Group and survivors of the two catastrophes that overtook the city in the first half of this century. Among these remnants are "Chrysanthemum Slope," Kikuzaka, and the alleys that run off it. This is the domain of wood, a world of pliant walls and intimate windows—and mold and damp and domestic discomfort. One of Hongō's many wooden buildings is the largest remaining three-story wooden building in the city. This is the Hongōkan, built in 1905 and still used as a lodging house for students. If one spends long enough looking at its front door, one half expects to see a student from a novel by Natsume Sōseki slipping into his clogs, a bundle of books under his arm, and clattering off to lectures at the university.

The university's prime requirement from Hongō has been to provide board and lodging and cheap books for its students. The lodgings have almost entirely disappeared now that students have accommodation on the campus in Komaba in Meguro Ward, but there are still several secondhand bookshops in the area. And then there are the inns, catering in the main to visiting academics, as well as to students celebrating all the many occasions that students have to celebrate. With their mortared walls and tiled and tiered roofs and wings and annexes, many of the inns have an elegant air, palm tree and podocarp and eight-fingered *yatsude* sprouting out of the sliver of land at their door.

Tokyo University itself is made up of a bleak, scruffy set of yellow-brick buildings, best seen when hidden behind its many ginkgo trees. As well as its Red Gate, the university has another beacon: the Yasuda lecture hall, founded by the head of the Yasuda business empire. When the students rose up in revolt in 1968, they occupied several campus buildings. But their stronghold was this, the university's main hall and the symbol of its links with the world of capitalism. It took 8,500 riot police, 700 police cars, 3 helicopters, 478 firefighting appliances, and 4,000 tear-gas canisters to prise them out after the fiercest and most famous battle of the university upheavals of the late sixties. The last students were dislodged and the occupation terminated at 5:46 P.M. on 19 January 1969 after a two-day-long police attack, the first event to be transmitted live on television. Many Japanese, with memories of the military fanaticism of the war years still far from buried, were shocked by the savagery of the fighting as they watched on television news. With bricks and burning beams hurled at the police and tear-gas canisters aimed at the students, the miracle was that no one was killed. The main casualty was the Yasuda lecture hall, which now stands an empty, unusable shell of a building.

# # #

Nezu, Sendagi, and Yanaka

Here on the back of Ueno's hill and in the valley beneath is the connoisseur's Tokyo: restaurants, shopping streets, old houses, and temples where impatient, arrogant, corporate Tokyo has yet to penetrate. But while escaping the neglect and torpidity that have infected some older parts of the city, Nezu and its surrounding areas have also managed to avoid excessive attention from the tyrants of trend and fashion. In other words, they have struck a happy balance between craving for the future and basking in the past.

Administratively speaking, Nezu and Sendagi belong to Bunkyō Ward, and Yanaka, on the hill, to Taitō Ward. There was once a river whose course is marked by the boundary between the wards. But administrative convenience is one thing; from other points of view these three areas belong together, especially as nowadays the Chiyoda subway line affords easiest access to all three. Nezu, which has long been famous for its shrine, gained notoriety of a different sort for a few brief decades of the nineteenth century. Houses of entertainment were opened here, bawdy houses to cater to the less spiritual impulses of worshipers at the shrine. The authorities blew hot and cold, but eventually, in the second year of Meiji, 1869, they gave their official blessing, and by the twelfth year of Meiji, there were no fewer than 574 women employed in the Nezu brothels. It was not long, however, before official minds were changed. The Nezu quarter was too near the newly installed Imperial University, where the flower of Meiji youth was supposed to be undergoing training in the ways of Western enlightenment. Plenty of records of the time—diaries, satires, and novels—attest to the fact that many of these supposed young paragons were undergoing training of a different sort in the Nezu bawdy houses. In 1888, the government called these affairs to a halt. The Nezu quarter was to be moved to the mosquito-infested flatlands of Susaki, in the east of the city. There is nothing now to suggest the presence in Nezu of a pleasure quarter, although the streets on either side of the main road (Shinobazu Street) as one walks north from Nezu subway station are old enough and narrow enough to suggest they may be hiding a few secrets of an amorous nature.

Further north along Shinobazu Street, past Nezu Shrine, we reach Sendagi, home of the shogun's falconers, and one of Tokyo's most famous slopes, Dangozaka, "Dumpling Slope." Anyone who has ever eaten *dango* will agree that they deserve the honor of having one of the city's gentle inclines named after them. The question, however, in the case of Dangozaka, is which came first: the name or the dumplings that are sold in the shops here. Some say that Dangozaka had its appetizing name bestowed on it because of a similarity between the way a slope slopes and the way a dumpling is shaped. The other party to this etymological dispute claims that the dumpling shops came first and the name later, which, after all, sounds more likely, as all slopes are more or less dumpling-shaped. Strictly speaking, Dangozaka is the slope to the left (looking north) at the crossroads by Sendagi subway station, but Dumpling Slope has followed dumpling shops up to the right (east) as well.

As if the dumplings were not enough, Dangozaka is also famous for its chrysanthemums—or, rather, was famous for them. From about the beginning of the nineteenth century, the cultivation of chrysanthemums became a flourishing business in the market gardens of Sugamo, Somei, and Hakusan, near here in the north of the city. Markets were held, and stall holders attracted customers by fashioning statues out of the flowers. Then in 1856, Dangozaka started its own chrysanthemum festival, which became a regular event held annually at the beginning of November. Commerce was no longer the main object. Instead, at Dangozaka customers paid to enter the booths and admire scenes from romances or battles or plays portrayed by chrysanthemum heroes and chrysanthemum heroines with papier-mâché heads. In the Meiji era Dangozaka's chrysanthemum festival was one of the city's most colorful annual events, and we are lucky to have a record of the festival preserved for us in one of the first Japanese novels to be written almost entirely in colloquial speech—Futabatei Shimei's *The Drifting Cloud.* The account is a highly amusing one, full of the sort of comments one might expect from a true son of the city (Futabatei was born in Edo in 1864): "What a crowd! Shaven-headed priests had come and long-haired men, men with half-shaven heads, and men with topknots. And they, too, had come, those beloved of the gods, the darlings of destiny, the men among men and objects of universal esteem, those cynosures of envy—I mean those who in days of yore were called liegemen, but who now are our so-called public officials, and who may in future generations be styled 'public servants.' Businessmen came and the meek and the humble.... Dangozaka was in a state of the wildest confusion. Flower-sellers stood by the usual signboards waving the flags of their respective establishments in the attempt to lure in customers."[4] Futabatei ends his description by stating, in a reference, perhaps, to the dumplings, that "there was not a single visitor who did not in fact seem more interested in food than in flowers." The chrysanthemums disappeared from Dangozaka in 1912.

Dumplings are still there for the eating in the shops that line Yanaka's main street, but beyond and behind them Yanaka is a land of temples. It was one of the areas set aside for temples after fires and urban expansion had prompted the shogunal authorities to move places of worship to the city outskirts. And they have stayed here ever since, even though the city swallowed them up long ago.

No fewer than three of Yanaka's temples have in their grounds a shrine of the same name: Kasamori Inari Jinja. One of these is Daienji, first temple on the left as you walk up the main road through Yanaka. Kasamori Osen (married name, Kurachi Osen) was a real person who died, surrounded by children and grandchildren, in 1829. In her youth in the 1760s, she had worked in a teahouse at the entrance to the grounds of Tennōji, Yanaka's largest temple. Among the customers at her teahouse, the Kagiya, was Suzuki Harunobu, Edo's most celebrated *ukiyo-e* artist, pioneer of the multicolored woodblock print. He chose Osen as the subject of one of his prints, and from then her fame knew no limits. There was much learned and spirited debate among the city's literati as to whether Kasamori Osen was more beautiful than Otō, the pride of the Asakusa teahouses, with Ōta Nampo, the poet and leader of literary circles, coming out in favor of Osen's rustic naturalness over Otō's cosmetic charms. It was not long before Osen found her way onto the stage, and by the middle of the nineteenth century, she had been made a tragic heroine who died of unrequited love. In fact, Osen at the height of her fame disappointed her platoons of admirers by falling to the blandishments of a certain Kurachi Seinosuke, son of one of the shogun's gardener-spies, the *niwaban*. Modest though it might seem to us, this was definitely a successful match for Osen, the daughter of a farmer.

Next door to the teahouse where Osen had worked stood a small temple, Tennōji Fukusen'in, which contained a shrine known as Kasamori Jinja founded by the Kurachi family. Like the shrine in Daienji, where we started off on this historical ramble, it was a very popular shrine because, as so often, of a play on words: *kasa*, written with a different character, means "syphilis" and *mori* can also mean "protection from." Osen had made Fukusen'in's Kasamori Shrine all the more famous. Daienji down the road wanted to share in the fame, and people's memories being infamously short, it was soon able to claim that it was the Kasamori Shrine blessed by the proximity of Osen. Later, further complications arose when Fukusen'in, along with most of Tennōji and its surrounding temples, was destroyed in the fighting on Ueno hill in 1868. It was rebuilt as Yōjuin on the other side of the hill, and the shrine was rebuilt there, too. Later still, another temple, Kudokurinji, was built on the original site of Fukusen'in, and the Kasamori Shrine was resuscitated yet again. That meant three Kasamori Inari shrines, each with claims to being the Kasamori Shine beside which Osen served tea to pie-eyed customers. Such is the havoc that beauty can wreak.

Tennōji, Yanaka's largest temple, was one of the busiest in the city. It was built here on the route that the thirteenth-century firebrand of Japanese Buddhism, Nichiren, used to take on his way to and from Kamakura. The followers of Nichiren have a long tradition of challenging the authority of the state, and the priests of Tennōji belonged to the most strident of the Nichiren groups. The Tokugawa shogunate was not known for showing tolerance toward dissenters, and when the head priest of Tennōji refused to comply with the shogunate's policy, he was banished and the temple put under the tutelage of nearby Kan'eiji, the Tendai-sect temple patronized by the Tokugawa family. This was in 1699. Later on, Tennōji became famous as one of Edo's three lottery sponsors (the others were the Fudō Temple in Meguro and Yushima Tenjin).

There were times when these were the only three places officially licensed to hold lotteries. But for much of the second half of the eighteenth and first half of the nineteenth centuries lotteries were staged all over the city. Indeed, in the 1820s hardly a day went by without a lottery being held somewhere. The original idea behind the lotteries was to provide temples and shrines with the opportunity to collect funds for the construction and repair of buildings. But before long they came to represent a steady source of income, and this is one reason why the government periodically banned them. Not all the lotteries conformed to the same system, and this could cause confusion, as we discover in that classic picaresque story of the Edo period, *Shank's Mare*, when Yaji, one of the heroes of the tale, picks up a little package that had been lying on the ground. He opens it and finds it contains "a wooden ticket marked with the number eighty-eight. Although there are no such things nowadays, the temples at that time used to hold lotteries, and apparently one of the persons in the crowd they had just passed had dropped his lottery ticket." Yaji and his companion Kita rush to the Zama Temple (in Osaka), where the draw is being held that day and discover that eighty-eight is the winning number. Delighted, they spend a night in drink and dissipation and return to the temple the next day to pick up their winnings, one hundred pieces of gold. The priests wine them and dine them and then obtain their consent to the payment of ten pieces of gold for the upkeep of the temple, five for the manager of the lottery, and another five for a ticket for the next lottery. Kita and Yaji hand over their little wooden ticket, and that's when they discover that a mistake has been made. "All the tickets were marked on the back with one of the twelve signs of the zodiac, so that there were twelve tickets each bearing the same number but with a different zodiacal sign. Kita had known nothing about this and had paid no attention to the mark."[5] Yaji and Kita leave the temple tails between their legs, braving the taunts of the crowd that had gathered and grumbling about the incomprehensible ways of Osaka.

The lottery at Tennōji was also quite an occasion. The draw attracted a large crowd, and a contemporary print shows a blindfolded boy, an acolyte at the temple, fishing out a tablet from a large wooden chest with a spiked rod. Priests and parishioners in their best clothes look on from within the temple, while the throngs wait outside, open-mouthed in anticipation and excitement. Typical of Edo, even more popular than the lottery, it seems, was betting on what number would be drawn. This was simplicity itself. It involved no buying of tickets (although there was no lack of shops selling them) and no fattening of already well-fed priests. And best of all, it was illegal!

Most of the buildings of Tennōji were destroyed as the Tokugawa loyalists retreated in front of the irresistible advance of the imperial troops during their last stand early in 1868. The pagoda was left standing, however, and became a well-known landmark. In 1891, the young writer Kōda Rohan built a novel around it, around its construction, in fact. The novel tells the story of a young carpenter, as talented as he is undiplomatic, who through sheer perseverance contrives to be entrusted the task of designing Tennōji's new pagoda. After countless struggles with his fellow men, his last battle is fought against the elements. No sooner is his pagoda completed than the temple is visited by a terrible typhoon. He passes a night of suspense, but daybreak reveals his pagoda still standing. It is ironic that this should have been the subject of the book, for in 1957, the pagoda was burnt down; two ill-fated lovers had set fire to it and then to themselves. Now plans are afoot to resurrect it.

Many of the greatest men and women of modern Japan are buried in Yanaka cemetery, and some of the wickedest, too, including Shimada Ichirō, who assassinated the home minister, Ōkubo Toshimichi, in 1878, and Takahashi Oden, who killed so many men—it was said—and was so wicked that several cemeteries claim the honor of containing her ashes. The story of Takahashi Oden was brought to the attention of a wider world in 1879 by a journalist and satirist, one of the very first of his breed, Kanagaki Robun, who lies buried in a nearby temple. In Yanaka cemetery is the grave of Futabatei Shimei, author of *The Drifting Cloud,* who died on board ship in 1909 on his way back from St. Petersburg, where he had been sent as correspondent by the *Asahi* newspaper.

Great writers are buried in Yanaka, and great writers lived there, too, in Yanaka and Nezu and Sendagi, among them a couple of men who helped to transform Japanese fiction, Mori Ōgai and Natsume Sōseki. Sōseki, on returning in 1903 from studies in Britain, was appointed professor of English literature at Tokyo Imperial University in succession to Lafcadio Hearn. He moved into a house here near the university, but when the rent was raised not long after, he departed for Waseda, where he had been born. It was during the three years he spent here that he wrote some of his most famous early works, including *I Am a Cat* and *Botchan.* Neko no Ie, the "Cat House," as it came to be known, has been moved plank by plank and carefully reconstructed in Meiji Village on the banks of Lake Iruka, north of Nagoya. Sōseki's Cat House is a large, wooden, one-story building with a veranda and a small maid's room.

About ten years earlier, Mori Ōgai had lived in the very same house, although not for long. A few months later, he had a second floor added to a house nearby and moved in there. He spent most of the remaining thirty years of his life in this two-story house in Sendagi, a stone's throw away from his beloved Dangozaka. Nagai Kafū, bard of old Tokyo, visited the house of Mori Ōgai, to whom he was greatly indebted, and described it in one of his journals: "Save for the hanging and vase in the alcove, the room was quite bare.... In the middle of it there was a desk, again bare, actually more like a table, a single board with four legs and no drawers, and no ornamentation."[6]

Ōgai had called his house Kanchōrō, "Tide-Viewing Tower," for it had once been possible to glimpse the shimmering waters of the bay from here, and Dangozaka had a second name, Shiomizaka, "See Tide Slope." Ōgai was very interested in the development of Tokyo. He felt that a centrifugal city like London was a more suitable model than a centripetal city such as Paris, for, despite the inconvenience of having to travel further from home to work, "the more people there are crowded together, the greater the danger of total congestion." The problem of distance, he suggests, can be overcome through the construction of "a tight network of horse-drawn trolleys and municipal steam trains," and, he adds for good measure, "of ring roads like those of Vienna."[7] Would Mori Ōgai consider his vision fulfilled if he saw Tokyo today?

If proximity to Tokyo University was one of the reasons many writers and scholars chose to live in Sendagi and Nezu, the nearby presence of the Tokyo School of Fine Arts helps explain why so many artists lived in Yanaka. The doyen of Japanese artistic circles in the Meiji era—art historian, critic, and author of several books in English, including *The Book of Tea*—was Okakura Tenshin. Tenshin, together with his friend the American scholar Ernest Fenollosa, set out to reexamine and reestablish Japan's artistic heritage and to encourage young artists to treasure traditional artistic forms and idioms while incorporating Western ideas and techniques. His influence was enormous, and it would be hard to imagine what art in modern Japan would be like without him. Tenshin was one of the men responsible for the founding, in 1890 on Ueno hill, of the Tokyo School of Fine Arts, which later became the Tokyo University of Art, Japan's leading college of fine art and music. For eight years, from 1898 to 1906, Tenshin lived in Yanaka, in a house at the foot of the hill, a house that was torn down when it became too old and expensive to look after.

One of Japan's finest sculptors was also drawn to the area. Takamura Kōun, who was trained in his native Asakusa in wood carving, developed and modernized traditional carving methods and, almost single-handedly, gave life back to the ossified sculpture of Japan. Two of his works in bronze can be seen in the parks of Tokyo. His statue of Saigō Takamori is in Ueno Park and the other, of Kusunoki Masashige, is in the concourse in front of the Imperial Palace. With the help of Okakura Tenshin, Kōun was appointed to head the department of sculpture at the Tokyo School of Fine Arts. Kōun's house in Sendagi was little more than half an hour's walk away. Kōun's son Kōtarō, who was also a sculptor, lived much of his life there, too, there and at his atelier a little way down the road. Kōtarō, however, is best known as a poet, author of the famous anthology *Chieko's Sky*. Both house and atelier were destroyed in the 1945 air raids.

Japanese writers and artists, denied their formal "schools" of the Edo period and before, have never been able to resist the temptation to form groups, clubs, circles, or associations. One of the keenest satires of this, as well as much else in the Japanese temperament, is the story *Kappa* by Akutagawa Ryūnosuke, yet another great writer who lived—and died (suicide, aged thirty-five)—in the area. Visitors to the site of his house, in Tabata, not one hundred meters north of Sendagi, can still see the wall that once surrounded his house. But then what's there in a wall to get excited about?

# # #

Koishikawa

Three men of uncommon vision united their fractured country at the end of the sixteenth century. Three women, a mother and two of her daughters, were united to, and united, the families of these three men. The mother, Odani no Kata, stories of whose beauty are corroborated by a portrait kept in a temple on Mount Kōya, was the younger sister of the first of the three men, Oda Nobunaga, who welded an alliance with a potential rival by marrying her off to him. Nine years, three daughters, and two sons later, the potential rival realized his potential, turned on his brother-in-law, and was in turn annihilated by him.

This was not an age when chances of a marital alliance were left to waste. Nobunaga before too long dispatched his sister, with her children, into marriage with another powerful lord, who, in 1583, exactly ten years after the fall of his predecessor, was defeated in battle and, before the arrayed might of his own and his enemy's armies, killed his wife, Odani no Kata, and then thrust the same sword into his own belly. The daughters escaped. The eldest of them became the mistress of her step-father's vanquisher, Toyotomi Hideyoshi, second of the three men who fought to unify the country. She was Hideyoshi's favorite. She was known as Yodogimi, one of the most famous figures in Japanese history. In 1593, she bore him a son, Hideyori, whom she loved passionately, and for whom she fought furiously and maneuvered valiantly, and together with whom she died in the burning mass of Osaka Castle in 1615.

And what does this all have to do with Koishikawa? As the flames devoured Osaka Castle, the glorious vestige of Toyotomi power, two figures were to be seen fleeing from the falling timber. One of them was a girl, Senhime, wife of the Toyotomi pretender, Hideyori—cousin as well as wife of Hideyori, because Senhime's mother was a younger sister of Yodogimi. The other was Senhime's father, Tokugawa Hidetada, who, together with his father Ieyasu, the first of the Tokugawa shoguns and the third of the three great unifiers, had led the troops investing Osaka Castle. Senhime was taken back to Edo and then married off once again, with no more success than before, for once again her husband died within a few years. Again she returned to Edo, where she built a house in Takebashi on the ruins of a mansion that had belonged to the Yoshida family. From here history fades into fiction, facts become fancifully embroidered. It is said that after two such short-lived, unsuccessful marriages, Senhime became infected with uncontrollable feelings of lust. "*Yoshida tōreba,*" it was said, "if you pass the Yoshida place," and everyone knew what this meant: that wanton woman, that nun who has failed to shave her head, will assail you. Out of these stories Kabuki plays were contrived. Poor Senhime! It is highly unlikely that there is any truth in all of this. When she died, in 1666, at the age of sixty-nine, she was buried in a temple named after her great-grandmother, Tokugawa Ieyasu's mother, Odai. Odai took the religious name Denzūin, and that is the name by which Muryōzan Jukyōji is still best known. The temple is at least a hundred years older than Odai, but it prospered as a result of Tokugawa patronage and came to be one of the biggest temples in Edo, with over a hundred buildings. Nowadays it is a small, insignificant place, but it still contains the grave of Odai and, beyond it, by the cemetery's far wall, the grave of poor Senhime.

Senhime's brother Iemitsu became the third Tokugawa shogun, but for a time the succession was very much in doubt. Their mother was planning to pass over Iemitsu in favor of a younger son. Iemitsu's wet nurse, however, was not the sort to stand idly by. She made her way down to the town by the coast beyond the Izu Peninsula where grandfather Ieyasu was living out his last years to warn him of what was about to befall his beloved grandson. Ieyasu was incensed, and he immediately had his son Hidetada promise to make Iemitsu his heir. Both Hidetada's wife, Tachihime (Yodogimi's sister), and this wet nurse were redoubtable women. They are said to have been responsible for the establishment of the rules that governed life in the shogun's inner chambers. On this occasion victory belonged to the wet nurse. Iemitsu never forgot his debt to this woman. He arranged for her to be given an audience with the emperor, who conferred on her a court rank and the name by which she is still known, Kasuga no Tsubone. When he became shogun, in 1623, Iemitsu gave her land in Koishikawa which came to be known by her name. To this day the district between Koishikawa and Kōrakuen is called Kasuga. Kasuga no Tsubone remained loyal to Iemitsu, and she died at her temple in Yushima, Rinshōin, refusing medicine and praying for Iemitsu's recovery from an illness he had caught. Her grave can still be seen in this temple, better known as Karatachidera, "Orange-Tree Temple," after its fence made of *karatachi*, the trifoliate orange tree.

The history of Koishikawa never takes us far from the suburban estates of the feudal lords, of which there were once so many in the area. Several of these are remembered in the names of local hills and slopes. There is, for example, Andōzaka, in Kasuga, named after the Andō family, lords of Hida in the north of modern Gifu Prefecture, and Harimazaka, running in between Koishikawa 4- and 5-chōme, site of one of the Edo compounds of the lords of Harima. But among these estates was one with a difference. This was the ironically named Kirishitan Yashiki (in Kohinata 1-chōme), "residence" of those few unfortunate Christians who were caught in Kyushu and brought to Edo before being killed. The prison was built in 1640, only a year after Iemitsu had closed the country to all foreigners save a handful of Dutch and Chinese. It was built by the man directly responsible for stamping out Christianity, Inoue Masashige, in a corner of the garden of his own Edo residence. The prison housed several Italian priests over the years. One of them, Giovanni Battista Sidotti, was keenly interviewed by the historian Arai Hakuseki. Another became a convert to Buddhism, took a Japanese wife and name, was allowed several servants, and lived to the age of eighty-five "under house arrest." The prison was destroyed by fire in 1729 and never rebuilt.

A more conventionally embellished Japanese garden was to be found in the estate of the first lord of Mito, eleventh son of Tokugawa Ieyasu. The garden was called Kōrakuen, "Garden of Pleasure Last," in reference to a famous aphorism enunciated by the Song-dynasty Chinese statesman Fan Zhongyan, "a gentleman should be the first to worry about the world's troubles and the last to enjoy its pleasures." The first lord's son, Mitsukuni, known as the Yellow Gate (after the Chinese name for his court title), devoted himself in his youth to the pursuit of the pleasures of the flesh but reformed in time to become one of the greatest patrons of scholarship of the Edo period. It was he who initiated the most ambitious intellectual project undertaken by the Tokugawa shogunate, the compilation of a history of Japan, *Dai Nihon shi,* a work so monumental that it was not completed until 1906, two hundred fifty years after it had been begun and two hundred years after Mitsukuni's death. As well as being an adherent of traditional ideas of imperial authority, Mitsukuni was an advocate of Confucianism, and specifically of the Zhu Xi school of Neo-Confucianism, fashionable at that time in Japan. Among his protégés was Zhu Shunshui, a Chinese refugee who had fled his country after the fall of the Ming dynasty. Mitsukuni was a great admirer of Chinese culture, and, with advice from Zhu, he incorporated into the Garden of Pleasure Last models of many of the most famous sites of China as well as those of Japan.

Although all around it has changed, the Kōrakuen garden is still there tucked away behind the domed baseball stadium of the Tokyo Giants. Another garden with strong links to the Tokugawa family lies a little more than a kilometer to the north, on the other side of Koishikawa. This is now the Koishikawa Botanical Garden, but it used once to be the shogunate's herb garden. Originally, it had belonged to the estate of Tokugawa Tsunayoshi. When his eldest brother died without an heir, the dog-loving Tsunayoshi became fifth Tokugawa shogun, moved into the castle, and decreed that his old estate should be made into the shogunal herb-garden. It was here that Aoki Kon'yō—Doctor Potato, as he came to be called—conducted his experiments into the suitability of the potato as a supplementary staple to rice. The son, according to one theory, of a Nihombashi fishmonger, Doctor Potato was the founder of that important branch of Edo-period intellectual endeavor, "Dutch learning," the attempt to find out about European civilization through the only channel that was open. He was also the teacher of the two leading lights of Dutch learning, Maeno Ryōtaku and Sugita Gempaku.

Alongside the garden stood a hospital for paupers, the only one of its kind in the city. The city magistrate, Ōoka Tadasuke, had ordered the installation of a suggestion box outside the central court house. The creation of a hospital to which admission would be restricted to the poor was one of the suggestions taken up by the authorities. And where better to build such an institution than next door to the herb garden, where all sorts of medical treatments were available, including ginseng from Korea? The patients were cared for by the doctor whose idea the hospital had been, and later by his descendants. The hospital was a great success, and by the end of the Edo period it contained as many as 117 separate rooms for patients. The herb garden's medical associations (although not the hospital itself) continued into the Meiji era. The main hall of Tokyo Imperial University's medical faculty was built here. And here it still stands, in the northwest corner of the botanical garden, one of the best surviving examples of early Meiji architecture in Tokyo.

Where all these gardens and the temple cemeteries petered out into the country, there lurked all manner of animals and apparitions which found their way into the names of the sloping roads. Up in Sengoku, in the northeast of what is now Bunkyō Ward but before the war was Koishikawa, is Nekomatazaka. A handful of derivations exist for this slope, but the preference of several of the old gazetteers is for the story of a gullible young monk returning from a wake, who on seeing two white eyes flashing in the dark took them to belong to one of the animals spirits that were known to haunt the district. He ran helter-skelter toward a nearby stream and plunged head first into the water. The slope became known after the sort of feline apparition, *nekomata,* that was held responsible for the acolyte's late-night bath.

The Japanese have always stood in awe of the bewitching power of certain animals, especially the fox, and there were plenty of foxes on the perimeter of the city. Foxes (*kitsune*) are experts at transformation of their identity. Here they have gone so far as to transform the names of two slopes (one in Kohinata, the other in Mejirodai) from the common-or-garden Kitsunezaka to something much more bewitching, Yakanzaka, written with different characters but having exactly the same meaning as Kitsunezaka. Where foxes are to be found, ghosts are surely not far away. Mejirodai, in the western extremities of old Koishikawa Ward, has a Yūreizaka, "Ghost Slope," marked as such on all the best modern maps of the city. The temple and graveyard that gave the slope its name disappeared long ago, leaving only the slope, and maybe a few ghosts as well. Another apparition lurking in the outskirts of town was the water sprite. The water sprites were to be found in the middle of Koishikawa, just south of the shogunal herb garden. Here there was a spring, refreshing water bubbling up, and a slope, known either as Kamurozaka (*kamuro* being another word for *kappa,* water sprite) or as Fukiagezaka, "Spout-Out Slope," referring to the waters that gushed up from the spring and provided the sprites with a suitable sort of home.

The animals are there, too: a "Frog Slope," Kaeruzaka, and a "Snowy Heron Slope," Sagizaka, both of them in Kohinata. Frogs and snowy herons can still occasionally be glimpsed, even in Koishikawa, but not oxen. Before the war, however, things were different. Oxen were often to be seen pulling carts down the city streets even as recently as the 1930s. The ox carts contained anything from barrels of saké to bushes and trees for a new garden. "It is one of the delicious sights of the city," wrote Katherine Sansom, wife of the historian, "to see the immemorial ox-transport of gay trees in full leaf which have come in from the country."[8] Behind Kōrakuen is a slope to the oxen, Ushizaka. Ushizaka's ox, however, was not an ox at all but a rock resembling the beast. The twelfth-century general and first of the country's military rulers, Minamoto no Yoritomo, fell asleep here on one of his expeditions. In his sleep, he dreamt he saw Sugawara no Michizane, the god of learning and the arts, in full regalia riding an ox. When he woke up, he caught sight of the rock that had become an ox in his dream.

Koishikawa had always had two faces: one was its temples and mansions on high ground, the other was to be found in the houses of the shopkeepers, traders, and sundry attendants to the military class in the valleys and back streets. Perhaps, then, it is not so strange that, despite its proprietorial airs, Koishikawa should have been in the vanguard of the fight for workers' rights. In 1918, the year of rampant inflation (the price of rice rose over 300 percent in six months) and obscene profiteering, workers in the country's largest ordnance factory went on strike. The factory was situated in Koishikawa, in Kōrakuen to be precise, where the Tokugawa lords of Mito once took leisurely and learned strolls round their garden and where now Giants and Tigers slug it out in the baseball stadium. Troops were called in, and the strike was soon snuffed out.

Things proved very different six years later when print workers at the recently formed Kyōdō Printing Company laid down their tools in protest against the enforcement of part-time working. The early twenties had seen the emergence of the country's first modern trade unions, and it was in response to a union call that the print workers went out on strike on 20 January 1926. The management's reaction was to dismiss the striking workers. The knee had jerked. The workers tried to occupy the print shop, but police stood at the gates and barred their way in. On two nights in the beginning of February, pitched battles occurred between workers and police. The number of arrested was so great that there was nowhere left to put them. A focus had been found for all the resentment and hostility that had its roots in the authoritarian nature of successive Meiji and Taishō governments and in the police repression after the Great Kantō Earthquake of a little over two years earlier. Entrenchment, increased bitterness, great hardship, suicides, and random acts of violence ensued. Attempts at arbitration failed. Eventually, on 18 March, a compromise was reached involving reinstatement of some of the workers and compensation payments of ¥120,000. The strike was a milestone, perhaps the most important in the history of Japanese industrial relations. It was followed, however, by a long series of reverses for workers' interests culminating in total repression. Part of the renown of the Kyōdō strike results from a novel written by one of Kyōdō's striking printers, Tokunaga Sunao. In the novel *Streets on Which the Sun Never Shines* Tokunaga describes the hardships that the strikers underwent, and, even if time has not dealt kindly with his book, its title has become a commonplace of the Japanese language. And Kyōdō the printer is still there, a whale surrounded by a shoal of lesser print shops here in Koishikawa's central valley.

# # #

Komagome

Like all cities great or small, Tokyo has its kitchen gardens in surrounding areas, in Ibaraki, Chiba, Saitama, and other nearby prefectures. In Edo times the city's kitchen gardens were here in Komagome and the surrounding areas of fertile land immediately to the north of the sprawling city. Komagome had its aubergines; in nearby Sugamo turnips were grown; Takinogawa, a little to the north, was known for its burdock; and Nagasaki, to the west, for its carrots. Radishes were cultivated in all these districts. These and the other villages of the north, part of the countryside in the beginning of the seventeenth century, had become, by the middle of the nineteenth, part of the city—the roads that connected them lined with houses, the vegetable fields behind the houses, less fields than patches. Along one of these roads, the Iwatsuki Kaidō, linking Edo with Iwatsuki (now in Saitama Prefecture), a market developed out of what was once just a resting place for farmers on their way into the city to sell their goods. The market became one of Edo's three biggest—along with those at Senju and Kanda. Because roots formed the preponderance of the produce on sale (chestnuts and mushrooms were also to be had), the market became known as Tsuchimono-dana, "Earth Goods Shops." And because it was at a crossroads, it was popularly called Tsuji no Yatchaba, the "Veggie Place at the Crossroads." As well as vegetables, the farmers of Komagome, Sugamo, and Somei specialized in plants for the gardens of the mansions of the feudal lords. If modern prices are anything to go by, we can infer that they did well out of the horticultural business, well enough, at any rate, to mount the exhibitions of "chrysanthemum sculptures" that were later amalgamated and moved to Dangozaka.

Where there were plants and vegetables and markets, there were certainly plenty of greengrocers. Most of them, no doubt, lived and worked, loved and died without a great to-do. But one of them had a daughter who unfortunately turned out to be among those people who by dint of strength of character or through some quirk of fate set themselves apart from the common run. Such a person was Oshichi, the greengrocer's daughter. Oshichi's love and folly and sad fate attracted the sympathy of the citizens of Edo and the attention of Ihara Saikaku, master storyteller and portrayer of the life of the common people, who made her fourth of his *Five Women Who Loved Love*.

"A fierce winter wind blew in from the northeast and clouds moved with swift feet through the December sky."[9] With these chilly words, Saikaku begins his account of the events surrounding the death of Oshichi, events that had taken place only a few years earlier. On the winter day in question (the twenty-eighth day of the Twelfth Month of 1682), fire broke out near Oshichi's home and destroyed much of Edo, including such faraway spots as the poet Bashō's cottage in Fukagawa. Oshichi and her family were forced to take refuge in a nearby temple, where the girl fell headlong in love with one of the young temple acolytes. Before many days had passed, however, the greengrocer's shop had been rebuilt and Oshichi had to return home. Unable to withstand this enforced separation, on the second day of the Third Month of the following year, Oshichi set fire to her own house, hoping thereby to be able to take refuge again in the temple where her sweetheart lived. She was caught *in flagrante delicto*.

"Even though a fire is set, should the criminal be fourteen years of age or under: Banishment to a distant island. But when fifteen years of age and over: Burning at the stake."[10] Oshichi had just turned fifteen, and so she suffered the full penalty imposed by a shogunate as afraid of arson and politically motivated rioting as it was of "natural" conflagrations in a combustible city. However, Oshichi's demeanor as she was paraded through the city with five other arsonists and at the Suzugamori execution ground a few days later was so noble and unrepentant and her face so young and fair that all who saw her felt pity for her. Her memory was cherished, and she became a sort of folk heroine.

The story is a startling one, and touching. Saikaku had little need to embellish it. He did, however, change the temple that gave shelter to Oshichi and her family. Saikaku's setting, Kichijōji, was one of the great temples of Edo—everyone had heard of it, even in his native Osaka—while Enjōji, the temple where the romance actually occurred (although there is not unanimity on this point), was a far more modest establishment. But it was there at Enjōji that one hundred ten years later a gravestone for Oshichi was erected. Later, it came to be believed that the Bodhisattva Jizō had, out of compassion for the young girl who suffered so harshly, himself taken on her burden of suffering, and so she came to be so closely associated with Jizō that eventually she was regarded as a manifestation of the deity. Now, beside her gravestone tucked in among the houses that surround the tiny Enjōji, stands an image of Jizō. Incense burns, the flowers are fresh, and people still occasionally come to offer a prayer at Oshichi's gravestone, among them, actors about to play her part on stage. Kichijōji itself has recently commemorated its connection with the tale by erecting a *hiyoku* stone—representing a pair of mythical birds whose bodies are welded together like those of young lovers.

Was there a fatal link between temples and fire? Almost twenty-six years before Oshichi was driven by fire into the arms of the temple acolyte, another strange story unfolded, this one involving not one but three young girls. The first of these three girls died lovelorn; the other two died shortly after putting on for the first time the same long-sleeved kimono that the first girl had once worn. The priests of Hommyōji in Hongō, where these unfortunate girls had lived, decided to do away with the evil garment once and for all by burning it. So burn it they did, but instead of being devoured by the flames, the material was whisked up by a strong wind and deposited first here and then there and then somewhere else, and each time it fell it ignited whatever it fell on. Before long the whole city was ablaze. The fire became known as the Long-Sleeves Fire (Furisode no Kaji), after the garment that wrought the destruction. And it all started at Hommyōji, a temple which moved in 1911 from Hongō to Sugamo, Toshima Ward, just north of Komagome.

The temples and shrines moved out of the center of the city to areas like Komagome, and with them moved some of those popular beliefs that meant so much more to the citizens of Edo than the dogma of established religion. Among the manifestations of popular religious sentiment are the miniature Mount Fujis, of which there are several in the north of the city, including one in the grounds of Hakusan Shrine and another in the precincts of the Fuji Shrine in Hon Komagome. In the Edo period, the worship of Mount Fuji became extremely popular among townspeople and farmers. The movement is said to have been founded at the beginning of the seventeenth century by a certain Hasegawa Kakugyō, who undertook various ascetic practices on the mountain and later formed his followers into associations known as Fujikō. In summer, pilgrims flocked up the mountain dressed in white, ringing bells, and chanting (some still do). But for those who could not make the climb, either for financial reasons or because they had not the strength of limb, these miniature Fujis were built, using lava transported from the mother mountain. There are at least a dozen of them dotted around Tokyo. Most of them are fenced off and covered with dedicatory stones, lichen, and shrubbery and festooned with sacred straw ropes.

In the days before pharmacists and bathroom cupboards stocked with medicines, an appeal to the gods offered one of the best chances of a cure. In 1891 a little temple called Kōganji moved from near Ueno to its present location in Sugamo. Together with the temple came a small image of the Bodhisattva Jizō, known as the Togenuki ("Splinter-Remover") Jizō. Despite its inconsequential size, this is one of the most popular statues in the city. Why? Because if you wash that part of the statue that corresponds to the part of your body that hurts, you will be cured. Another temple, again not far from Komagome, has images that minister to the faithful in the same sort of way. The two Niō (protective deities) that stand guard outside Tōkakuji in Tabata are known as the Red-Paper Niō. Stick a strip of red paper on one of the two statues and that part of your body will be cured of pain. Like the Splinter-Remover Jizō and the Red-Paper Niō, the Earthenware-Bowl Jizō of Daienji in Mukōgaoka bears no lack of testimony to its continuing popularity as a healer of woes, physical as much as spiritual. The Earthenware-Bowl (Hōroku) Jizō provides an efficacious cure principally for headaches and also for any pain afflicting the neck or upwards, including throat, mouth, eyes, and nose. Place one earthenware bowl with your name and address and the nature of your ailment written on it on Jizō's head, and await disappearance of symptoms.

These images are among many in the city that have retained their claim to curative powers, despite competition from Chinese and Western medicine. Other traditional remedies have not done so well. No one believes any longer (as far as I know) that clutching the railings of Nihombashi will cure whooping cough, or that Kyōbashi will have a similar effect on headaches. Both beriberi and the gates between one quarter and another are things of the past; so too, presumably, is the belief that to touch the bars of these gates while making the appropriate wish will cure one of beriberi. And as for that awful disease known as *kinketsubyō* ("money-lack disease"), to which we are all permanently prey, who among us still believes that an offering at the Koishikawa Ushi Tenjin Shrine—the shrine named after Ox Slope—will deliver us of this affliction?

7

Minato Ward
and the South and
Southwest

Shiba

Shiba is a place that has been twice transformed. In the Edo period it was a city of temples, with Zōjōji as its citadel. There were hundreds of temple buildings congregated around Zōjōji in the area now known as Shiba Kōen, as well as refectories and boarding houses for thousands of priests and novices. Zōjōji was set just back from the Tōkaidō, the "East Sea Road" to Kyoto, so there was a ceaseless flow of pilgrims and travelers and mendicant monks, as well as one of the city's busiest *monzen* ("before-the-gate") markets selling every variety of local delicacy and pseudo-Buddhist trinket imaginable. Storytellers would set up shop and mountebanks would draw swords to catch the eye and impress on the crowds the efficacy of mountain herbs from Etchū province or toad oil from Mount Tsukuba. On each side of Zōjōji were the mausoleums of the Tokugawa shoguns, set in large compounds with black-lacquered gates, long Praetorian rows of bronze lanterns, and the rococo decoration on beams, trellises, transoms, joints, and coffers in which the Tokugawa delighted. The woodwork was alive with Chinese lions, peonies, pines, and cranes, and the Tokugawa three-leafed mallow crest. Behind the temple and these shrines was a pagoda, a lotus pond with an island shrine to the lute-playing goddess Benten, and a thickly wooded slope, from the top of which one had an excellent view all the way from the nearby shores of the bay to the hills of the Bōsō Peninsula on the far coast. All of this, all these temples and shrines, were enclosed within walls.

The year 1868 brought the fall of the Tokugawa, the restoration of imperial rule, and Shiba's first transformation. The rulers of Meiji Japan moved quickly to deprive the Buddhist temples of much of their wealth and to forestall any possible challenge to their power from that quarter. Shiba was affected more seriously than other areas because it contained, as well as the extremely wealthy and powerful Zōjōji, the mausoleums of the deposed shoguns. The government expropriated much of the temple's spacious grounds and turned them into a park, one of Tokyo's first. The Shiba mausoleums were not destroyed, although they were not as well cared for as in earlier days. They were objects now of tourism, not pilgrimage. Basil Hall Chamberlain, in the 1913 edition of *Murray's Handbook,* described them as being "among the chief marvels of Japanese art."[1]

Whatever their state of repair, at least in those years between 1868 and 1945 they still existed, and the ground on which they stood was a park in the original sense of the word *kōen:* a garden for the public. The second great transformation to befall Shiba left it bereft of its shrines, virtually all of which were destroyed in the air raids, and with a park in name but not in reality. A luxury hotel, a golf club, a bowling alley, and various other establishments have made of Shiba Park a very unpublic sort of garden. And in 1958 Shiba's new landmark appeared, to make nonsense of all beneath it and consign the shoguns to the history books once and for all. One is tempted to say that the shoguns would turn in their graves if they knew of Tokyo Tower, but the truth is much more unkind. Not only did they turn in their graves, they were actually turned out of them. They were in the way: in the way of the hotel, in the way of the golf club, in the way of Tokyo Tower—in the way, in other words, of development-besotted Tokyo and of people who wanted to make money. They had been embalmed, and now their mummified bodies were disinterred, examined by scientists and historians, and reburied in a modest graveyard behind Zōjōji's main hall.

Tokyo Tower's main purpose is to beam the waves that carry television pictures to houses in the east of the country. It was decided to construct it here in Shiba because this is allegedly the place most advantageous to the propagation of electric waves. Shiba has several other connections with electricity. Indeed, one might even be justified in calling Shiba the home of Japanese electronics. NEC, the Nippon Electric Company, has its headquarters in Shiba. Oki Denki, makers of advanced electronic equipment, are based in nearby Shibaura. And as for Tōshiba, its full name is Tokyo Shibaura Denki. Shibaura in fact lies on reclaimed land just to the south of Shiba Park. It was one of the first of Tokyo's industrial zones, its growth spurred by the wars with China and Russia either side of the turn of the last century. It was completely flattened in the air raids of 1945, but its resuscitation and growth were once again fueled by war, this time the Korean War.

Shibaura, the cradle of Japanese electronics, is a far cry indeed from Shiba, the citadel of Tokugawa Buddhism.

# # #

Shinagawa and Takanawa

Within walking distance of the enormous seminary at Zōjōji in Shiba, where three thousand novices and more were studying for the priesthood, were the brothels of Shinagawa. In an age notable for its religious laxity, it is unlikely that many of the novices were content to remain celibate, or faithful to the embrace of a fellow monk. So to Shinagawa they went. They could be there and back in an evening, while the journey to the licensed quarter at Yoshiwara or one of the unlicensed quarters of Fukagawa would involve time and expense, subterfuge and danger.

The other patrons of the inns of Shinagawa were the samurai, many of whom came from the residence in Mita of the great lord of Satsuma. There was another Satsuma residence nearer still, in Takanawa, and other powerful lords from Kyushu like Arima and Hosokawa had mansions in the south of the city, near Shinagawa and at the head of the road back home. The men of Kyushu, and especially those of Satsuma (Kagoshima Prefecture), were known for their rough tempers and rude tongues, as well as for their courage and independence. It was as well to keep out of their way, as a British merchant called Richardson discovered one day in 1862 on the Tōkaidō near Yokohama when he failed to do just this. The lord of Satsuma was passing by with his retinue, and Richardson was hacked to death for his impudence.

With warriors and priests as its main customers, the atmosphere in Shinagawa was different from that of Edo's licensed quarter, Yoshiwara, bastion of the effete culture of dilettante townsmen who lived by the pen and the abacus, not the sword. Nevertheless, in their dress, speech, and mannerisms, the girls of Shinagawa wanted nothing more than to be considered the equals of their vaunted colleagues. Yoshiwara was known as Hokkoku, the "North Country," and Shinagawa as Nangoku, the "South Country." In the early part of the Edo period, the authorities had tried to restrict the activities of the waitresses of Shinagawa's inns to serving food and drink. But they met with little success. In 1718 they decreed that each inn was to be allowed two *meshimori onna,* "serving girls," a quaint euphemism for the women who served a lot more than just rice. This regulation applied not only to Shinagawa but to all inns outside the city boundaries yet within a ten-kilometer radius of Nihombashi. The best way of controlling prostitution inside the city is by licensing it outside was what the authorities seemed to be saying. In the case of Shinagawa, the authorities soon found themselves altering their regulations in order to suit the arithmetic of reality. In 1764 it was decided that the inns of Shinagawa were to be allowed five serving girls each. And by 1843, when the authorities once again decided to put a stop to frivolity and idle pleasure, either the number of inns had risen drastically beyond the theoretical maximum of ninety-three or each inn had many more than five. How else to explain that the total number of serving girls had reached 1,358?

Not all the patrons of Shinagawa's inns came in search of distraction. Shinagawa was the post station at the end of the first of the fifty-three stages on the Tōkaidō, the East Sea Road, which connected Edo with Kyoto and Osaka. Its inns therefore were for travelers. The East Sea Road was one of four great highways that led out of Edo, and travelers to or from distant provinces, especially if they were feudal lords, were compelled to take whichever of these highways served their part of the country. The East Sea Road was by far and away the busiest of the country's highways, and Shinagawa, correspondingly, far busier than Senju, Itabashi, and Naitō Shinjuku, the other three towns that served as first post station on their respective highways.

Travelers bound along the Tōkaidō for the west of the country left Edo by Takanawa Gate, the foundations of which can still be seen on the east side of the Daiichi Keihin Road by the north exit of Sengakuji subway station. This was the city gate, but Edo was a large city and it soon learned to sprawl. Takanawa was "where the suburb of Sinagawa merges into the city, much as Kensington straggles into London."[2] From Takanawa Gate to Shinagawa, the Tōkaidō skirted the bay, whose waters lapped the shore where the Yamanote Line now runs. Traders set up stalls between the road and the sea, while on the land side of the road a small escarpment made it easy to cut off this main approach to the city to any invading force from the west of the country. The first of the hills between Takanawa and Shinagawa was Yatsuyama, and beyond it, behind Shinagawa, was Gotenyama.

Both these hills suffered severe depredations when it was decided to build a series of fortified islands to protect the city from Black Ships and other foreign flotillas. "On the coast of the bay," wrote Henry Heusken, Dutch interpreter to the first American consul, Townsend Harris, on his entry into Edo in 1857, "Shinagawa is protected by five batteries, the first four on islands, preventing thereby any communication with the capital, and the fifth one at Shinagawa."[3] There were to have been twelve of these gun emplacements, making a formidable double row of barriers against intruders. The work was carried out in great haste and fury under the direction of Egawa Tarōzaemon, a military expert and shogunal official. In the space of a year and a quarter from August 1853, just a month after the departure of Commodore Perry and his Black Ships, five of the emplacements were completed and two were half built. But that was as far as Egawa and his five thousand men got. Only the third and the sixth still stand. The land used to build the batteries was taken from these two hills, and Yatsuyama virtually lost its contours altogether. Gotenyama's contours can still be discerned, south of Shinagawa Station. But the hill is no longer crowned by the cherry trees that made its blossoms among the city's most famous and prompted the author of the *Illustrated Gazetteer of Famous Places in Edo* to write this about them: "The blossoms of the Third Month swirl like clouds and fall like snow. Their scent is carried far by marine breezes until it impregnates the sleeves of the divers for the fruits of the sea."[4] In 1863 this hill so beloved of the citizens of Edo was chosen as the site of the new British legation, and the minister was about to move in where it was burnt down by a group of protesters that included a hotheaded young man from Chōshū who was later to become prime minister and linchpin of the pro-Western party in government, Itō Hirobumi.

Between Gotenyama and the sea stood the first of the three districts of the Shinagawa post station. This, the northernmost, was known as Kachi Shinjuku, the "New Lodgings within Walking Distance" (of the city), where the pick of the serving girls were to be found. This corresponded to the modern Kita Shinagawa 1-chōme. Beyond this was Kita Honjuku, modern Kita Shinagawa 2-chōme, and on the further bank of the Meguro River, furthest and cheapest, was Minami Honjuku—now Minami Shinagawa 1- and 2-chōme. Shinagawa was only about eight kilometers from Nihombashi. This made it the ideal place for that favorite Japanese pastime: sending off departing friends, and its obverse, greeting friends who are arriving. The Dutch merchants on their quadrennial trips from Nagasaki were among those so treated. "At about half past six," wrote warehouse-master Fischer about his visit to Edo in 1820, "we reached the Sinagawa suburb, where our Yedo friends were waiting for us, to spend a last evening together and to say farewell."[5] So in days when life was lived at a more leisurely pace, Shinagawa was often far enough for the first day's journey.

Although such things can hardly be measured, the Tōkaidō was probably the busiest highway not only in Japan but in the whole of the world. From Shinagawa to Kanagawa and beyond, both sides of the road were lined with shops. Each of the post stations had plenty of inns, and each inn had touts calling for customers and making a great clamor. Each station also had to provide a certain number of horses and grooms to walk the horses back after a "ride," and legions of porters who hired their services out to foot-weary travelers. In the first decade of the nineteenth century, Jippensha Ikku published a picaresque tale, a *Pickwick Papers* of the East Sea Road, relating the misadventures of Kita and Yaji, two amorous, accident-prone townsmen from Edo. Their story, *Shank's Mare*, includes dozens of tips on how to poke fun at a samurai and escape unharmed, how to fall foul of hucksters, and how to slip up in the dark and rouse the whole house while on an amorous foray, as well as innumerable encounters with extortionist chair-bearers and argumentative grooms. The citizens of Edo loved it. They idolized the author and embarked by the hundreds of thousands on vicarious journeys along the great highway.

Like Kita and Yaji, most users of the highway spent most of their time walking, straw sandals on their feet, straw hats on their heads, and straw capes on their backs to keep themselves dry and keep out the cold. They carried spare sandals with them, and in summer they wrapped up their capes and walked in the shade of the cryptomerias and pine trees that lined the road, the surface of which consisted of packed earth. When it rained, the going got heavy, but because of the scarcity of wheeled transport, it seldom became impassable.

Of the two greatest obstacles the traveler faced, the greater of the two was presented by rivers in flood. With their short, steep courses, rivers flood easily in Japan, easily and briefly. The waters soon subside, allowing the bearers to resume their lucrative work carrying travelers over the wide, rock-strewn riverbeds. The other obstacle was provided by the feudal lords and their retinues. The most powerful lords traveled with an escort of up to one hundred thirty footsoldiers and three hundred servants and porters. All sorts of essential equipment accompanied them on their journeys to and from Edo, including tea-ceremony utensils, pickles, birds in cages, and even lacquer lavatories. The Maeda lords went so far as to have spring water from their native province of Kaga brought along with them. At the head of these processions marched soldiers twirling long, plumed lances in the air and jangling the metal-studded hems of their trousers.

The processions were impressive affairs. They had precedence over all other traffic, and other users of the road had to make way, to bow in respect, and to avert their eyes (just what the British merchant Richardson neglected to do). Each time a procession passed through one of the post stations, heralds announced its approach with the cry "*Shita ni iro!*" ("Down on your knees!"). But Henry Heusken relates how "our heralds continually repeated the 'shita ni iro,' kneel down, even in the remotest parts of the forests or on the tops of the mountains where there was no one, as if the trees and plants should pay homage to the Embassy of the Republic Par Excellence."[6]

At the end of the day, the lord and his retinue stopped at the nearest post station, the lord himself staying in the official inn, of which each station had at least one. The retinues, however, were often so large that there was not room for all of the men in the inns, and they had to be billeted in private houses. "Commuting seasons" existed, when many of the lords were required to make the journey to Edo, where they would spend the next year as virtual hostages of the shogun. The fourth month was a time of much toing and froing and consequently of great confusion on the road and at the stations. All that was needed to cause a human traffic jam the like of which even mechanized Tokyo is not capable was a river in flood and a couple of large processions converging on the same ferry or held up in the same post station.

It was little comfort in the Edo period to be a lord or a man of high estate when traveling. As befitted a society of ranks and classes, there were all types and standards of litters and chairs depending on the wealth and status of the traveler, the only constant being their extreme degree of discomfort. The lords were carried in *norimono*, cooped up in these heavy lacquered boxes with tiny windows and matted floors, a pole threaded under the "eaves" of the roof and carried by four bearers. Those lucky enough to be of more modest status were carried in the less infernally restrictive *kago*, litters borne by two porters hired with the chair at a post station who trotted along with rhythmic grunts like college joggers in modern Japan and a jerky running action that threatened to dislocate the traveler's body at every joint. Early Westerners in Japan suffered agonies of discomfort when they were forced by the dictates of protocol to squeeze their bodies into these little boxes in which they could neither sit up for lack of headroom nor lie down for lack of legroom. We can be sure that Japanese found it uncomfortable, too. Riding would seem to have been the perfect answer, but no, it, too, was dangerous because of the high-peaked saddle and large stirrups. The idea of shodding a horse with iron horseshoes had not occurred to the Japanese, and so horses (like humans) wore straw sandals.

Traveling was painful and dangerous, but then those were painful and dangerous times for some—and painful in the extreme for those who ended their lives at the Suzugamori public execution ground. This was one of two in or near Edo, the other being at Kozukappara to the north of the city. When a heinous crime was committed by a servant against his master or by a liege-man against his lord, then not only was the perpetrator of the crime held responsible but the head of the family, too. Execution was the punishment, and executions were normally carried out at the city jail in Kodemmachō, but crucifixions and burnings at the stake were reserved for Suzugamori. The conspirator Marubashi Chūya, the lovelorn arsonist Oshichi, and the star-crossed murderer Shirai Gompachi all met their ends here. The decapitated heads of criminals were exposed to public view for three days, notices of their crimes being affixed to the pole bearing their heads. This was the chilling, gory sight that greeted travelers after weary days of walking up the East Sea Road to Edo. Not far beyond Suzugamori, Shinagawa began, and beyond Shinagawa lay Edo itself.

The convulsions of the Meiji Restoration put an end to the feudal system; railways followed soon after, and they put an end to the East Sea Road. But there is no such easy end put to the oldest profession. The inns became brothels, the serving girls rented out rooms, and their clients were no longer priests and samurai but workers from the factories that began appearing in the area. In early Meiji days, as fishing in the bay began to become less economical, Shinagawa became famous less for its fish than for its *nori* seaweed. Encroaching industrialization put an end to Shinagawa's *nori*-culture, and soon began to change the face of the area.

# # #

Akasaka and Toranomon

The city's confused state has long been one of its glories. High on a hill overlooking Akasaka is a gate which, like Akasaka itself and Toranomon, commanded an entrance across the outer defense of Edo Castle. It was a smaller affair than the other two large barbican gatehouses, and it had a substantial earthen rampart leading across the moat, built to confuse the view of an invading force. For this it was called the "Confusion Gate," Kuichigai-mon. The landscape here has changed little. The gate itself has confused the issue by disappearing, but its earthen rampart now carries a road out from a part of town still named after its feudal landlords. Kioichō was occupied by the vast residences of the Kii, Owari, and Ii families, all of them collateral branches of the Tokugawa.

Like the other feudal lords, these three families had other estates in the city, even larger but at the same time just as austere and spartan. The main Kii residence in Edo lay opposite Confusion Gate on land where that peculiar piece of architectural confectionery, the State Guest House, now stands. It was here that Yoshimune, the eighth and most capable of the Tokugawa shoguns, spent part of his youth. Third son of the lord of Kii, it was only through a coincidence of deaths that he came to spend most of his life in Edo Castle, serving as shogun from 1716 to 1745. The huge grounds of his estate were put to urgent use shortly after the restoration of authority to the imperial family. In 1873, when the emperor Meiji's residence in the grounds of the old castle burnt down, the Kii residence was transformed into the Akasaka Detached Palace, a temporary abode for the emperor until, fifteen years later, something better was ready for him in the castle grounds. In 1909, the final transformation occurred when the palace we see there today was built. The State Guest House is, ironically, one of the few notable buildings of any size and age left in the center of Tokyo, but notable chiefly as a curious architectural symbol of cultural aspirations. It has in its time been put to various uses. It served as venue for the meetings of the Higashikuni cabinet in the months immediately after the end of the war, as part of the National Diet Library, as headquarters for the committee arranging the 1964 Olympic Games, and as venue for the summit meeting of leaders of the seven industrialized countries.

The stretch of road leading down from Confusion Gate is known as Kinokunizaka, the "Kii Province Slope." But it was once also called Akasaka, "Red Slope," on account, it seems, of the many madder plants that grew here, from whose roots a purplish red dye was obtained. This, then, is the origin of one of the modern city's most famous place names, plausible, but a little pedestrian. It is not a particularly old or important name. But it had its gate, and the gate seems to have been one of Edo's finest. It was built in 1636, and guarded by an assortment of gunners, lancers, and archers. In fact, it was really two gates. One small one led into a large courtyard, on the right of which was a second-larger gate with a guardhouse built on top of it. On the outside of the gate was a *mitsuke,* "lookout tower," one of the thirty-six guarding the castle.

The Tokugawa shoguns liked nothing less than a straight road, which they saw as an invitation to marauders and rebels. The road that now leads directly southwest from Akasaka Mitsuke, Aoyama-dōri, did a little zigzag in the Edo period and then wound its way round and behind where the Akasaka police station now stands. On its way, it passed through a post station, Omote Demmachō, behind which, in the early Edo period, there was an intriguing little district called Akasaka Furoyacho, the "Akasaka Bathhouse Quarter." We read in one of the city's old gazetteers that, "There were once many bath-houses and women of pleasure here."[7] This was on the north side of the Ōyama Kaidō, predecessor of Aoyama-dōri, in Moto Akasaka 1-chōme. To the south was a district with a name much older than that of Akasaka, Hitotsugichō, a village that existed before the arrival of Tokugawa Ieyasu in 1590. But now our only reminder of the village is in the name of a road, Hitotsugi-dōri, one of Akasaka's most animated, running along the west side of that little network of streets which is the hub of Akasaka's nightlife.

On the west side of Hitotsugi-dōri, where now we find Akasaka Junior School, a shrine once stood. The Toyokawa Inari stood in the grounds of the Edo residence of a most remarkable man, perhaps the only administrator of the city with the strength of mind and wisdom to rise above the stifling system and impose his ideas to improve the lot of the people who lived there. In this, Edo's Dick Whittington was given protection and encouragement by the shogun Yoshimune. Ōoka Tadasuke, lord of Echizen, was magistrate of the city for nineteen years, from 1717 to 1736. During this time, he introduced all sorts of reforms, organizing the fire fighters, improving construction methods, and handing down judgments of proverbial wisdom. The town of Toyokawa lay within his fief, not far from Nagoya, and, as was the custom, he had a branch of Toyokawa's main shrine built on his estate. With the construction of the school, the shrine was moved into the grounds of a nearby temple, Myōgonji. And that is where it stands today, its many images of foxes, symbol of the deity Inari, each with a morsel of fried tofu, the fox's favorite food, placed in front of it by the proprietors of nearby bars.

Although Akasaka has always been basically a part of the samurai city, the two or three streets that run south from Akasaka Mitsuke between Hitotsugi-dōri and the main road, Sotobori-dōri, and the alleys that link them have a different flavor to them now, as they did in the Edo period. The difference in flavor then was literal. There seems to have been a little nexus of brothels here, unlicensed houses, where the entertainment on offer was preceded by a meal of barley gruel. Among the other inhabitants of this commoners' enclave were several dyers and Akasaka Hikojūrō, a maker of sword guards. If we followed the road that led then as it does now due west next to the hill on which the TBS studios stand and took a turning in to the left, we would have reached the tutelary shrine both of Akasaka the place and of Yoshimune, the man whose name is perhaps most closely connected with the place. The buildings of Hikawa Shrine have a starkness and simplicity that reflect Yoshimune's stern character; they are the original ones, built under the shogun's direction in the 1730s.

On the TBS bluff itself, there once stood a barracks and before that an army prison and before that the estate of the Asano family, lords of Aki. The Asano contribution to Akasaka was not inconsiderable. Yoshinaga, the first Asano lord of Akō, a province in the west of modern Hiroshima Prefecture, was given the task of building a link in the outer web of moats around the castle. He set his retainer Yashima Chōun to work, and what Chōun came up with, after much difficulty, was a weir situated roughly at the crossroads in front of the Patent Office. But he got more than he bargained for. Water soon built up on the Akasaka side of the weir, and before very long a lake had formed. This lake became known, rather prosaically, as Tameike, "Storage Pond," but it was the dominant feature of the landscape in this part of town. In the early part of the Edo period, it was large in size (almost a kilometer long and shaped roughly like a gourd) and its waters were clean enough to serve as drinking water for the locals, home for fish, and a swimming pool for the third shogun. On its south bank, Yashima Chōun planted a hackberry as a reminder of all the trouble that he had gone to. In later years, the tree acquired unusual powers. "People with toothache pray to this tree," we read in the gazetteer *Gold-Dust Tales of Edo,* "and when they have recovered, they plant a toothpick at its roots."[8] The road along the north side of the American Embassy, which once bordered the lake, is still called Enokizaka, "Hackberry Slope," even though both hackberry and slope have gone. Gone, too, are the paulownia trees that once decorated the banks of the lake and the lotus plants that performed a similar function in the lake itself. Gone, indeed, is the lake. Over the centuries it became smaller and dirtier. An archery range and a riding ground were built on land reclaimed from it. It shrank into a mere stream in the Meiji era, when the weir was razed. In 1910 the stream was drained, and Sotobori-dōri, the "Outer Moat Road," built down the course of the outer moat itself.

Downstream from the weir, the moat took a sharp turn round the estate of the Naitō family (and later the site of Japan's first technical college) before reaching Toranomon, the "Tiger Gate," one of four at the cardinal points of the compass, each of them protected by a mythological animal. It was said in the Edo period that on one side of Tiger was Monkey and on the other Elephant. Monkey is the messenger of Sannō Gongen (just as Fox is the messenger of Inari), and Sannō Gongen is the god enshrined in Hie Shrine, perched on a hill looking north toward Akasaka Mitsuke and south over Tameike. The shrine's festival has since the seventeenth century been one of the city's two greatest. Held on alternate years with Kanda Matsuri, these two festivals alone were allowed to parade their floats through the castle grounds and past the admiring eyes of the shogun's ladies. In all there were some fifty floats, some of them decorated with striking models of animals and divine figures, Monkey again to the fore. Elephant belonged to another shrine. "Mount Elephant Head" is the name of a hill, shaped something like an elephant's head, that juts into the Sanuki plain of northern Shikoku. And near the top of this steep hill is one of the country's most celebrated shrines, Kompira-sama. The shrine fell within the domain of the Kyōgoku family, who, like Ōoka Tadasuke and his Toyokawa Inari, built a subsidiary shrine in the grounds of their Edo estate here just outside Tiger Gate. From the 1810s on the shrine was opened to the public on the tenth day of each month, when it invariably attracted a great crowd. People still visit the shrine, now known by its official name of Kotohiragū, on the tenth of the month, the festival day of Kompira-sama. The shrine, which seems in permanent danger of being crushed by the buildings around it, is protected by one of the city's most attractive monuments, a *torii* arch erected in 1821 and still standing many conflagrations later. On its two copper-plated posts are the four Chinese geomantic animals: the blue dragon (east) and black tortoise (north) on one post and the red phoenix (south) and white tiger (west) on the other.

Akasaka has prospered well under their protective gaze, and never more so than toward the end of the nineteenth century. Around this time, businessmen, journalists, and above all politicians and government officials began to find Shimbashi rather too exclusive and expensive and decided they wanted somewhere less formal where they could discuss their business affairs and be entertained by geisha. They chose Akasaka, which was, as it still is, conveniently near their offices and not so far from Shimbashi that they could not go there later if need be. By the turn of the century, the restaurants of Akasaka had all but eclipsed those of Shimbashi, and the geisha of the two areas were locked in fierce rivalry. If Shimbashi had its Okoi, then Akasaka could boast of Manryū, for whose dreamy face on a poster Mitsukoshi is supposed to have paid ¥100 (at a time when a middle-ranking government official was earning ¥45 a month). Postcards of Manryū of the Harumoto house sold like hotcakes, and the sentimental propensities of the newspaper-reading public were stretched to new bounds when Manryū sold all her property to find the ¥12,000 she needed to redeem herself and marry the gallant student from Tokyo University who had saved her life during a flood in Hakone.

# # #

Aoyama and Harajuku

In the merry-go-round world of Aoyama and Harajuku, one might be forgiven for thinking that the past never existed. Life seems to be a succession of present points, oblivious of anything before and heedless of anything after. But Aoyama and Harajuku do have a history, not a history of long urban exploitation but rather one of gradual urban encroachment. Indeed, they have a prehistory, if one counts the archaeological finds in the grounds of Yoyogi Hachiman Shrine.

For present purposes, we will look no further back than the eleventh century, when Harajuku was a post station (*shuku*) on the Kamakura Kaidō, the road from Kamakura up to the semiautonomous north of the country. The redoubtale general Minamoto no Yoshiie was on his way back from his campaign of subjugation in the north. He decided to strike camp here at Harajuku, and he lined his troops up along the road as it wound its way down from the temple of Ryūganji to the Kumano Gongen Shrine, which to this day is the "parish" shrine of the area. For one of those reasons that are now lost in the dust clouds kicked up by the march of history, the image of the troops lined up along the road stuck, and the hill here became known as Seizoroezaka, "Muster the Troops Slope."

In 1590, when Tokugawa Ieyasu made his ceremonial entry into his capital-to-be, Edo, there were but a cluster of villages in the area. Ieyasu chose to give some of the land here to one of his close advisers, Aoyama Tadanari. Land was not in those days the object of idolatry that it is today, and Ieyasu told his retainer to take as much land as his horse could cover in the area outside Akasaka Gate. Aoyama flogged his horse on until it was on its last legs. Eventually it collapsed at a place that came to be known as Hizaorizaka, "Knee Snap Slope." In memory of the horse, a shrine was built here, the Komadome Hachiman Jingū, "Colt-Stop Hachiman Shrine," which was popularly called the Yabure Hachiman, or "Collapse Hachiman." The Knee Snap Slope now goes under the name of Nogizaka, but it is still at a corner of the district known as Aoyama after its longtime landlord.

Aoyama Tadanari had indeed helped himself to a good chunk of land, most of it high ground well suited for the residence of a feudal lord. Across the middle of his land ran the Ōyama Kaidō, which once led to Ōyama in the Tanzawa hills and is now known in this part of town as Aoyama-dōri. As is the way with families the world over, the Aoyama family split into branches, with one branch taking the land north of the highway (Kita Aoyama) and the other taking the lion's share, south of the road (Minami Aoyama). But not all this land was for the exclusive use of the Aoyama. Ieyasu had put under Tadanari's care one hundred lower-ranked shogunal officials, and they had been given quarters on Aoyama land. The district where they lived, on the south side of the Ōyama Road, came to be known as Aoyama Hyakuninchō, the "Hundred People's Quarter." When Hidetada, the second Tokugawa shogun, died, the hundred officials were so overcome by grief that they shaved all their hair off their heads. And when the Seventh Month came round, they hung lanterns from poles outside their houses. Each year they did this in the Seventh Month, the month of *obon,* and eventually it became an annual custom. The lanterns, hung high over each house, looked like stars when seen from afar. One night many years later, Ietsugu, the seventh shogun, was on his way back to the castle from Meguro. He saw the Star Lanterns of the Hundred People's Quarter and was so impressed that he gave each official a gift of silver. The custom of hanging out lanterns in the month of *obon* lasted until the end of the Edo period.

There were all sorts of other petty officials who lived on the Aoyama estate. The residents of Aoyama Osōjimachi, for example, were humble cleaners, thirty of them, who had followed Ieyasu from his home province. The twenty-five carpenters who lived in Aoyama Otedaikumachi and the fifty laborers who lived in Aoyama Gojūninmachi were moved to the area in 1683 from other parts of town. So although most of Aoyama was occupied in the Edo period by the suburban residences of feudal lords (and by paddy fields), all sorts of people lived there. All sorts indeed. The largest of the few townspeople's districts here was Kubomachi. Part of Kubomachi was occupied by gentlemen from Iga province who put their nefarious skills in spying at the service of the shogun. Other inhabitants of the area included vegetable wholesalers, who prospered increasingly as time went by, until the farmers took to selling their products themselves along the Ōyama Road. This practice led to several disturbances. There were quite a few low-ranking samurai living in the area. Many of them were worse off than the townspeople and had to earn a living by making umbrellas or engaging themselves in some other sort of cottage craft. The countryside had retreated, and some feudal lords, notably the powerful Ii of Hikone, had their suburban mansions on the far bank of the Shibuya River, which once flowed through Harajuku.

After the Meiji Restoration, Aoyama and Harajuku were transformed by mulberry trees, by graves, and by soldiers. One of the earliest and more eccentric policies pursued by the Meiji government was the planting of mulberry trees with the aim of garnering foreign currency by exporting silk. The policy was hasty and badly conceived. In 1873, it was revoked, and three years later the last trees were uprooted. Never again was Aoyama-dōri to be lined with mulberry trees. Today Aoyama is perhaps better known for trees of a different hue: the cherry trees that grow in its cemetery. Aoyama Cemetery is one of four (Yanaka is another) that were created by the Meiji government as the nation's first public cemeteries. Over one hundred thousand people are buried there, including many foreigners, and enough of the country's political and military leaders and leading intellectuals to be able to stitch together a history of modern Japan.

The departing feudal lords had left behind them the spacious grounds of their large suburban mansions. South of Aoyama-dōri, the Aoyama land had been transformed into the cemetery. To the north a military college was built, and a large parade ground was staked out in 1889. There, every year on his birthday, 3 November, the emperor Meiji would review the troops in front of a large and unabashedly patriotic crowd. These were just two of the many military facilities that appeared in the area. In 1909, the parade ground was moved further out to Yoyogi, to the south of the large tract of land on which the Ii mansion once stood. Here, in 1910, for the first time ever in Japan, man took to the air. Flight Lieutenant Tokugawa piloted his craft for three kilometers, rising seventy meters above the ground, and then landed safely again.

The Ii family lands had become the property of the imperial household. When the emperor Meiji died in 1911, they were chosen as the site of a shrine to be built in honor of his memory and that of his consort, the empress Shōken. Work on the shrine was finally finished in 1920, and on the appointed day, the ceremony of enshrinement was held. A new road—Omote Sandō, the "Outer Approach Road" —had been built and a bridge over the railway line, but on the day of the ceremony part of the bridge collapsed, causing injuries and a few fatalities. Several officials of the city government were arrested, and it soon became clear that they were involved, together with city councillors and others, in an extensive network of bribery and corruption. The upshot of one of the city's most serious scandals ever was the resignation of the mayor.

The shrine was given an enormous chunk of land, an inner preserve (*naien*) and an outer preserve (*gaien*) which together cover 125 hectares. The inner preserve contains over one hundred thousand trees, most of them camphors and other broadleaf evergreens. But the most famous of them all, the original Tree of Ages (which is what Yoyogi means) was destroyed when a B-29 bomber fell out of the skies on top of it. The shrine buildings, too, were destroyed in the air raids, and the present ones were not completed until 1958. By then, all sorts of other changes had befallen this part of town, and the biggest change of all was already in the planning stage.

The Occupation forces had requisitioned the Yoyogi Parade Ground and there had established quarters for military personnel and their families. The barracks were called Washington Heights. When Tokyo was chosen as host city for the 1964 Olympic Games, the Japanese authorities asked for the land and the buildings back. The barracks were used as lodgings by the athletes, and on the land Tange Kenzō built his pavilionlike stadiums. When the games were over, further transformations ensured. NHK moved from its cramped offices in Shimbashi to land behind the stadiums. Much of the athletes' village was torn down to make way (what a grand rarity!) for a park, Yoyogi Park, and a new road was built between the stadiums and the park. Perhaps it is the speed and totality of these changes that has nailed Harajuku so firmly to the eternal present. Certainly, it was the presence of a large number of foreigners that set the area off on its westerly cultural course in a swirling sea of American, French, and British currents.

# # #

Shibuya

The story of Shibuya starts stormily and ends romantically. Its early days, before ever it was known as Shibuya, are colored by two men, both of whom bequeathed their names to the area. The first of the two was born the son of a retainer of the father of Japan's first shogun, Minamoto no Yoritomo. The story goes that this retainer one day caught an armed intruder in his lord's quarters. He brought the man in front of his lord, and as a token of his valor had the robber's name, Shibuya, bestowed on him.

Shibuya and his wife were childless. They prayed to the god Kongō Yasha Myōō, who answered their prayers and gave them a son. Out of gratitude, they chose the first and last syllables of the god's name and called their son Konnō, to which name later they added the suffix *maru*. Konnōmaru was the epitome of the eastern warrior, loyal, brave, and a little too quick to draw his sword. In a celebrated night attack, Konnōmaru infiltrated the residence of Yoritomo's brother Yoshitsune in an attempt to kill him. The attempt failed, and we hear nothing more of Konnōmaru. But his descendants continued to rule over the area from the fortified homestead he had built in his domain. A few of the stones that supported this building can be seen in the grounds of a shrine that commemorates Konnōmaru. The shrine, Konnō Hachiman-gū, still exists, and its main hall retains the same form and structure as it had in the seventeenth century. Indeed, it is the only building with such pretensions to age in this upstart part of town. In the grounds of the shrine stands a cherry tree, a descendant of a tree planted by Yoritomo as a token of his appreciation of Konnōmaru for his loyal service.

What the Shibuya family thought of their near-neighbor Owada Dōgen we shall never know. It is unlikely to have been favorable. Owada Dōgen was a thirteenth-century highwayman, member of a clan that had risen in revolt against the shoguns in Kamakura. He lurked here in this secluded valley, picking off travelers as they made their way west along the road to the mountains. When he, too, finally was picked off, he left behind him his name. Dōgenzaka is the name of the hill where he committed his nefarious deeds, and, until 1970, Owadachō was the name of the district to the south of his hill.

The road along which Dōgen plied his deadly trade became known in the Edo period as the Ōyama Kaidō. It led from Aoyama Gate out of the center of the city, following the path of the modern Aoyama-dōri to Shibuya and then on to Sangenjaya, Futago Tamagawa, and through Sagami Province to Ōyama in the Tanzawa hills. Although this was not one of the four great highways that led out of Edo, it was nevertheless an important road with its share of travelers, including white-clad pilgrims on their way to pray at Afuri Shrine, on the top of Ōyama. As the travelers made their way out from the center of the city along the Ōyama Kaidō, they passed between long walls that hid the spacious grounds of the suburban villas of the feudal lords. They followed the road down the slope known now as Miyamasuzaka to a bridge over the Shibuya River and then up the slope named after Dōgen the highwayman. The Shibuya River is the same river that, as the Furukawa, flows through Hiroo and Azabu and out into Tokyo Bay.

Shibuya was in the Edo period on the extreme outskirts of the city. It was a meeting point between town and a country, and it is as a junction, in every sense of the word, that Shibuya has grown up and prospered over the centuries. Although, in the Edo period, most of the southwestern suburbs of town were taken up by the villas of the feudal lords, the Ōyama Kaidō had several temples and townspeople's districts along its route through the Shibuya valley. During all these years the most heavily built-up district in the area was Miyamasuchō, along the slope of the same name. At the beginning of the nineteenth century there were one hundred seventy houses here, most of them rented by carpenters, day laborers, and hawkers of vegetables. The vegetables these men sold were grown in the fields on the other side of the river: carrots, aubergines, onions, radishes, and trefoil.

When the shogunate finally fell in 1868, the new government had more land on its hands in its capital city than it knew what to do with. In this part of town, it turned much of the land it had automatically inherited from the lords of the now defunct feudal system into mulberry groves and tea plantations. This was part of an ill-fated attempt at revenue raising. The tea bushes were planted on a gentle hillside on the far side of the Shibuya River. The tea grown there was called Shōtō tea. It was served in the teahouses of Miyamasuchō and elsewhere, and in its day was quite widely appreciated. But its day was soon over. In 1889 the Tōkaidō railway line was completed, and top-quality tea from Shizuoka and Uji was transported in abundant quantities to the capital. The Shōtō tea plantations disappeared, but they left behind their name. Not long after, Shōtō became an expensive residential district, and so it is today.

In the 1890s a small but growing band of writers, government officials, and army top brass chose to live in Shibuya. Among the writers was Kunikida Doppo. He described the Shibuya of his day and the countryside beyond in lyrical terms: "From out of Shibuya onto the high ground, the main road crosses Komaba, curving its way around the groves of oak trees. Over there I can see a stream following its meandering course through the paddy fields. Downriver on the near bank water mills are busy at work. The horizon is fresh and clear, and in the distance the rolling wooded hills so characteristic of the Musashi Plain stretch as far as the eye can see."[9] Kunikida Doppo lived in a Shibuya in transition. The rice mills were still there, and among his neighbors were several dairies. He himself lived in a thatch hut near the banks of the Udagawa, the stream he is presumably referring to in the passage quoted above. But about a decade later, a military prison was built near the site of his hut, and barracks were put up in several parts of what is now Setagaya Ward. In 1907, a tramway, the Tamagawa Densha, was built linking them to Shibuya Station. The

Tamaden, as it was called, was supposed to make money not so much by conveying people as by carrying gravel from the bed of the Tamagawa to Shibuya Station. But this proved to be something of a miscalculation. For soldiers and students at the veterinary and agricultural colleges down the line, as well as picnickers and sightseers, the Tamaden was a boon, and its four carriages were filled with passengers.

At the bottom of Dōgenzaka, the military police had their offices, and from there up the hill prostitutes operated out of little hovels in the district so aptly named Owadachō after the old highwayman. Eventually, in 1912, the prostitutes were sent packing, off to Asakusa, where they made their home near the Twelve Stories tower. The authorities had decided to clean up Shibuya, and this they did by creating a geisha district in the area known as Maruyamachō, up and behind Dōgenzaka. Here, the environment for entertainment was more rarified. There was a valley with an ancient spring, Shinsendani, the "Valley of the Sacred Spring." Not long after, Shibuya got a second entertainment district, just down the hill from Maruyamachō. This was Hyakkendana, the "Hundred Shops." The two districts reflected nicely the ambivalence of Shibuya. Maruyamachō was quiet and dignified, just the place for the top-drawer residents of Shōtō. Hyakkendana, in contrast, was more extrovert and raucous. Its roughly rectangular shape, with a bisecting central road, was said to have been modeled after Saruwakachō, the famous late Edo-period theater district in Asakusa. It had theaters and a cinema, and some of the country's first strip shows. Nowadays, it bears that peculiarly unloved look of a district given over to love hotels.

Even before the Great Kantō Earthquake of 1923, and before the Hundred Shops was complete, Shibuya was one of the city's busiest suburban centers. In 1921 it contained nearly five hundred restaurants and eighty-six geisha houses, as well as about four hundred geisha. An average of thirty thousand people used Shibuya Station every day, and five hundred people got on and off trams there every hour. A year before that, the station had moved two hundred meters north to its present location. The new tracks were built overhead, reputedly so that the emperor could pass without having to stop his carriage at the railway crossing (although surely it would have been easier to halt the trains). Over the next few decades, the terminals for the Tōyoko and Inokashira lines were completed, and in 1939, the year that the Ginza subway line was extended to Shibuya, all these stations were brought into one big building. Japan's first composite station was born.

If Shibuya had already been a thriving suburban center before the 1923 earthquake, it grew all the greater and more populous thereafter, when people flocked to the west of the city from the ruins of the old downtown. It was during these years of hectic growth that Shibuya's most memorable story unfolded. The story concerns a dog, Hachikō, "Lord Eight," a pedigree Akita. Every day, Hachikō would accompany his master, Professor Ueda Eisaburō of the Imperial University, down from his home in exclusive Shōtō to the station, and then return to pick him up in the evening. One day in May 1925 the professor failed to return. Hachikō waited in vain. His master had died. Every day he returned to the station and waited. Eventually, the professor's family gave Hachikō to relatives in Asakusa. But Hachikō, undaunted, would set off stubbornly each morning in the direction of Shibuya. Rather than chain him down all day, the professor's relatives sent Hachikō off to live with a mutual friend in Yoyogi. And from there the dog would saunter down to Shibuya Station and await the professor's return. Everyone got to know and love Hachikō. His fame grew immensely, and when he fell ill he was treated by his master's former colleagues at the Imperial University. In 1934, a year before his death, Hachikō was a puzzled onlooker at an elaborate ceremony. Hisako, the professor's granddaughter, unveiled a bronze statue of the nation's most famous and beloved dog.

But even this great symbol of trust and affection failed to outlive the war. It was melted down for metal. It would, in any case, have been damaged beyond repair during the air raids of 1945, when nearly all of Shibuya was burned to the ground. In the first year or two after the war, the station square and surrounding streets became the site of a black market controlled by Chinese from Taiwan. The Taiwanese moved in in numbers and they made Shibuya something of a Chinese enclave. When the police tried to move them out, they resisted. Bloody skirmishes ensued (this was in July 1946), and several people were killed or injured. Today, the mood of the times is different, but there are still many Chinese in Shibuya, and some of the city's best Taiwanese restaurants.

And finally, the romantic ending. When the foreign troops that had been billeted in and around Shibuya departed for home, they left behind them many a broken heart and hand unable to write love letters in English. A certain gentleman trained in the composition of English and French set up shop to help the girls and women so handicapped and so inscribed his name in the last chapter of the annals of Shibuya's history. However, the story has an unromantic twist in its tail. The shop and the lane on which it once stood, Koibumi Yokochō, "Love Letter Lane," have been swept away and replaced by a modern building and a sign.

# # #

Roppongi and Azabu

Cities spread inexorably outward, greedily munching up the land as they go. Behind them, they leave a trail of place names like debris to remind us of what once was. In this part of Tokyo, we find a dense growth of trees and plants and animals that have worked their way into local lore and the local place names. Azabu, it is said, is a place where once the hemp (*aza*) grew thick (*fu-eru*). Here in ancient times, there was a collection of settlements at least as old as those that grew together to become first Edo and then Tokyo.

At the center of these little villages was a temple, Zempukuji, that some say is the second oldest in this part of Japan, after the temple to Kannon in Asakusa. Whether Zempukuji was indeed founded in the ninth century by the Buddhist saint Kūkai is highly debatable, but there is no doubting that the temple was in existence and thriving in the thirteenth century, when it was visited by another of the great apostles of Japanese Buddhism, Shinran. He converted the temple's young abbot Ryōkai to his own brand of Pure Land Buddhism, and before leaving the temple, he planted his staff upside down into the ground. "If my teachings prosper and find favor with the people," he declared, "then my staff will strike root and grow into a flourishing great tree." Mock though one may at such a story, the old ginkgo tree that still stands in the grounds of the temple on the left of the main gate is thought to be about seven hundred fifty years old, which is just the right age for the story. But miracles do not end there. This, the oldest tree in Tokyo, had been designated before the war a natural monument of national importance. During the air raids of 1945, however, when the temple buildings were burnt to a cinder, the tree was badly scalded and appeared so thoroughly dead that it had its designation lifted. The move turned out to be premature. The tree burst back into life and was made a natural monument all over again, as well it might be.

This part of town is full of trees that have left their mark. The pine tree that has given its name to a slope just above Zempukuji has not weathered as well as the ginkgo, being already in its fifth generation. But it has proved very fertile in the number of stories it has spawned. These involve scholars, generals, and poets, and all of them purport to tell us why there should be something special about this "one pine," *ippon no matsu*. But the story that strikes most insistent and true concerns a woman who lived nearby whose heart and head and every thought was consumed by jealousy. "She would deliver countless curses," according to one of the old gazetteers, "and each curse she accompanied by hammering a nail into the aforementioned pine, which came to be known as the Pine Tree of the Mother-in-Law's Mark."[10]

One pine tree standing by the road seems to have made a great impression on passers-by, but so, too, did six pine trees (or alternatively, one pine tree with six shoots) that adorned the crest of a hill not far north of here. The six trees—some say pine and some not—are thought to have been situated where the Roi Building now stands, but all trace of them disappeared long ago. In 1818 it was stated in an official document compiled for the shogunal authorities that the type of tree and date of disappearance were unknown. The trees have disappeared; the name has remained. And Roppongi, "Six Trees," has become the epitome of brash, modern, vibrant Tokyo. But there is a variant, more elaborate derivation for the name which connects it to the names of six feudal lords who had estates in the area: Uesugi (upper cryptomeria), Kutsuki (rotting tree), Takagi (tall tree), Aoki (green tree), Katagiri (wayside paulownia), and Ichiryū (one willow).

Either way, the Six Trees of Roppongi are one of the Seven Wonders of Azabu. The only trouble with the Seven Wonders of Azabu is that although they crop up here and there in the old gazetteers of the city, they are never the same seven, and indeed sometimes they seem to add up to a lot more than seven. Wondrous indeed are the Seven Wonders of Azabu. Of the seven (or however many you care to count), the most wondrous concerns a monster toad that devoured two of the servants of a retainer of the shogun. This man decided to vanquish the toad and avenge his servants, but before he had a chance to put his plan into action, the toad appeared to him in a dream, apologized for his evil deed, and promised by way of contrition to protect the house from fire. And when, in 1821, a fire did engulf the area, the flames miraculously stopped when they reached the man's house. From that day on, his family was able to make a pretty penny selling talismans showing the toad, protection against fire.

Most of the other wonders are something of a disappointment. Mamianazaka, the slope that runs alongside the Soviet Embassy, was named after a badger, we learn, that was spotted by the third Tokugawa shogun, Iemitsu. He was on his way to the shogunal medicine gardens, which stood, until they were moved to Koishikawa at the end of the seventeenth century, by the temple of Myōshōji, in Minami Azabu.

This part of the city is indeed full of intriguing place names. Behind the Roppongi crossroads, there are Imoaraizaka, "Potato-Wash Slope," at the bottom of which a potato market was held in the autumn, and Udonzaka, a nearby slope named after an *udon* noodle shop. Other names, such as Higakubomachi, "Sun Hollow Quarter," down by the Swedish Center, reflect the lay of the land here, all dimples, crests, and unexpected hollows. The feudal lords in the seventeenth century built their suburban villas on the high ground, leaving the more fertile land in the valleys to the farmers, the townspeople, and the temples. These were the older districts, the old settlements from pre-Edo days, and it is fascinating to see how even today they have retained their commercial, plebeian roots, with shops and restaurants clustered around the gates of temples like Zempukuji. The shopping street here by Zempukuji still goes under its old name of Azabu Jūban, "Azabu Number Ten." It was called number ten because, when the banks of the Furukawa were strengthened in 1675, the river was split up into sections, and this was the tenth upstream from its mouth.

From 1723 until the fall of the feudal regime in 1868, the main attraction in this part of town was a *baba,* an exercise ground for horses, situated in the district known today as Higashi Azabu. The finest horses from Sendai were traded at a market here, and the tailors of the area became renowned for their Edo-style jodhpurs, which were known as *jūban hakama.* Both the horse ground and the district's name, Jūban Babachō, were discarded at the end of the Edo period, but the local residents were so attached to the old name for their district that, in 1962, it was resuscitated, and the city had its Jūban Babachō back again. Not for long: soon after, officialdom triumphed once again, and the name disappeared for all time.

Compared with the flourishing little communities of Azabu, Roppongi, on the crest of its hill, was a bit of a late starter. The road that now runs (under the expressway) from Akasaka to Shibuya was not built until well into the Meiji era, around the turn of the century. The main thoroughfare ran, as so many did at the time, along the crest of a ridge, from Aoyama-dōri round and down toward Shiba and the huge Zōjōji Temple complex. In the seventeenth century the road was thought rather lonely and dangerous, so a temple or two were built near the modern Roppongi crossroads, and a little market, and a couple of shops and inns took root at the temple gates.

Azabu's wealth of temples and its situation near the southern approaches to Edo made it one of the obvious sites for the consulates of foreign barbarians, when Japan was gingerly opening its doors in the late 1850s. It was in fact in 1859 that the American legate Townsend Harris moved into his new official quarters in the grounds of Zempukuji, a move accomplished after long months of wrangling stuck out in the seaside town of Shimoda. Among the other consulates lodged in Azabu temples was that of Prussia. One evening, early in 1861, Henry Heusken, Harris's young Dutch interpreter (the shogunate carried on all business with the foreign barbarians in a stilted form of Dutch, learned from traders in the seventeenth century, which they insisted was the correct form of the language), was on his way back home to Zempukuji from the Prussian consulate when he was struck down and killed by fanatic xenophobes. Heusken was a cheerful, intelligent young man, and his death was a worrying blow to the small foreign community.

From then on for the next hundred years, the history of Azabu and Roppongi, like that of the whole nation but more so, is one of martial deeds and the military men that brought them about. The first of those whose name lives on in the area is Prince Arisugawa. A plump little man of unmilitary bearing, he enjoyed a dazzlingly successful career and died while at the pinnacle of the military command in 1895. For many years he lived in a house here in Azabu built on what had once been the grounds of the Nambu family, lords of a large fief in the north of the country. In 1934 the former Arisugawa residence was handed over to Tokyo city and turned into a public park.

Another military man whose whole life was connected with this area is perhaps the most celebrated and certainly the most revered of all Japan's modern military leaders, Nogi Maresuke, who as commander of the Third Army captured Port Arthur from the Russians in 1905 after losing sixty thousand of his own troops. Nogi was born in Roppongi in the estate of the powerful lord of Chōshū, whose samurai contributed so much to the fall of the shogun. He lived much of his life near the barracks of his troops in the part of town now known in his memory as Nogizaka. It was here in his house that he and his wife committed ritual suicide as the emperor Meiji's body was carried in an ox-drawn catafalque out of the gates of the Imperial Palace.

There were barracks on both sides of the road that leads down from Nogizaka to the Roppongi crossroads. On the east side, where the Defense Agency now stands, the first infantry regiment of the First Division was stationed, and on the west, on land now occupied by Tokyo University, the third infantry regiment had its home. Roppongi was, in other words, a garrison town; and it remained that way after the war. The Occupation forces took over the land that had been occupied by the third regiment and built there the Hardy Barracks.

By now we have most of the elements that have made modern Roppongi the hub of nightlife that it has become. We have the young people, most of them still in military khaki. We have the diplomats from the embassies, which continued to find Azabu congenial terrain, and the well-heeled businessmen and their families, who nestled down comfortably beside the diplomats. But there was still one great inconvenience, at least for most Japanese—transport. In 1964, the Hibiya Line was completed and the problem solved. From then on, Roppongi never looked back.

# # #

Meguro

At the beginning of the seventeenth century, soon after the Tokugawa had made Edo their capital, one of Ieyasu's closest advisers, the abbot

Tenkai, decided that the new city needed greater protection than the castle could ever afford it. He decreed that five temples should be established on the outskirts of the city, each temple to house an image of Fudō with different-colored eyes, each image representing one of the five elements. The temples became popular places of pilgrimage and recreation in the Edo period, in particular the Black-Eyed (Meguro) Fudō, which once stood some way outside the city limits. A. B. Mitford records his impressions of Meguro as it was in the Edo period. "As we draw near to Meguro, the scenery, becoming more and more rustic, increases in beauty.... Close at our feet runs a stream of pure water, in which a group of countrymen are washing the vegetables which they will presently shoulder and carry off to sell by auction in the suburbs of Yedo."[11]

At length, Mitford reaches the village of Meguro, at the gates of the temple to Black-Eyed Fudō. "Meguro is one of the many places round Yedo to which the good citizens flock for purposes convivial or religious, or both; hence it is that, cheek by jowl with the old shrines and temples, you will find many a pretty tea-house."[12] The "purposes religious" that Mitford refers to were not the normal perfunctory prayer at a temple or shrine. In the grounds of the Meguro Fudō was a pond, the pond of purification, into which water gushed (as it does to this day) from the pouting mouths of two bronze dragons. Penitents, ascetics, and all manner of pious folk would come to the temple and stand under the water in order to purify the soul as the body was cleansed, the colder the day the more efficacious the cleansing.

Mitford mentions Meguro and its scenery by way of introduction to his real destination: a grave and a gravestone, behind which lies a classic old tale with all the romantic ingredients. The story concerns a certain Shirai Gompachi, and, like other stories of its kind, the people it describes are real people, and the events, dramatic elaborations of real events. The events in question occurred in the 1670s, when the country had yet to finally resolve the problems caused by a large military class left with no wars to fight. Quarrels were a common occurrence, and the swords the samurai carried meant they often ended in death. This was just what happened when two samurai, retainers of Ikeda, lord of Tottori, took to arms to resolve an argument. The vanquished died, the vanquisher fled, taking with him his son, Gompachi.

So much is historically verified. From here on we follow the embroidered version presented on the Kabuki and Bunraku stages and in Mitford's book. On his way to Edo, Gompachi puts up at an inn, where bandits plan to add him to their list of victims. Forewarned by a beautiful young girl the bandits have been holding, he slays them and escapes with the girl. She returns to her home; he presses on for Edo. In Edo, he falls in with Banzuiin Chōbei (this much is certainly fiction; Chōbei had been killed twenty years earlier) and joins Chōbei's valiant band of townsmen (who were actually common rogues and ruffians). He takes to frequenting the licensed quarter, and there in one of the most famous houses, the Miuraya, he meets the girl whom he saved from the bandits. Her family have fallen on bad times. She has been forced into the life of a courtesan and has taken the name Komurasaki. The two fall in love, a passion of truly Wagnerian intensity. Komurasaki, however, is the prize possession of Yoshiwara's most expensive house. Gompachi's passion drives him to visit her every day, but the expense is crippling, and he soon finds himself resorting to criminal ways. He robs and murders, loitering in dark street corners and picking off his victims at will. Chōbei disowns him. But like a tiger who has tasted blood, he is not to be stopped. Eventually he is caught and executed at the public execution ground in Suzugamori. His head is exhibited for all to see, and learn. But Chōbei takes pity on him, retrieves his body, and buries it here in Meguro. When Komurasaki hears of the fate of her love, she is driven into a frenzy of distress. She escapes out of the licensed quarter, finds her way to Meguro, and, unable to recover from her grief, stabs herself over the grave of her beloved Gompachi.

Touched by her fatal loyalty, the people of Meguro buried her next to her lover, and over their graves placed a *hiyoku* stone, a memorial of two birds who fly as one, their bodies united in conjugal embrace. When Mitford visited the grave ("The key is kept by a ghoulish old dame, almost as time-worn and mildewed as the tomb over which she watches."), it was situated in the grounds of a nearby temple. The temple is no more, but the grave and its *hiyoku* gravestone can still be seen just to the left when facing the main gate of the Meguro Fudō.

8
Shinjuku Ward and the West

Ushigome, Ichigaya, and Yotsuya

According to the exhaustive Meiji-era guide called *Tokyo annai,* "Ushigome was from ancient times pastureland, a place where cattle grazed."[1] It is one of several place names in Tokyo with pastoral origins. Others like Magome and Komagome derive not from cattle but from the horses that grazed the land there. The common denominator of each of these names, *kome* (or *gome*), refers to a gathering of animals in a herd. Cattle have not been grazing in Ushigome for many a century. There were probably few of them left when the head of the Ogo family moved here from his home on the skirt of Mount Akagi, northwest of the little settlement called Edo at the mouth of the Sumida River. He settled in Ushigome, taking the name of the district as his own and building a homestead where the temple of Kōshōji now stands in Fukuromachi, just south of Kagurazaka. He, or a descendant, established a shrine nearby, Akagi Jinja, which remains one of the larger of the many shrines in the area.

In the 1630s, much of the land here was assigned to the military class. While there were several large suburban estates belonging to the feudal lords in this outlying part of the city, most of Ushigome and the contiguous, and overlapping, district of Ichigaya was staked out for the humbler military servants of the shogunate, the men who worked in the various offices of the Tokugawa government. The accommodation that these men and their families enjoyed was a lot better than their incomes would allow, and better, too, than what the townsmen had to put up with. That we can tell from the size of their plots of land, most of which can comfortably fit a decent-sized home in the modern city. We are fortunate today that, together with the townsman's part of Kanda, this is another district where the old names of the quarters have been preserved.

There is a fascination, therefore, to the map of this part of town, for it still tells us much about the city's history. We find here, for example, Tansumachi, district not of makers of *tansu* (chests of drawers), but of administrators and comptrollers of the shogun's furniture and military ordnance. This was where they lived. In a nearby district, Nandomachi, lived their colleagues, the *gonandogumi dōshin,* accountants to the shogun, who checked expenditure on clothes, furniture, and others of the shogun's appurtenances. What the accountants thought of their next-door neighbors in Yamabushichō, the history books do not tell us, but since Yamabushichō was named after its erstwhile residents, *yamabushi,* or mountain ascetics, we can imagine the accountants were relieved when a fire in 1732 forced the *yamabushi* to pick up their conch shells and esoteric spells and move to Shitaya.

Many of the names here have intriguing derivations, not least of them Kagurazaka, which means "Slope of the Music of the Gods," an enchanting name indeed. Why it should be so named has never been satisfactorily explained, but one theory has it that when nearby Ichigaya Hachimangū, one of Tokyo's oldest shrines, held its festival, the portable shrines and floats and bands of musicians passed down the slope on their merry, meandering way through the streets of the area. They stopped here for a rest, and left behind in this name a reminder of their visit. On the crest of the hill is a temple dedicated to Bishamon, one of Buddhism's protective deities. Opposite Bishamon's temple is a maze of alleys full of steps and corners and dead ends that contains the last few traditional restaurants that in the Meiji and Taishō eras made Kagurazaka the preeminent geisha quarter of the Yamanote hills. There had been an unlicensed pleasure district here in the Edo period, but for the first few decades of the Meiji era, there was little more than a handful of geisha houses. Then, in the 1890s, when the country was flush from its victory over the enfeebled Qing dynasty in China, money started pouring in, and new houses were opened on the hill. Before long, Kagurazaka had become Yamanote's equivalent of Shimbashi and Hamachō. Its situation here in the west of the city meant that it was not damaged during the 1923 earthquake, and its prosperity continued for many more years. It was particularly lively on festival days of the Bishamon temple, when night stalls lined the steep slopes of the hill. And it had a notable collection of variety halls, each of which specialized in one of the traditional arts of entertainment, dancing, chanting, or joke telling.

This had long been considered the center of Yamanote. It was here at Kagurazaka and the Ushigome Gate and bridge over the outer moat that goods for the military districts were unloaded from boats that had made their way up the Kanda River. It was a busy market, often referred to as the place where the two parts of the city met, Shitamachi and Yamanote. The porters who loaded the vegetables, viands, and other provisions off the boats were known as *karuko,* a name that has been preserved in the slope—Karukozaka—that runs parallel to Kagurazaka, as well as in the name of the quarter, Agebamachi, the "Unloading Quarter," by the now unhappy pool of water at the Iidabashi crossroads.

There were many lesser retainers of the shogun living in Ushigome, and there were a few townspeople here, too, most of them in the *monzenmachi,* the districts at the gates of the many temples that had been moved here in the first half of the seventeenth century. But there were, too, several powerful feudal lords, who had been given land here on which to build their suburban estates. Iemitsu, the third Tokugawa shogun, had granted land just a little way beyond the top of Kagurazaka to Sakai, lord of Wakasa. He was a regular visitor to the Sakai estate, paying over a hundred visits, it is said. No doubt most of these visits had as their aim the enjoyment of the garden that the Sakai had built. It was supposed to be one of the most beautiful in Edo, with its pond, its tea hut, and its shrine to Confucius. But one visit was rather more hasty. This was in the First Month of 1657, when the whole of the city, including the shogun's castle itself, was being burnt to cinders by a dozen dreadful fires that had sprung up in different places. Iemitsu sought refuge here in the grounds of the Sakai estate. His guard flung up an impromptu palisade to protect their lord, thrusting their spears into the ground in a circle. In later years, when the city had been rebuilt, this moment of desperation was remembered, and the lord Sakai built a fence round his estate with tree trunks fashioned to look like the lances of the shogun's guard. The incident became a part of the local folklore; to this day the district in which the Sakai estate stood is called Yaraichō, the "Palisade Quarter."

The next gate south from Ushigome along the outer moat was at Ichigaya. For some reason, this gate closed a lot earlier than the others, at four in the afternoon. A bell was sounded at this time each day in the nearby shrine of Ichigaya Hachimangū to let everyone know that the gate was about to close. This shrine, which now looks out no further than the rear of the buildings in front of it, once gazed gracefully and proudly from the top of its steep hill east toward the center of the city. Its grounds contained a stage and stalls where tea was served, and at the bottom of the steps were the houses of some of the city's better-known prostitutes. At the entrance to the shrine stood a copper arch. It was completed in 1804, the work of the head of the smiths of Kajichō in Kanda. He carved on one of its two posts his own name as well as that of the men who donated the funds for its construction. It is therefore a valuable document of sorts, and one that is there to be seen today by anyone who cares to make the ascent of the steep stone steps that lead up to the shrine.

Just behind the shrine in the Edo period stood the vast grounds of the main compound, the *kami yashiki,* of the lord of Owari, whose family was descended directly from Tokugawa Ieyasu. After the Meiji Restoration, this land was given to the government, which established here in 1875 the Officers Academy for the army. When this was moved away to Zama in Kanagawa Prefecture in 1937, its place was taken by the Army Ministry and the office of Chief of Staff, which had stood until then in front of the new Diet building in Kasumigaseki. No more fitting a place could have been chosen for the military tribunal at the end of the war, when the allied leaders tried to apportion the blame for a national nightmare. And perhaps it is fitting, too, that this should now be the headquarters of the Self-Defense Forces. It was here that the writer Mishima Yukio attempted to inspire the soldiers into revolt on 25 November 1970. When his grand gesture met with hoots of derision, he committed suicide as best as he could in keeping with the correct precepts.

The Owari had another huge compound, their suburban estate, on land not far to the northwest of here on the very outskirts of town. It was situated in a district called Toyama, and it, too, became a military academy under the Meiji government. Now the Toyama estate is the site of one of the city's largest metropolitan housing projects. In between these two Owari compounds that had become military academies was more land that had belonged to feudal lords. This was put to different use, as a prison. Ichigaya Daichō and Tomihisachō were for many years the site of a prison, two prisons, to be precise. One had been moved there in 1875 from its old site in Kodemmachō, the old Edo prison. The other came from Kajibashi, near the site of the compound of the city magistrates. Executions, which had once taken place on Edo's northern fringes at Kozukappara, were now held here. This is where the wicked killer Takahashi Oden met her end, as well as Kōtoku Shūsui and the eleven others who were convicted of plotting to dethrone the emperor in 1911.

The lords of Owari, together with two other families descended from Tokugawa Ieyasu, had had their main Edo mansions in the grounds of Edo Castle, but they were all moved out after the fire of 1657. To compensate for this estrangement, they were given much more land on which to build several separate estates. Two of them, the lords of Owari and Kii, had subsidiary compounds within the outer moat just south of Yotsuya Gate. The lord of Kii was given land for his main estate just outside this same gate on the south side of the Kōshū Kaidō, the highway that led first to Naitō Shinjuku and then to the mountain province of Kōshū. This later became the Akasaka Detached Palace, home for many years for the Meiji emperor. Although a railway line and a road separated them, the emperor had as his neighbors on the northwest side the inhabitants of one of Tokyo's three large slum districts. It was known as Samegahashi Tanimachi, the "Shark River Bridge Valley District," and it was situated in one of Yotsuya's four valleys along the course now taken by the road that runs through Wakaba 2-chōme. (The other two slum districts were Mannenchō, northeast of Ueno Station, now Higashi Ueno 4-chōme and Kita Ueno 1-chōme, and Shin'amichō, just south of Hamamatsuchō Station in Minato Ward.) Why the bridge in this valley was given the name of Shark River Bridge, no one really seems to know. One theory, not a very convincing one, is that the priest of a local temple, while out riding a famous horse called Samé, took a tumble and fell into the river here. Other theories exist, but none of them explain why the name is written with the homonymous character for "shark." One of the slum's most famous inhabitants was a former Shimbashi geisha, Hanai Oume. She opened her own house of assignation in Hamachō but fell victim to the wicked machinations of one of her employees and eventually lost patience and killed him. She was sentenced to life imprisonment, but sixteen years later, in 1903, was pardoned and released. By then she was a celebrity. Kawatake Mokuami and other famous playwrights had written dramas about her life and deeds. She ended up playing the part of herself, but she died in poverty in the Shark River Bridge slum in 1916 at the age of fifty-two.

The name Yotsuya is written with two characters that mean "Four Valleys," and indeed four valleys have been found to explain the name, one of which was the Shark River Bridge Valley. Two of the other three, however, lie rather too far afield—Myōgadani in Bunkyō Ward and Sendagaya in Shibuya Ward—for this theory of the name's derivation to be acceptable. In fact, it seems that the original characters used to write Yotsuya meant "Four Shops." This makes more sense, especially as the four shops have been traced and they all stood in the area. One of them, Bokuya, sold saké from premises in Shiochō, and another, Nunoya, also in Shiochō, sold paper and cloth for one hundred twenty years until 1818.

In the streets behind these shops there once lived a samurai named Iemon and his gentle wife, Oiwa. Iemon was an unrepentant philanderer and a high liver who was habitually short of cash. With an equally evil neighbor as his accomplice, he plotted to murder Oiwa and marry the neighbor's granddaughter. The neighbor poisoned the unsuspecting Oiwa with an awful potion that horribly disfigured her. Iemon finished her off, tied her body to a door, and floated her away down the river that ran past their home—only for Oiwa's vengeful ghost to rise from the watery depths one fearful night and exact a chilling revenge on her persecutors. This was, at any rate, the story as Tsuruya Namboku IV wrote it in his celebrated play for the Kabuki stage, *The Ghost Story of Yotsuya*, and it is supposed to be based on real events. Oiwa lived in Yotsuya, in Samonchō. On the site of their house is a shrine where Oiwa is worshiped as a manifestation of Inari, the rice deity. Kabuki actors traditionally come to offer a prayer at her shrine before playing her part on stage, and perhaps unhappily married women come to worship and seek comfort.

In the Edo period, Yotsuya stretched as far west as a gate at the city confines, Yotsuya Okido, and that is about as far west as it stretches today. The gate, by the modern Yotsuya 4-chōme crossroads, was built in 1616. Here goods in transit to and from Edo were checked, although the inspection was a rather desultory business. The gate was pulled down in 1792, but the inspection post remained until the advent of the Meiji government.

Not even the name is left now. But then if there is one thing which this part of the city does not lack, it is old place names. For this we must be thankful, but it is hard not to wish, futile though that wish might be, that there were just a little more left than names on the face of a map.

# # #

Shinjuku

The five gentlemen of Asakusa might have thought of a better name when, in 1698, the authorities granted them permission to open a new post station on the Kōshū Kaidō, the road to the mountain province of Kai west of Edo. But instead they chose Shinjuku, "New Lodgings," which came to be Naitō Shinjuku, after the Naitō family, lords of Takatō, part of whose suburban estate was requisitioned for the new post station. The five gentlemen of Asakusa came, in fact, from Yoshiwara, where they were brothel owners. They had argued in their petition that it was too much to ask a fully laden horse to walk in one day the sixteen kilometers from Nihombashi to Takaido, first stop on the Kōshū Kaidō. And they had therefore proposed the construction of a new post station just beyond the city confines west of Yotsuya. But their concern was not for the well-being of horses. Three of the other four highways out of Edo had, just outside the city boundaries, a post station that was really more of a brothel district. They thought the Kōshū Kaidō should have one, too, even though it was much the least traveled of the four.

Their petition was granted, and they moved their business from the licensed quarter of Yoshiwara. But they must have regretted their move, for twenty years later, the Naitō Shinjuku post station was closed down. Again, a petition had been presented, this time by a retainer of the shogun whose brother had disgraced the family name by getting into a brawl in a brothel. Together with the petition, the man had presented the severed head of his brother, whom he had forced to commit suicide. This was just the sort of pretext that the officers of the eighth shogun, Yoshimune, had been looking for. The doors of the inns and brothels of Naitō Shinjuku were barred. Half a century and many vigorous petitions later, they were reopened. Tanuma Okitsugu, the shogun's councillor of state in the 1770s, was a man of a different stamp. Never averse to a good business deal—and a bit of pleasure—himself, he ordered the post station to be reopened in 1772 so that the authorities could levy an appropriate sum in taxation.

Eighteen years later, there were a full fifty-two inns where prostitutes, known euphemistically as "serving girls," served up the same sort of fare as at Yoshiwara but without all the rigmarole and expense. Indeed, the poor women of Shinjuku were regarded with some contempt by their peers in the licensed quarter. A reference in a famous ribald tale to "flowers in the horse dung" became a stock-in-trade epithet. A century and a half later, however, the tables were turned when Yoshiwara was destroyed by fire after the Great Kantō Earthquake of 1923, and Shinjuku prospered at its expense. Indeed, the prostitutes of Shinjuku survive to this day, just, having moved in 1958 from their old haunts in Shinjuku 2-chōme to that inviting little web of back alleys known as Golden Gai.

The location of Naitō Shinjuku can be easily traced from the present pattern of roads. It began just west of the city confines at Yotsuya Okido and stretched about a kilometer west along what is now Shinjuku-dōri as far as a point called Oiwake (the Shinjuku 3-chōme crossroads), where the Kōshū Kaidō made a left turn and parted company from the road to Ōme. Teahouses, inns, stores, and brothels lined the road in Naitō Shinjuku. To the north were the temples of Taisōji, famous for its statue of Emma, lord of hell, and its market, and Jōkakuji, where the women of Naitō Shinjuku were disposed of if they should die while in the custody of the innkeepers. On the south side, the post station was lined by an aqueduct built in 1653 to supply the south and center of the city with drinking water. It tapped the water of the Tama River and so was known as the Tamagawa Jōsui. It was built by two brothers, experts in riparian engineering, but expert though they may have been, they ran into an age-old problem. They had exhausted their budget before finishing their work. Eventually, they were forced to sell their own house to raise the necessary funds. So well did they do their work, however, that the aqueduct they built remained an important conduit of water for the city until the early 1960s.

The Tamagawa Jōsui flowed along a course that is marked nowadays by the north wall of Shinjuku Gyoen. And this in turn occupies land that had once been the suburban estate of the Naitō family. In 1872, after the fall of the feudal regime, the Naitō estate became the property of the government, and an agricultural station was established here, where the first experiments in Japan were conducted on the raising of livestock and the growing of fruit. A college was built here that later moved to Komaba and became the agricultural department of what is now Tokyo University.

To the west of Naitō Shinjuku, near the Oiwake junction, stood a famous old temple, Tenryūji, whose bell, known as *oidashi kane,* the "chasing-out bell," was struck thirty minutes or so before the city gates were closed to allow revelers in the post station brothels time to get back home. Outside the gates of this temple lived a little community of storytellers, dancers, drummers, and other streetside entertainers. There were performers of *kappore,* a kind of dance popular in the late Edo period, and *chokobure* chanters of the Ahodara Sutra, a liturgical satire chanted by mendicant monks. However, the day of the Ahodara Sutra was soon over, and in 1887, the area by the temple gate, through which Meiji-dōri now runs, became the site of cheap lodging houses, indeed something of a slum.

Until the 1920s, Shinjuku was regarded as being one of the more distant, unattractive parts of the city. It was described in the following terms by Sōma Aizō, a baker who had the prescience to open a shop in Shinjuku: "In those days [ca. 1907] Shinjuku looked so miserable that there is nowhere to compare with it now. As for any notion of rustic suburban charm, it could not have looked more dreary, and if you walked just a little way in from the road, you would come upon open-air toilets."[2] Sōma's main bakery had been in the more salubrious district of Hongō, near the gates of the Imperial University. But business at the Shinjuku branch soon picked up, and he began serving Indian curry and Chinese dumplings, and never looked back. Today, his shop, Nakamuraya, is still there. When Sōma opened his bakery in Shinjuku, one of his neighbors was Takano Kichitarō, a dealer in raw silk from Chōfu, who had opened in 1885 a little shack where he sold watermelon, persimmons, and other fruit to the local farmers and stable lads and the men who floated timber down from Ōme to Fukagawa. His shack prospered and grew, until by the 1920s it became one of the three main ice-cream parlors of the city. Like the Nakamuraya, it survives to this day, not far from the site where it first started up. Another shop whose name stands out in the annals of Shinjuku is the bookshop Kinokuniya. But until 1927, Kinokuniya had sold not books but charcoal. It had been one of the many charcoal shops whose black facades lined the Ōme Road between the Oiwake intersection and Shinjuku railway station.

Shinjuku Station was built in 1885. It stood on the Shinagawa Line, which ran from Shinagawa to Akabane and linked the only two trunk lines in the east of Japan, the Tokaidō and Takasaki lines. There had been much opposition to the construction of the railway. Farmers in Meguro feared that birds would perch on the electricity cables and then swoop down and damage their crops, while the innkeepers and brothel owners of Shinjuku insisted successfully that the station be built in the village of Tsunohazu, four hundred meters or so west of their district, so that it would not damage trade. Just a few years later another railway line was built, linking Kōfu and Shinjuku. The plan had been to build it along the Kōshū Kaidō, but opposition had been fierce, and eventually a route was chosen through the woods of Musashino and away from habitation. By 1895, this line had been extended to Ushi-gome and then Iidabashi, although only after more protests, which were eventually overriden by the emperor Meiji himself, who condescended for a tunnel to be built under the grounds of the Akasaka palace.

Both these lines were open only to freight trains, the Kōmu Line carrying textile products from Hachiōji and the Shinagawa Line, coal and kindling from the north. It was no wonder, then, that the area to the east of Shinjuku Station became an important center for charcoal and coal merchants. But in 1906, the lines were nationalized and opened to the transport of people. Trains remained infrequent, and this led to long waits in the waiting room drinking tea, and to plenty of accidents at the level crossings just north of the station, where a man would draw a rope across the Ōme Road at the approach of a train and hope that the traffic would be so good as to stop.

A tramline was built to Hanzōmon in 1903. In 1915, the Keiō Line, first of the modern private railways, was extended to Shinjuku. And it was followed twelve years later by the Odakyū Line. By then Shinjuku Station had been rebuilt in an early example of the Egyptian-influenced modern style. But in Shinjuku's rapid transformation from backwater to busiest station in Japan by 1928, one event above all others played a central role, and that was the Great Kantō Earthquake of 1923. The fires that engulfed nearly all of the old center of the city scarcely affected Shinjuku. Massive numbers of people moved westward from the devastation of Nihombashi, Kanda, Asakusa, Honjo, and Fukagawa. Suddenly, Shinjuku's position at the junction of two key railway lines made it irresistibly attractive to the commercial forces that have drawn the contours of modern Japanese cities. Mitsukoshi and Hoteiya, later bought by Isetan, led the department stores into Shinjuku. The Teitoza and the Moulin Rouge were among the first theaters. By 1930, there were two hundred coffee shops in Shinjuku employing two thousand waitresses. The price of land in Shinjuku rose remorselessly, and even the Great Depression made barely a ripple, leading a newspaper reporter to talk about "this monster, Shinjuku."

In 1945, the monster was soon resurrected. On 25 May that year, the whole of Shinjuku was destroyed in an air raid, save only for Isetan department store. Three days after Japan's surrender on 15 August, the following advertisement appeared in the *Asahi* newspaper: "Urgent notice for factories under conversion and industrialists.... We are accepting large quantities of manufactured goods at 'reasonable prices.' Anyone interested should proceed urgently with samples and estimates of factory prices to 1–854 Tsunohazu, Yodobashi Ward (site of Urui residence), Shinjuku Market of Kantō Ozu Group."[3] This bureaucratically couched notice sounded the start of trading life in postwar Tokyo. Anyone with a pot or a pan or any odds and ends from wartime factories rushed to Shinjuku, and within a few days the road from the station to Isetan was lined with stalls, crates, newspapers, cloths, anything on which to place a few chattels for sale. *"Hikari wa Shinjuku yori,"* "Light Shines from Shinjuku": this was the sign adorned by 117 naked light bulbs proclaiming Ozu Kinosuke's black market, which came to acquire the grandiose name of Ryūgu, "Dragon Palace," Market. Other markets, too, were formed, on the south and west sides of the station. Initially, the police gave their tacit consent, and Shinjuku became the largest black market center of Tokyo.

However, the day of the black market was short-lived. In 1948, much of Ozu's market was swept away to the area of Golden Gai behind Hanazono Shrine, while a couple of the other black markets were brought together on the grounds of the tram terminus, but Isetan moved in in 1965 and built an annex there. Golden Gai, however, has managed to survive, despite the never-ending threat of development, a threat that seems to grow more serious by the year. A compound of the black-market stalls and the dives of the prostitutes from Naitō Shinjuku, the area was originally known as Hanazono Gai and also catered to American servicemen until 1958 and the banning of prostitution. In 1965, it gave itself the new name of Golden Gai, and since then the denizens of the tiny bars of this beehive of nighttime fun have been for the main part newspaper reporters, writers, and others who live off their wits and their nerves and so remain thin enough to fit through its doors.

At the heart of postwar Shinjuku lies Kabukichō. But what can Kabuki have to do with this brash, sometimes sleazy center of nightlife? In the years immediately after the end of the war, the chairman of the local residents' association (in the days when Kabukichō had such a thing) put forward a proposal to build a high-class (*kaori takai*) entertainment district. He won the cooperation of the most prominent local landowner and set about building theaters, cinemas, dance halls, and a Kabuki theater, to be called the Kikuza. In honor of this, it was decided to call the area, most of which had been occupied by a school before the war, Kabukichō. This was, however, a miscalculation. The resources were simply not available at the time to build a Kabuki theater, and anything that smacked of traditional culture was viewed with suspicion by the occupying forces. They preferred to promote Japan's first strip show, *The Birth of Venus,* which was held at the nearby Teitoza. Little was revealed except for veils and bras amid the giant tree trunks that formed a frame for the show, but this was enough to cause quite a stir at the time.

There was to be no Kabuki in Kabukichō. The funds that were available came largely from Overseas Chinese sources. The Chikyū Kaikan, "Globe Hall," was built in the center of Kabukichō by Overseas Chinese interests. This hall, which stands on the south side of Kabukichō's central square, contains what used to be one of the city's leading cinemas. The Chikyūza was the first cinema in Japan to show many important European and Russian films. It helped, until its closure in 1958, to make Shinjuku, and in particular Kabukichō, a favorite haunt for intellectuals, students, and, in the 1960s, hippies and other members of the radical young. Anyone could—and at times it seemed that most did—make their intellectual home in Kabukichō. Hoodlums, gangsters, and pimps were no strangers either. And while Kabukichō's more intellectually inclined visitors have tended to disperse over the last ten or fifteen years to the quieter waters of Golden Gai and even to other parts of the city, the more shady elements have moved in and stayed. Sex, the promise of it, became Kabukichō's great lure. In the early 1980s, in particular, the statistics of sex in Kabukichō grew beyond all bounds: 20 general porn parlors, 13 peep-show parlors, 17 sex shops, as well as strip shows, no-panties coffee shops, to make a total of 132 purveyors of porn in Kabukichō 1-chōme alone. New legislation was introduced in 1985 to clean up. Turkish baths were to be called "Soaplands" and were to close at midnight. These and other measures, however, had little more than a distorting effect, with the pursuit of illicit sex now being carried on more assiduously than ever, but out of the public view, so to speak, in apartments and hotels.

In sharp contrast to the effervescence and decadence of Kabukichō and the rest of Shinjuku to the east of the station, the west side is severely modern and austere, dominated by the skyscrapers that stand on land that had, for the first sixty years of this century, been occupied by the Yodobashi water purification plant. These buildings, which have been so aptly described as urban grave markers, are soon to be joined by Tokyo's city hall. Tokyo, it seems, has no more time for Shinjuku's flowers blooming in the horse dung.

Metropolitan Tokyo

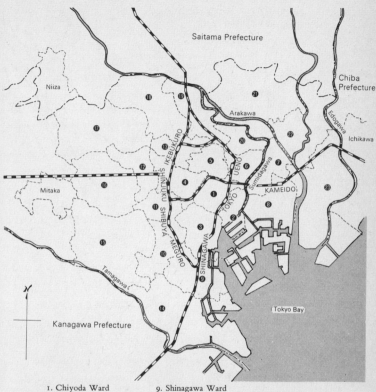

1. Chiyoda Ward
2. Chūō Ward
3. Minato Ward
4. Shinjuku Ward
5. Bunkyō Ward
6. Taitō Ward
7. Sumida Ward
8. Kōtō Ward
9. Shinagawa Ward
10. Meguro Ward
11. Shibuya Ward
12. Nakano Ward
13. Toshima Ward
14. Ōta Ward
15. Setagaya Ward
16. Suginami Ward
17. Nerima Ward
18. Itabashi Ward
19. Kita Ward
20. Arakawa Ward
21. Adachi Ward
22. Kasai Ward
23. Edogawa Ward

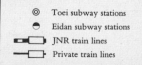

◎ Toei subway stations
● Eidan subway stations
JNR train lines
Private train lines

The Edo Area (c. 1480)

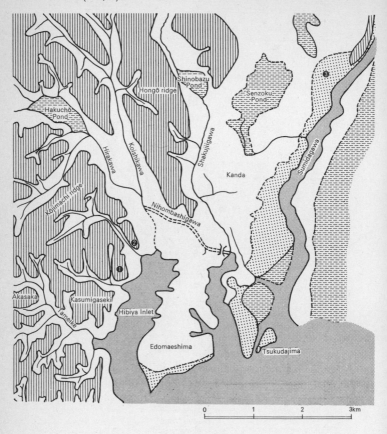

1. The Imperial Palace, after 1868.
2. Edo Castle (first built by Ōta Dōkan in 1457)
3. Sensōji (founded late seventh century?)

▨▨▨	Tableland of the Musashi Plain
⠿⠿	Alluvial deposits of dry land
▦▦	Alluvial swamp lands
☐	Old alluvial plains
═╕╞	The diverted course of the Hirakawa

The Defenses of Edo Castle (c. 1644)

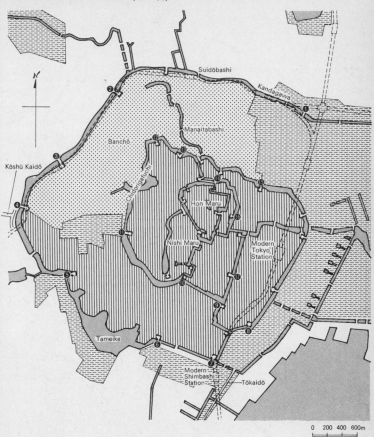

Suidōbashi

Kandagawa

Manaitabashi

Banchō

Kōshū Kaidō

Chidorigafuchi

Hon Maru

Nishi Maru

Modern
Tokyo
Station

Tameike

Modern
Shimbashi
Station

Tōkaidō

0 200 400 600m

1. Sujigaibashi Gate
2. Ushigome Gate
3. Ichigaya Gate
4. Yotsuya Gate
5. Akasaka Gate
6. Toranomon
7. Onaribashi Gate
8. Sukiyabashi Gate
9. Hibiya Gate
10. Outer Sakurada Gate
11. Hanzōmon
12. Tayasu Gate
13. Shimizu Gate
14. Hirakawa Gate
15. Kandabashi Gate
16. Ōte Gate
17. Babasaki Gate

|||||| Daimyō districts

∷∷∷∷ Hatamoto districts

▭▭▭ Townspeople districts

-=[_]=- Modern train lines

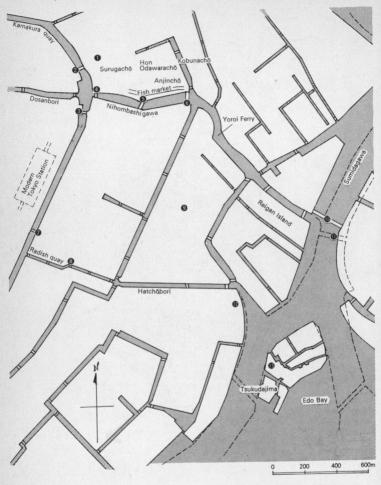

Edo Port (c. 1800)

Kamakura quay

1 Surugachō
Hon
Odawarachō
Kobunachō

2
Dosanbori
4
Anjinchō
5 Fish market
Nihombashigawa
3
6

Yoroi Ferry

Modern
Tokyo Station

9

Reigan Island

Sumidagawa

7
Radish quay
8

11
11

Hatchōbori

12

13
Tsukudajima
Edo Bay

N

0   200   400   600m

1. Gold mint
2. Tokiwabashi
3. Gofukubashi
4. Ichikokubashi
5. Nihombashi
6. Edobashi
7. Kajibashi
8. Kyōbashi
9. Residence of Yoriki
10. Eitaibashi
11. Modern Eitaibashi
12. Teppōsu Inari Jinja
13. Ishikawajima Detention
   Center

Notes

From Edo to Tokyo

1. Rutherford Alcock, *The Capital of the Tycoon,* 2 vols. (1863; reprint, New York: Greenwood Press, 1969), p. 123.

2. Statistics taken from Naitō Akira, *Edo to Edo-jō (Edo and Edo Castle) (Tokyo: Kajima Shuppankai, 1966), p. 137*

3. R. H. Blyth, *Japanese Life and Character in Senryu* (Tokyo: Hokuseido Press, 1960), p. 21.

4. Clara Whitney, *Clara's Diary* (Tokyo: Kodansha International, 1979), p. 253.

5. Alcock, *Capital,* p. 128.

6. Robert Guillain, *Le Japon en guerre* (Japan at War) (Paris: Stock, 1979), p 159.

Chiyoda Ward

1. Philipp Franz von Siebold, *Manners and Customs of the Japanese* (1841; reprint, Tokyo: Tuttle, 1973), p. 93.

2. Murai Masao, *Edo-jō* (Edo Castle) (Tokyo: Chūō Kōron-sha, 1964), p. 99.

3. Fosco Maraini, *Meeting with Japan* (New York: Viking Press, 1960), p. 87.

4. Laurence Oliphant, *Elgin's Mission to China and Japan,* 2 vols. (1859; reprint, Hong Kong: Oxford University Press, 1970), 2:123.

5. Maraini, *Meeting,* p. 63.

6. Whitney, *Diary,* p. 183.

7. Leon Zolbrod, *Takizawa Bakin* (New York: Twayne, 1967), p. 88.

Chūō Ward

1. Charles Dunn, *Everyday Life in Traditional Japan* (London: B. T. Batsford, 1969), p. 175.

2. Kitahara Susumu, *Chūō-ku no rekishi* (The History of Chūō Ward) (Tokyo: Meicho Shuppan, 1979), p. 71.

3. Whitney, *Diary,* p. 111.

4. Ibid., p. 16?

5. Siebold, *M̶̶̶̶* ?1.

6. Ibid., p. 8?

7. Ibid., p. 88.

8. Iwaki and Sh̶̶̶ *i-shō fūshi manga,* p. 12?.

9. Katherine Sansom, *Living in*

Tokyo (London: Chattus and Windus, 1936), p. 13.

10. Edward Seidensticker, *Kafū the Scribbler* (Stanford, Calif.: Stanford University Press, 1965), p. 129.

11. Ibid.

12. Mary Fraser, *A Diplomat's Wife in Japan* (Tokyo: Weatherhill, 1982), p 48.

13. Ernest Satow, *A Diplomat in Japan* (1921; reprint, Tokyo: Tuttle, 1973), p. 21.

14. Donald Keene, *Appreciations of Japanese Culture* (Tokyo: Kodansha International, 1971), p. 179.

15. Whitney, *Diary*, p. 192.

TAITŌ WARD AND THE NORTH

1. Keene, *Appreciations*, p. 160.

2. Translated from *Edo meisho zu-e* (Illustrated Gazetteer of Famous Places in Edo), quoted from *Edo meisho ki* (A Chronicle of Famous Places in Edo) by Imai Kingo (Tokyo: Shakai Shisō-sha, 1969), p. 161.

3. Translated from *Shimpen Edo sunago onkoshi* (New Gold-Dust Tales of Edo), quoted from Imai, *Edo meisho ki*, p. 160.

4. *Meiji Taishō zushi: Tōkyō* (An Illustrated History of Tokyo in the Meiji and Taishō Eras), 3 vols., ed. by Ogi Shinzō and Maeda Ai (Tokyo: Chikuma Shobō, 1978), 2:40.

5. A. B. Mitford, *Tales of Old Japan* (1871; reprint, Tokyo: Tuttle, 1966), p. 131.

6. Ibid., p. 126.

7. Whitney, *Diary*, p. 36.

8. Mitford, *Tales of Old Japan*, p. 66.

9. Seidensticker, *Kafū the Scribbler*, p. 143.

KŌTŌ WARD AND THE EAST

1. Statistics from Guillain, *Le Japon*, p. 251. Other sources give differing numbers.

2. Translated from *Shimpen Edo sunago onkoshi* (New Gold-Dust Tales of Edo), quoted from Imai, *Edo meisho ki*, p. 50.

3. Translated from *Edo meisho zu-e* (Illustrated Gazetteer of Famous Places in Edo), quoted from *Edo no tabemono* (Foods of Edo) by Hirano Masaaki, in *Edo shinise chizu* (Maps of Edo's Established Shops), ed. by Edo Bunka Kenkyūkai (Tokyo: Shūfū to Seikatsu-sha, 1981), p. 123.

4. Imai, *Edo meisho ki*, p. 55.

5. Translated from *Edo meisho ki* (Notes on Famous Places in Edo) and quoted from Imai's book of the same name, p. 50.

6. Seidensticker, *Kafū the Scribbler*, p. 33.

7. Basil Hall Chamberlain and W. B. Mason, *Murray's Handbook for Travellers in Japan*, 9th ed., rev. (London: Murray, 1913), p. 135.

8. Ibid., pp. 126–27.

9. Ibid., p. 66.

10. Seidensticker, *Kafū the Scribbler*, p. 116.

BUNKYŌ WARD AND THE NORTHWEST

1. Alcock, *Capital*, p. 117.

2. Quoted from Mori Ogai, *Gan* (The Wild Geese). Translated from a sign on Muen Slope, near the supposed setting of his novel.

3. Ibid., 3:38.

4. Quoted from the translation by Donald Keene of a passage from *The Drifting Cloud* in Donald Keene ed., *Modern Japanese Litera-*

ture (New York: Grove Press, 1956), p. 63.

5. Jippensha Ikku, *Shank's Mare,* trans. by Thomas Satchell (1929; reprint, Tokyo: Tuttle, 1960), pp. 34647.

6. Seidensticker, *Kafū the Scribbler,* p. 68.

7. *Meiji Taishō zushi: Tokyo,* 1:144.

8. Katherine Sansom, *Living in Tokyo,* p. 87.

9. Ihara Saikaku, *Five Women Who Loved Love,* trans. by Wm. T. de Bary (Tokyo: Tuttle, 1956), p. 159.

10. Ibid., quoted from an essay by Richard Lane therein, p. 257.

MINATO WARD AND THE SOUTH

1. Chamberlain and Mason, *Murray's Handbook,* p. 116.

2. Alcock, *Capital,* p. 110.

3. Henry Heusken, *Japan Journal 1855–1861,* trans. and ed. by Jeanette van der Corput and Robert Wilson (New Brunswick, N.J.: Rutgers University Press, 1964), p. 139.

4. Imai, *Edo meisho ki,* p. 241.

5. Seibold, *Manners,* pp. 1023.

6. Heusken, *Japan Journal,* p. 135.

7. Translated from *Shimpen Edo sunago onkoshi* (New Gold-Dust Tales of Edo), quoted from Imai, *Edo meisho ki,* p. 197.

8. Imai, *Edo meisho ki,* p. 198.

9. Hayashi Rokuro *et al., Shibuya-ku no rekishi* (Tokyo: Meicho Shuppan, 1978).

10. Imai, *Edo meisho ki,* p. 214.

11. Mitford, *Tales of Old Japan,* p. 42.

12. Ibid., p. 49.

SHINJUKU WARD AND THE WEST

1. Tokyo Shiyakusho, *Tokyo annai* (Tokyo Guide) 1907 (reprint Tokyo: Hihyosha, 1986), vol. 2, p. 217.

2. Shinjuku no Rekishi o Kataru Kai, *Shinjuku-ku no rekishi* (Tokyo: Meicho Shuppan, 1977), p. 136.

3. *Edo Tōkyō gaku jiten* (Dictionary of Edo Tokyo Studies) (Tokyo:Sanseidō, 1987), p. 166.

Index